WOMEN, EUROPE AND THE
NEW LANGUAGES OF POLITICS

Politics, Culture and Society in the New Europe
Series Editor: John Gaffney, Aston University, Birmingham

This is the first textbook series in Europe explicitly cast in a trans-European mould, eschewing either a West or an East European perspective. The series is distinguished by three major preoccupations: sensitivity to the comparative perspective; a concern to widen the political debate through its theoretical emphasis; and a commitment to extend the paradigm of politics research to include cultural studies approaches. The series will include studies of individual countries, chiefly France, Germany, Italy, Spain, Britain and Russia; comparative European perspectives and studies of the European Union; and treatment of key themes including democracy, political leadership and youth culture.

Forthcoming titles:

Democracy and Modern France by Nick Hewlett

Industrial Relations in France by Nick Parsons

The New Social Democracy in France by Ben Clift

Youth and Society in Post-War France by Chris Warne

WOMEN, EUROPE AND THE NEW LANGUAGES OF POLITICS

HILARY FOOTITT

continuum
LONDON • NEW YORK

CONTINUUM

The Tower Building, 11 York Road, London SE1 7NX

370 Lexington Avenue, New York, NY 10017–6503

First published 2002

British Library Cataloguing-in-Publication Data
A catalogue record for this book is available from the British Library.
    ISBN 0–8264–5296–5 (hardback)
        0–8264–5297–3 (paperback)

Library of Congress Cataloging-in-Publication Data
Footitt, Hilary.
    Women, Europe and the new languages of politics / Hilary Footitt.
        p. cm. — (Politics, culture, and society in the New Europe)
    Includes bibliographical references (p.) and index.
    ISBN 0–8264–5296–5 — ISBN 0–8264–5297–3 (pbk.)
        1. Language and languages—Political aspects. 2. Women legislators—Language. 3. European Parliament. I. Title. II. Series.

    P119.3 .F66 2002
    306.2′082′094—dc21   2001047376

Typeset by CentraServe Ltd, Saffron Walden, Essex
Printed and bound in Great Britain by
Biddles Ltd, *www.biddles.co.uk*

For Lena Powell: the first one, with love

CONTENTS

PREFACE

In this book, I hope to contribute to two ongoing debates: one about the presence and activity of women in politics, and the other about the part which language plays in shaping and developing our political activity.

We can approach or 'read' politics of course in a variety of ways, focusing for example on ideology, or political organizations and structures, or leadership styles, or the media. The starting point for this book is the belief that a study of language is a vital and productive way to help us to understand politics. By paying attention to the languages of politics, to the ways in which we constitute what we call 'politics', I believe that we may be able to cast new light on some of the key questions which concern us today. How do we make representative democracy more inclusive, so that more of us are involved in a democratic process? How do we understand citizenship in a world in which some of the traditional landmarks are disappearing in a haze of globalization? How do we define some of the transnational political spaces that we already inhabit, like the EU, and do these definitions provide any new ways of imagining communities to which we might belong?

At the centre of this exploration of the languages of politics are the women who participate in one of these transnational political sites, the European Parliament. In this book, women are neither victims of the political process, nor marginalized from it. They are the principal actors who, the book surmises, may be able to show us some 'new' languages of politics if we take the time and trouble to hear the ways in which they are talking. I am arguing that we can 'read' distinctive political languages of women: the ways they understand their job in the European Parliament, their 'narratives of representation'; where they locate the citizen in Europe, their 'grammars of citizenship'; and what they understand about operating in a transnational context, their 'imagined communities' of Europe. These are the languages of politics that I shall examine in this book.

A study of this sort is modest in ambition. It does not purport to challenge the roots of political and social inequality. It does not suggest ways to eliminate the problems we face in adapting our political activity to a fast-changing world. It does aim, however, to do two things. Firstly, the book emphasizes the position of women as potentially prime contributors to developing our understanding of democracy. Secondly, it seeks to encourage us to pay attention to the languages we use in constituting politics, and indeed to begin to see language as an integral part of the creative process of political relations.

In a world of shifting roots and multiple identities, the stories we tell, the ways we understand relationships between us, and the communities we imagine ourselves belonging to are of ever-increasing political importance. Language narrates the stories, positions us in relationships, and frames our imaginings. And women, this book suggests, are particularly gifted political linguists.

ACKNOWLEDGEMENTS

This book would not have been written without the kindness and professionalism of women Members of the European Parliament. I come away from the experience with a renewed belief not only in representative democracy, but in the potentially crucial part that women can play in it.

Dr Maria Allen, Marianne Sharpe, Inge Kruse and postgraduate students on the bilingual translation course at the University of Westminster participated in the interviewing and translation processes, and I would like to thank them all.

I am grateful too for the financial support which this book received from the Nuffield Foundation and the University of Westminster.

John Gaffney, the editor of the series, and the two original readers of the project, were extremely helpful in providing focus and direction to the work.

On a personal level, Lena and Martin Powell have encouraged me warmly throughout. Above all, Richard Footitt has accompanied this project every step of the way and I owe him an enormous debt of gratitude.

ABBREVIATIONS

ARE   Radical European Alliance

EDA   European Democratic Alliance

EDN   Europe des Nations

ELDR   European Liberal, Democratic and Reformist

EP   European Parliament

EPP   European People's Party

EU   European Union

EUL   European United Left

FE   Forza Europa

IND   Non-attached

MEP   Member of the European Parliament

NGO   Non-Governmental Organization

PES   Party of European Socialists

Union   Union of Europe

. . . it is only words that can construct a world that makes sense.

Kate Atkinson, *Behind the Scenes at the Museum*

CHAPTER 1

WOMEN, LANGUAGE AND POLITICS

At the outset of a study of this sort, I want to ask the questions: Why bother to bring women, politics and language together? What is there that could be particularly useful in such a potentially difficult combination? This chapter tries to answer these questions in three ways. Firstly, it reviews aspects of the current relationship between feminism and politics. Then, it considers how language has become a key domain of politics. Finally, it suggests what some of the implications might be of bringing together women, language and politics.

FEMINISM AND POLITICS

The only thing that feminists appear to agree on these days is that 'feminism' is a tricky term to define. In the late 1990s, writers signalled how problematic this was with book titles which emphasized the diversity of the term 'feminism': *Feminisms* (Kemp and Squires, 1997), *Intersecting voices: dilemmas of gender, political philosophy, and policy* (Young, 1997). By the time we had reached the cusp of the millennium, commentators were either looking back with puzzled sorrow – *Critical Condition: feminism at the turn of the century* (Gubar, 2000), *Promise of a Dream: a memoir of the sixties* (Rowbotham, 2000) – or giving their books more crisply challenging titles: *What is Feminism?* (Beasley, 1999), *Why Feminism?* (Segal, 1999).

Doubtless this telegraphic titular questioning had much to do with a publishing market in which feminist academic writing was deemed to sell poorly, and with a media context in which feminism was often dismissed as belonging to a 'bra-burning' and irrelevant past, or was blamed for having pushed things 'too far in the other direction' (Fawcett, 2000), with men perceived as losing out to women at work, in schools and in personal relationships.

What is undoubtedly true is that the visceral link between feminism and politics – a link born in the 1960s and established as the women's liberation movement developed beside the broad left movement of political protest – has been apparently irrevocably severed. So complete is this divorce between the two, that it has become normal within university departments to ghettoise any putative relationship in (often unpopular) optional courses entitled 'Women and Politics', 'Feminism and Politics'. As Anne Phillips eloquently suggests, even for the sympathetic 'the political' is often viewed today by feminists as a 'dreary universe' in which they would simply prefer not to engage (Phillips, 1991: 4). It is reasonable for us to ask how this separation between feminism and politics has occurred, and to wonder whether it really matters. Is it still important for us to bring feminism and politics together, and if so, how is this to be accomplished in the coming years?

Surprisingly, perhaps, there is a fair identity of view on the history of feminist theory from the 1960s up to today. Julia Kristeva (Kristeva, 1981) famously argued that there had been three generations of feminist thought. The first, in the 1960s, used, she suggested, a 'logic of identification', and pursued a largely liberal, egalitarian agenda. The second rejected the equality narrative as profoundly patriarchal, and sought to emphasize the difference between men and women, proclaiming the need to create women-based counter societies. The third stage, which others have labelled 'post feminist' (Moi, 1985: 13), called for the abandonment of any totalizing, universal accounts (including that of essentialist feminism) and advocated a deconstruction of theory itself. Whilst Lynne Segal (Segal, 1999) has called for a greater understanding of the continuities between generations of feminists, and a more historically contextualizing view of feminist theory, the three 'waves' which Julia Kristeva identified are still a helpful basis from which to view feminist theory.

For 1960s feminists, Simone de Beauvoir's classic 1949 formulation: 'One is not born, but becomes a woman' (de Beauvoir, 1974) carved out a clear starting point where biological 'sex' would be strongly distinguished from societally and culturally conditioned 'gender'. The implicit presumption of a sexually undifferentiated human nature focused attention on the political, societal, psychological and cultural norms which had produced the perceived inequality of women. Hence feminists in the late 1960s and 1970s studied sites of oppression, ways in which women had been and were being conditioned to be unequal. The (now) classic texts of this period – Shulamith Firestone (1972), Germaine Greer (1970), Juliet Mitchell and Ann Oakley (1976), Mary Daly (1973), Kate Millett (1971) – reflect these assumptions, arguing passionately as they do that women are victims of identities imposed on them by hostile environments. Inevitably, the message is political – if we change the environments in which women operate, they will suffer less from their condition, indeed they may be freed or liberated. Marxist and socialist feminists in this period nuanced this interpretation by locating sexual oppression as one dimension of class power. The radical feminist approach, developing in the late 1970s and early 1980s, focused more pointed attention on patriarchy as a total system, with men defined as the 'main enemy' (Delphy, 1984). Whatever the definition of the culprit, however, it would be fair to say that feminist theory at this stage generally took female oppression as an unproblematic universal given and sought to change those environments – defined in the specific, or in Marxist/socialist or radical terms – which had produced the historic downgrading of women.

By the end of the 1970s and through the 1980s, this political engagement with the sites of oppression came under sustained attack from two quarters. Firstly, and doubtless as a reaction to the formerly negative presentation of the position of women, writers began to carve out positive and active portrayals of women and their potentialities, moving attention away from the oppression of women onto the innate 'otherness' (and often implicit superiority) of women. These writings tended to focus on the bodies of women, and on the radical potentialities of their mothering role. The celebration of gender difference – through Adrienne Rich's 'lesbian continuum' (1977), Catherine MacKinnon's anti-pornography writing (1987), and 'maternalist' political thinkers like Carole Pateman (1988) – arguably drew attention away from the environments of oppression, and centred it in historically and politically decontextualized areas where the essential nature of women could contribute to a fundamental rethinking of the bases of society. Carol Gilligan's enormously influential *In a Different Voice* (Gilligan, 1983) is a typical product of this period, positing as it does a different style of moral reasoning and ethical understanding between men and women.

At the same time as the male/female 'difference' debate was in full swing, the universal oppression thesis that had characterized the first stage of feminist theory was also being challenged by the rise of feminist groups which differed strongly from their predecessors of a decade before. Women who were black, women who were not Western, in short women who did not fit into the 1970s' white woman activist/scholar framework, argued with increasing intensity that the accounts of oppression that had been given them did not fit with the race, ethnic or class particularities of their own situations. In 1982, for example, American 'women of colour' produced an anthology of their work tellingly entitled *All the Women are White, All the Blacks are Men, But some of Us are Brave* (Hull et al., 1982). Thus, from a general concentration on universal external sites of oppression, feminist theory in the late 1970s and through the 1980s turned to celebration of essential difference, and to a sometimes uneasy embrace of the cultural diversity of women's experience.

For both broad groups, identity – whether female as opposed to male, or in terms of ethnically diverse femininities – was key, and it was in this fertile terrain of identity that the influence of French philosophy was to be particularly formative in the mid 1980s through to the 1990s. As they sought to confront issues of identity and feminism, feminist writers and commentators were increasingly attracted to the analytical tools of post-structuralist theories. Derrida's deconstructionist methods, with their emphasis on 'différance' as the inevitable deferral of meaning, challenged descriptions of identity based on experience, which failed to acknowledge that meaning was produced through shifting and multiple discourses. There was in fact no universalizing category 'woman' on which feminism could be based, and no totalizing category of 'power' against which it could be set. As the traditional sociological grounds on which identity might be understood began to crumble, so French feminists in particular turned to Lacan's psychoanalytical post-structuralism in search of a feminine imaginary, a difference which could both draw on the body and propose an alternative and subversive poetics. Hélène Cixous, Luce Irigary and Australian philosophers like Elisabeth Grosz and Moira Gatens (Beasley, 1999) began, in rather different terms, to describe a corporeal and more intimate feminism, where theories of the body, and ways in which we socially produce ourselves through our bodies, replaced an interest in social and political external contexts.

Foucault, using the tools of post-structuralist analysis in a socio-historical context (Foucault, 1980), directed other feminist thinkers towards a notion of the body, and of sexual identity, as an ever shifting and unstable category, radically dependent on changing contexts which are themselves the product of competing sets of regulatory discourses. One of the most influential of the 1990s' feminist theorists, Judith Butler (Butler, 1993), used this genre of analysis to argue that there is no stable feminine identity, but rather a 'gender performativity' through which, by repetition and re-enactment in cultural performances, something akin to sexual identity is temporarily established.

The shift in feminist focus over the last decade of the twentieth century has thus been very considerable. A move away from external sites of oppression to the intimacy of the personal. An attention to words rather than things. A replacement of agreed categories – 'woman'/'power' – by a theoretical consensus that categorization is a doomed a priori exercise. A locus of academic interest based largely in the humanities and arts rather than the social sciences, with symbols and representation prioritized over material or societal concerns. Inevitably in this situation, the gap between feminism, as defined in the 1990s, and politics (understood as some form of collective engagement with change) now appears to be enormous. Sandra Kemp and Judith Squires introduce their late 1990s collection with the nail-in-the-coffin argument that the reflexive has now taken over from the political:

It is significant that the focus of ... questioning is not primarily the central question of early second-wave feminism – 'what is to be done?' but rather the more reflexive, 'what is the basis of my claim to knowledge' and 'who is the "I" that makes such a claim?' This shift from the overtly collectivist and political to the more individualist and philosophical might be viewed negatively as a shift from insurrection to introspection, or positively as the coming of age of feminism as an intellectual endeavour, or perhaps more neutrally as simply symptomatic of the 1990s. However one views the development, it is clear that epistemological, ontological, and representational questions currently serve as a key locus of feminist concern ... (Kemp, 1997: 8)

Quite so, we may say, and what does it matter anyway? In fact, I would argue that it matters a great deal. To begin with, there is a major problem in the way that theories are being described here. Theories do not, after all, appear only or primarily in relation to other theories. Theories are themselves, we might suggest with Foucault, radically contextual. They are discourses produced in relation to particular constraints, both responding to these constraints and constituting new productive contexts. The narratives of feminism are produced by political discourses as much as any other narratives, and contribute, whether we like it or not, to the formulation of new narratives. Put more simply, theories of feminism do not exist in a political vacuum, and they are not innocent of consequences. Juliet Mitchell, for example, memorably argued that feminism had contributed to new forms of capitalism by focusing on gender and its implications to the ultimate downplaying of class and key socio-economic variables (Mitchell, 1986). Whether this is an overstatement or not, the necessity to understand theory as being produced by and producing broader political contexts is indisputable.

The so-called feminist turn away from politics towards the epistemological and ontological which Kemp and Squires (1997) identify might, for example, be constructed as part of a much more general shift away from political and collective engagement in the 1990s which has been provoked by a number of quite different factors. The feminist concentration on the intimate and personal is perhaps not that far removed from the general 1990s' growth in personal affirmative strategies, from self-help books through to alternative religious experiences, all of which tend to prioritize the intimate and eschew the collective and institutional. The disengagement from collectivist political action which feminist commentators describe, and sometimes decry, might be more helpfully constructed as part of a general disengagement from the political process which of course has led many writers in the West to talk of the need to reconceptualize democracy and citizenship. Rather than feminism 'coming of age' in the linear and decontextualized formulation of Kemp and Squires (1997), we might describe feminism currently as being part of a more general 'age of the personal rather than the collective'.

Similarly, the grappling with multiple identities in feminism, which would appear to undermine the very notion of collective action, is not peculiar to feminism. It could indeed be helpfully represented as part of the context of so-called globalization, with globalization's conflicts between apparent homogeneities and very clear particularisms. What is happening in feminist theory is necessarily linked to other movements which affect all areas of our lives. The *European Journal of Women's Studies*, for example, recognized that the context in which feminism is now being constructed is an essentially mobile one when it called for papers for its Special Issue of August 2002 with the words: 'The traffic in feminism . . . the circulation of people, ideas, representations, and practices of feminist movements in post-World War II Europe and between Europe and other parts of the world'.

We cannot detach ourselves from the variety of contexts in which we operate and which we in our turn help to formulate. Feminism then is arguably both influenced by and a constitutive part of the context of power relations, whether it likes it or not. An understanding of this argues for feminism being necessarily involved in politics and power relations. What Joan Tronto called 'The power of context and the context of power' (Tronto, 1993: 4) is key to any strategic engagement in the questioning of definitions, boundaries and agendas, and it is this, we might argue, which is the business of any politics. In this context, feminist engagement or non-engagement with the political is in the nature of a non-choice.

The more salient point here is whether there is any collective praxis in feminism today, any way of defining women as a group, so that they can consciously operate to change the discursive framework of politics. In practice, defining feminism for collective action has not been easy. Leila Rupp and Verta Taylor (Rupp and Taylor, 1999) discussed these difficulties precisely in the context of multiplicity and diversity – the rise of a variety of feminist movements all over the world, which have appeared in response to different stimuli and which address very different issues. Again, it should be noted that these problems are not particular to feminism – the difficulties in defining group identities for action are common across a range of groups today – but they still present real challenges for feminism if women and politics are to be brought together.

Currently, there are two principal ways in which feminists are trying to bring a collective 'woman' into political action. We might schematize these as the 'multiple identities' strategy and the 'contingent identity politics' strategy, and both are worth examining in more detail.

The first, the 'multiple identities' strategy, implies a basic recognition and acceptance of the varied and many identities of women, as opposed to the old binary male–female divide. Elizabeth Spelman argues that it is a mistake to isolate gender from identities of race, class, age, sexuality, ethnicity and so on: '. . . though all women are women, no woman is only a woman. Those of us who have engaged in it must give up the hunt for the generic woman – the one who is all and only woman, who by some miracle of abstraction has no particular identity in terms of race, class, ethnicity, sexual orientation, language, religion, nationality' (Spelman, 1990: 187). The instability of gender as a category is, as she rightly points out, no less true of the other identities (class, age, sexuality and so on) we all own. This approach is an attractive one which seeks to keep diversity at its centre but encourage political engagement to change discriminatory structures and practices. It is at this point, however – how 'multiple identities' translates into collectivity for action – that there are inevitably some problems. Iris Marion Young, for example, argues that there could be a number of collective positions for women: a passive social construction of individuals for example, or a group that recognizes an active commonality around certain issues. One way of actualizing Spelman, she suggests, is for feminists to embrace coalition politics, accepting thereby (and she borrows from Jean-Paul Sartre's notion of serial collectivity) a view of 'gender as seriality':

> Feminist organizing and theorizing thus always refers beyond itself to conditions and experiences that have not been reflected on, and to women whose lives are conditioned by enforced heterosexuality and to a sexual division of labor, who are not feminist and are not part of feminist groups. We should maintain our humility by recognizing that partiality and by remaining open to inquiring about the facts of the series beyond us. (Young, 1997: 36, 37)

In a sense, this optic could complement some of the research which has been carried out on the construction of identity in social movements, with its understanding of collective identity as being embedded in multiple and different layers – organizational, movement and solidarity (Gamson, 1991) – which may or may not be closely integrated, depending on the movement and the issue involved.

The second strategy, 'contingent identity politics' in the context of an evolving feminist struggle, is in effect identity politics through action. Nancie Caraway, for example, posits a form of coalition politics, with the process of coming together for activity providing the collective identity 'woman' for common action: 'Identity politics advances a space for political action, praxis. . . . These emerging theories are about the fluid construction of identity.' By coming together and 'doing', you assume, at least temporarily, the label of feminist in relation to a specific issue – 'feminists in solidarity' (Caraway, 1991: 201). Such an approach necessarily involves accepting the arbitrary nature of political actions and activities – and indeed Caraway's vocabulary ('movement', 'alchemical', 'crossover') underlines the contingent nature of the process she is describing.

Both approaches – 'multiple identities' and 'contingent identity politics' – still seem to pose problems for those of us seeking to define a collective category which could operate to change structures and policies. The (multiple identities) strategy focuses attention on the diversity of our membership of a variety of groups. This allows us to understand our political engagement in an open way, and also to retain a notion of the complexity of operating politically with others. What is gained from this strategy in our understanding of openness and complexity, however, may be lost if our objective is to challenge some of the competing discourses and power relations today. At its worst, such a strategy could lead us to a strictly individual consciousness, with more and more of our overlapping identities proving politically problematic, or, at the other extreme, to a bewildering number of different political coalitions. In this scenario, one of the two extremes, political passivity or political hyperactivity, might well come to replace a strategic engagement with change.

There are equally problems with the other strategy, 'contingent identity politics', solidarity through action. As Caraway expresses it, this feminism in solidarity is effective in relation to the issues it chooses to address. It is, however, wholly dependent on the play of changing circumstance and differing personalities to identify what the points of action should be. To this extent we might argue that it is an essentially arbitrary strategy. The real danger in accepting this type of approach may well be therefore that some of the key sites of power which should be challenged by feminists are actually left unscathed and intact.

In making generalizations about women, and constituting some sort of collective category for political action, we are thus in something of a theoretical impasse, and it is an impasse, as Anne Marie Goetz has suggested (Goetz, 1991), which might well prevent us from addressing the ways in which structures of power are constituted, and in which they might be changed.

As one way out of these dilemmas, Iris Marion Young has argued persuasively that we could adopt what she calls a 'pragmatic' stance: 'By being "pragmatic" I mean categorising, explaining, developing accounts and arguments where the purpose of this theoretical activity is closely related to those problems' (Young, 1997: 16). In other words, a specific problem is identified and stimulates the development of accompanying feminist arguments. In this strategy, there is a readiness to accept the fluidity of collective identity, and an acceptance of the need to adopt whatever analytical methods and theoretical insights might seem best suited to the particular problem on which we are focusing. Rather than bringing feminism and politics together by seeking to conceptualize an a priori collective 'woman', multiple or contingent though this identity could be, we might pragmatically choose to assume a grouping around a specific problem, and then seek to theorize out from the experiences offered by this particular problem.

The pragmatic approach is the one that I am taking in this book. The collective 'woman' I have pragmatically defined as the centre of our project is constituted by those women who are Members of the European Parliament at a particular time. The problem I am addressing is the way in which this collective 'woman' engages in politics in a particular site, the European Parliament. The results of this focus will hopefully contribute to some of the broader issues raised by theories of feminism and politics.

By suggesting that we look at women in what is in effect a site of 'formal politics', we are of course entering a space which has been seen as especially intransigent to feminist enquiry and concerns. As Phillips puts it: 'Certainly, the politics portrayed to us via the daily newspapers and television accounts remain overwhelmingly masculine in personnel and style; while in some parts of the world, women face direct attacks on recently achieved civil rights by parties and governments resisting the implications of sexual equality' (Phillips, 1998: 1).

Arguments about what constitutes 'formal' as opposed to 'informal' politics, about where exactly the 'public' space of politics is, are at the heart of feminism's traditional political concerns, and we shall be discussing this in more detail in Chapter 3. One of our difficulties is, as Squires sensibly argues, that present descriptions of women in politics are deeply paradoxical. When feminists talk about women and politics, they claim both that women are excluded from politics and that feminism is fundamentally political. In doing so, they are employing the term 'politics' in radically different ways: 'The apparent tension between the claim that "feminism is politics" and that politics has been exclusively limited to men lies in the different notions of politics employed here . . . the apparently paradoxical nature of these two statements subjects the political itself to scrutiny' (Squires, 2000: 3).

By bringing women and politics together in the site of the European Parliament, I am in practice conflating these two definitions of politics. The collective 'woman' we are looking at is in a transnational site which is seen as one of so-called traditional 'formal politics'. My contention, however, is that women in this formal politics site are helping to redefine what 'politics' is by their participation. The ways in which they are 'doing politics' are in fact opening up the term to a different set of interpretations and practices. In the typology that Kathy Ferguson (Ferguson, 1993) and

Judith Squires (Squires, 2000) propose, for example, the approach in this book problematizes the notion of politics. Methodologically, it straddles both a 'reversal' strategy (reconfiguring the political to make it more open to gender specificity) and a 'displacement' strategy (deconstructing the discursive regimes) (Squires, 2000: 3). It asks us to pay attention not to the site itself and the role women play within it, but rather to the ways in which women are currently configuring 'politics' in this site, and configuring 'politics' so that it might become more open to the participation of many others.

Bringing feminism and politics together, I have been arguing, is actually inevitable. The real problems lie, however, in defining a collective 'woman' for engagement in politics. By taking a pragmatic approach to this, and choosing a specific political site, we will be defining a particular collective 'woman' in relation to a specific setting – women in the European Parliament – and we hope that this will help us to work outwards from the specific problem and thence be able to make some contribution to broader theoretical issues. The choice of such a 'formal' politics site lies at the centre of ongoing discussions about what constitutes the 'political' for feminists. My contention in this book is that a readiness to pay attention to how women currently 'do politics' in the European Parliament will be useful both in reconfiguring politics and in displacing the political.

To be successful in this endeavour, I believe we must look at the languages of politics. As Kathleen Hall Jamieson suggests, we need to be 'reclaiming language. . . . Language is a tool that changes our focus and our perceptions' (Jamieson, 1995: 192).

LANGUAGE AND POLITICS

Of course language, in the sense of the meaning of words, has always been of concern to political commentators. The semantics of politics – 'democracy', 'citizenship', 'freedom' and so on – was of very considerable interest to political philosophers in the late nineteenth century and throughout the twentieth century. For some, the meanings of these words have been seen to be empirically verifiable as 'true' (Easton, 1968). For others, particularly in the 1970s and 1980s, there was a more relativistic, contextualist approach, which suggested that political meanings are dependent on specific polities, and on the contexts in which they operate (Sartori, 1984; Ball et al., 1989).

More recently, just as feminist theory has been profoundly influenced by French post-structuralist philosophers, so discussions about the meaning of politics have begun to reflect the perspectives of Derrida and Foucault. In this perspective, definitions of politics are neither empirically verifiable, nor relativistically produced by different political contexts. Rather, language has come to be viewed by such political scientists and commentators as an active component in actually constituting the political process. Language itself is a domain of politics. Michael Shapiro, most notably, argues that we must 'textualize' the political arena (Shapiro, 1989: 13), and 'read' the polity (Shapiro, 1992). In this sense, language is an active element in politics:

> If we neglect the political relations that are discursive, that are in what we speak and how we speak, we have seriously diminished the arena of political action. Innovative political action, which has a constitutive effect on political life, consists in linguistic action, in changing the rules that link what we say to our experience. . . . Politics and language are intimately commingled . . . one must analyse language as a domain of political relations. (Shapiro, 1981: 233)

This political standpoint, which emphasizes the constitutive activity of language, has been strongly influenced by the work of two important theorists, Jürgen Habermas and Mikhail Bakhtin. Habermas (Habermas, 1986) most notably developed the concept of the public sphere as a structure within civil society. Beginning with an etymology of the terms 'public' and 'private', Habermas examined how the vocabulary of inherited political categories had helped to create our understanding of the public sphere. For Habermas, the modern bourgeois public sphere is the place in which private individuals come together to exercise their reason in public. Public opinion is the outcome of all the dialogues between these individuals. This notion of the public sphere most importantly emphasizes the power of words, the political implications of language. The discourse model Habermas presents is the 'ideal speech situation' in which interaction can take place without the intrusion of power relations, and where rational discourse can overcome distorted communication.

Bakhtin (Bakhtin, 1981), from a rather different theoretical basis, called for an awareness of language as one of the areas of class struggle. For Bakhtin, texts are heteroglossic, and the many voices contained in them show that any text is made up of a number of other texts or scripts, which can programme us in particular directions, or help us to innovate in new ways. His work on heteroglossia in the novel, for example, argued that some of the English comic novels of the nineteenth century are like 'an encyclopedia of all strata and forms of literary language' (Denith, 1995: 196), showing the diverse forms of social life in conflict at that period.

Ken Hirschkop, reinterpreting Bakhtin through the more contemporary perspective of Habermas, argues that discourse is an active element in the reinvigoration of the democratic agenda (Hirschkop, 2000). The relationship between language and democracy is a vital one in this analysis. The novel, for example, can provide a place in which we see how issues of identity and difference in society can be played out. The public square can be understood in the same way as the public sphere. Discourse, language, helps us to accede to a 'participatory description' of the world: 'It remains only to emphasise how little this historical vision has in common with the purely formal democracy on offer from the liberal state. The democracy of carnival is indeed a collective democracy, grounded in civil society, in which the abstract identity of the citizen is replaced by that of one who eats, drinks, procreates and labours. Utopian in the extreme, it describes a condition in which history is directly experienced in the texture of public social life' (Hirschkop and Shepherd, 1989: 35).

Thus, from an argument over the 'real', empirically verifiable, meaning of key political terms, many political scientists and political philosophers have moved to a position where language is itself a political institution worthy of study, either as a domain of politics, or as a major constitutive part of the political process.

Applying these perspectives to politics, analysing the ways in which language is a political domain, or how exactly it operates as a constitutive element of the political process, is more problematic. There is in fact a range of approaches and methodologies from which we might choose, and all have yielded useful insights to this discussion of language and politics. Each of these approaches contains elements of the other, but the methodologies each uses are strongly influenced by the major disciplinary focus of their exponents, whether this is political science for example, linguistics or ethnography.

For those writers particularly concerned with the understanding of specific political practices, or the construction of different political leadership styles, attention tends to be concentrated on language as a framing device or as a set of characteristic rhetorical practices. Kathleen Hall Jamieson in the United States, for example, has worked extensively on the 'packaging' of the President in successive presidential campaigns (Jamieson, 1996), and on ways in which democratic systems can be influenced by specific media constructs (Jamieson, 1992). In her work on the mayoral race in Philadelphia in 1991, and the health care reform debate in 1993/4, Jamieson has sought to investigate (Jamieson and Capella, 1997) the ways in which the press frames political debates, and the consequences of this on readership perceptions. She takes a 'framing' methodology in her work, a term she uses to describe the structuring of texts – 'news frames are those rhetorical and stylistic choices . . . that alter the interpretation of the topics treated . . .' (Jamieson and Capella, 1997: 39).

In the UK, John Gaffney has done a great deal of work on the languages of political leadership in Europe, arguing that polities function through underpinning myths, and that it is by analysing language that we will begin to understand the nature of these myths: 'wider questions should ... be asked about how a polity functions or is "reproduced" culturally ... how language functions as a vehicle for the discursive deployment of the myths underpinning a polity' (Gaffney, 1991: 3). For both Jamieson and Gaffney, media constructs and cultural myths are constituted by the conscious use of frames and rhetorical devices. As Gaffney suggests in his study of the discourses of communism and socialism in contemporary France: 'we shall be concerned to reveal the rhetoric of the texts to be examined. This will be studied in terms of the texts themselves rather than in terms of audience response. The rhetorical effects of our texts, therefore, will be inferred from their rhetorical qualities' (Gaffney, 1989: 34). Both see language as operating at a symbolic level in politics and being elucidated by a detailed study of rhetoric: 'the proper analysis of political language is interpretative ... the study of political discourse is not a science but an art, akin to literary criticism' (Gaffney and Drake, 1996: 14).

In comparison, people formed primarily by the discipline of linguistics have approached the bringing together of politics and language in slightly different ways, focusing as one might expect, less on the rhetorical/ literary aspects of communication styles, and more on pragmatics (how speakers and hearers interact), semantics (vocabulary/lexis and its meaning), and syntax (the way in which sentences are organized). Paul Chilton and Christina Schaffner (Chilton and Schaffner, 1998) have helpfully set out what they see as three broad approaches taken by writers from the tradition of linguistics; approaches influenced, as they suggest, by the particular historical legacy and cultural specificity of the countries concerned. They argue that there is a 'French School' which has tended, on the one hand, to work on 'political lexicometry', using computer aids to look at the frequency of particular terms across a large corpus of texts – speeches by the Communist Party, for example – in order to adduce differences and changes over time. Another tendency in this 'French School', they suggest, has been to follow Althusserian notions of the 'state apparatus' and produce detailed accounts of the functioning of political systems. In comparison, what they describe as 'German approaches' have developed a historical and often word-centred methodology, reflecting critically on the strategic use of certain keywords in the achievement of political ends. The third group, those using 'Anglophone approaches', have been strongly influenced by the 'functional' linguistics of Michael Halliday which has made the link between linguistic form and socio-political activity. A very influential grouping in this Anglophone School is that of the Critical Discourse Analysts, most notably Norman Fairclough, who argue that detailed discourse analysis is an engaged and committed activity, hence the adjective 'critical'. By analysing discourse, they claim, we are actively intervening in social processes.

Fairclough, for example, in his book on 'Blairspeak', *New Labour, New Language?* (Fairclough, 2000) looks at the communicative style of the British Prime Minister, at the political discourse of the 'Third Way', and at the ways in which Labour governs through language. In a classic summation of how his approach in critical discourse differs from that of a political scientist, he claims: 'Many political theorists and analysts recognise the importance of language in politics and government, especially in contemporary societies. But there is an important difference between much of this work and the approach I have adopted. It is one thing to recognise that language is important, it is another thing to see the detailed analysis of texts as important ... texts are processes in which political work is done' (Fairclough, 2000: 158).

The third methodological approach, what we might broadly call ethnosemantic, integrates language and culture in a tradition developed within cognitive anthropology. This method depends on reviewing linguistic categories provided by informants in order to make sense of their particular cultural worlds. Here, 'cover terms' and 'semantic relationships' (Spradley, 1979) are elicited so that an understanding of informants' 'interpretive frames' (Agar, 1973) can be formulated. David Silverman, for example, has applied this type of methodology to show how particular political discourses – 'whole-patient medicine', or 'democratic decision-making' – can influence vital policy implementation areas (Silverman, 1993: 187). Michael Agar argues that what is being uncovered in this method is 'languacultures', ways in which cultures interpret themselves through language (Agar, 1994).

What these three very different approaches share in bringing language and politics together is an interest not in the meanings of key political terms, but rather in language itself as a vital domain of political life. Starting from this basic recognition, we might focus attention on political frames and rhetoric as one means of configuring the political space. We might engage in a detailed linguistic analysis of the language of texts as a way of concentrating on the textual process through which political work is 'done'. Or, we might take a more anthropological approach, and pay particular attention to the language which chosen informants use to construct their specific political cultures. Later in this chapter, I shall discuss in a little more detail the ways in which this book will be borrowing eclectically from these three approaches in order to develop a methodology which responds to the aims of the project. For the time being, we need to note that there is a recognition in each of these approaches that an attention to language will not of itself change the material bases of sexual and economic exploitation. A study of language will not 'magic away' the forms of inequalities in society which feminists, for example, at different times and in different places have been decrying. But, in these approaches, changing politics, changing political cultures, is being understood as vitally linked to understanding and changing languages.

WOMEN, LANGUAGE AND POLITICS

The field of research into women and language is already a well-developed one. In fact, women and language, or, to put it more formally, language and gender research, seems to have had a troubled relationship with the politics of feminist engagement (Bucholtz et al., 1999: 3). Just as the relationship between feminism and politics has passed through a number of stages, so the interest in women and language has reflected a similar changing debate, moving from acculturation, to male/female difference, then to diversity and onwards to postmodernist concerns with discourse, performativity and shifting identity.

Feminist linguists have typically translated the question that Simone de Beauvoir (de Beauvoir, 1974) originally asked, 'Are there women?', into the linguistic, 'Is there a woman's language?', with responses dividing into 'yes' – and it is the language of the dominated – or 'yes' – and it is a different language, the language of a particular subculture.

Some of the key women and language texts of the 1970s argued that there was indeed a woman's language, and that it was the language of powerlessness and subordination. Robin Lakoff in *Language and Woman's Place* (Lakoff, 1975) suggested that the speech style of women (tag questions like 'isn't it?', etc.) indicated a hesitancy and tentativeness of style in comparison with that of men. Dale Spender in her influential *Man-made Language* (Spender, 1980) argued from a broader contextual framework that women were linguistically positioned as 'deficient', as 'muted' and 'unnamed'. In a later revisiting of this agenda, Deborah Tannen claimed (Tannen, 1990, 1994) that, rather than an intrinsic different, and powerless woman's language, there were cultural differences – differences which have arisen from the ways boys and girls are educated and socialized, and from our consequent expectations of them. For Tannen, the power-lessness that Lakoff sees in the way women talk is actually a more positively rendered difference in orientation – status for men, connectivity for women – a distinction which implicitly relates to Carol Gilligan's earlier work (Gilligan, 1983) on women and moral choices.

Influential as these books were, they were subjected to critique and extension through the 1980s, with the dominant themes of the discussion being that of contextualization and multifunctionality, mirroring the diversity/identity debates of feminism itself. Deborah Cameron and Jennifer Coates, for example, argued that monolithic analyses of 'women's language' and 'men's language' fail to recognize the real diversity of speech styles which exist in relation to different contexts. Jennifer Coates' work on 'Gossip Revisited' (Coates and Cameron, 1988) looked at the cooperative strategies women used together in single-sex talk, and Deborah Cameron (Cameron, 1998) pointed out that particular linguistic elements, like for example the infamous tag question, could have a multiplicity of different functions according to the specific contexts in which they were used. Thus, from the generalization of all women as linguistically powerless (the 'dominance' approach) or essentially different (the 'difference' approach), the debate has started to move into the sort of recognition of diversity with which feminist theory itself is grappling.

Whilst much of the headline-grabbing research has been about women's conversation – spoken interaction, with variations of the traditional methods of empirical linguistic research – a powerful influence on debates about women and language has come from cultural studies and contemporary psychoanalytic theory, in particular from the work of writers like Luce Irigaray, Hélène Cixous, and Julia Kristeva. Reacting against the Lacanian school of psychoanalytic theory, Irigaray has claimed that there is a quasi-anatomical link between the female body and a pluralist feminine language (Irigaray, 1977), whilst Kristeva has called for a new feminine writing – 'écriture féminine' (Kristeva, 1974, 1984) – which can replace the male symbolic order with that of the female.

In practice, these insights of the French psychoanalytic school, whilst giving value to certain putatively feminine qualities, have been less easy to integrate into a developing debate on gender and language. Arguably, it has been with the more general postmodernist emphasis on the discursive production of identity that the question of a woman's language has moved away from the dominance/difference debate, towards an understanding that language itself, like identity, is subject to fragmentation and role-playing, 'performativity' in Judith Butler's terms (Butler, 1993). The notions of identity as unstable – 'fragmented' (Johnson and Meinhoff, 1997: 228) – and performed in different ways at different times and in different contexts, has been increasingly reflected in discussions of gender and language. As Aki Uchida summarised it (Uchida, 1998: 291):

> The issue at hand is not whether we should take the dominance/power-based approach or the difference/cultural approach or both approaches to analyze sex differences in discourse. Rather, it is how we can come up with a framework that allows us to see gender as a holistic and dynamic concept regarding language use – a framework that allows us

to see how we, in the social context, are DOING gender through the use of language.

Today, approaches to the question of language and gender reflect the general mixture of methodological strategies we saw in relation to language and politics. Work derived from sociolinguistics thus stands alongside the research of anthropologists, cultural studies specialists and ethnographers, who are all, in different ways, exploring women and language. As Susan Gall memorably suggests, it is not always clear that all these specialists mean exactly the same thing when they talk about the 'voice', 'words', 'silence' and 'language' of women: 'On opening a book with a title such as "Language and Gender", one is likely to find articles on pronouns, pragmatics, and lexical variation jostling unhappily with articles on textual gynesis, Arabic women's poetry, and the politics of gender self-representation' (Gall, 1995: 169).

However puzzling these different and parallel approaches are, they also offer new possibilities for bringing women and politics together through a study of language. Just as approaches derived from political science, linguistics and ethnography can all contribute to understanding language as a vital domain of politics, so the range of disciplines currently engaged in looking at women and language can offer us insights into the ways in which women are, to quote Uchida, 'doing gender through the use of language'.

CONCLUSIONS

I have suggested that one way in which to advance the feminism/politics argument is to take a pragmatic approach and examine a collective 'woman' constructed in a particular setting – in this case women representatives in the European Parliament. In the terms used by some linguists and ethnographers, this group might be considered as a potential 'speech-community' or 'subculture'.

Given the range of perspectives we have seen which are being developed to examine language and politics and language and women, it seems reasonable for us to take advantage of this richness by adopting an eclectic approach to the analysis of women's languages in politics. Like Shapiro, I am going to be viewing the polity of the European Parliament as a text in which we should be able to 'read' the languages of women. This 'reading' will imply, as Jamieson and Gaffney contend, that we should be strongly aware of the frames that are being used, and of the rhetorical devices within the texts, that we should be taking a literary, interpretative approach to our material. Like Gaffney, my approach to the languages of women in the European Parliament is a fundamentally interpretative one. At the same time, the insights of linguistic-centred discourse analysis suggest that there could be some profit in applying a more detailed linguistic analysis to some of our material, so that this interpretative design is complemented by a simple quantitative analysis. Finally, an ethno-semantic understanding of the subculture of women in the European Parliament would encourage us to see women MEPs (Members of the European Parliament) as informants who can talk to us directly about aspects of their own culture.

The mixing of methodologies inevitably suggests that we can with profit examine different types of material: written speeches, for example, set alongside interviews and discussions with women Members of the European Parliament. This deliberate mixing of types of material and methodologies is of course by no means new. As Sara Mills has argued (Mills, 1999: 93):

> A combination of quantitative and qualitative research methods is probably more useful . . . for example, a sociolinguistic empirical piece of research could possibly isolate the most important variables, and come to some general tentative conclusions about interaction. However, the next stage might involve following it up with a questionnaire or a series of interviews . . .

I shall then be using a literary, interpretative framework – 'reading' the languages of women as narratives, grammars and imaginings. The material (which we shall look at in more detail in the following chapter) will be composed of speeches by men and women in the European Parliament, as well as a set of interviews with women MEPs. In 'reading' this material, we shall use some of the insights of ethno-semantics – domains and cover terms, for example – and some of the techniques of linguistic discourse analysis, in particular that of transitivity analysis.

It seems inevitable that we will need to embrace an eclectic approach if we want to explore a rich and diverse set of documents, both written and oral. If language is a vital and creative domain of politics, and if we believe that women are making a particular contribution to it, we should have no hesitation in being methodologically adventurous. A readiness to experiment methodologically is after all in the best traditions of feminist scholarship. Linda Singer memorably proposed the image of the 'Bandita' for the feminist writer, an intellectual outlaw who raids the texts of others and takes what she finds most useful: 'The remains recycled make a different map, and mark new intersections between discourses, disciplines, forms of "knowledge"' (Singer, 1993: 22). The spirit of Bandita discovery is one that I feel is particularly suited to the bringing together of feminism and politics through language.

CHAPTER 2

WOMEN IN THE EUROPEAN UNION

I have argued in the previous chapter that language can be considered to be a constitutive element in politics, and that one potentially productive way of exploring women's engagement in politics today is to examine how they are 'doing politics' through language. The women whose languages we are going to study are political representatives in the European Parliament. For some readers, the choice of the European Parliament as a site for this consideration of women's languages of politics will seem doubly strange. Firstly, as we have already seen, formal politics of the type conducted in political assemblies like the European Parliament have been treated with suspicion, if not despair, by many feminist commentators. Secondly, if women have often seemed marginal to national formal politics, they have been almost invisible in the world of international formal politics. On both counts, therefore, the focus I am using here may appear to be particularly bizarre.

In this chapter, I shall be explaining why I believe that the European Parliament is a potentially fruitful site for a study of women's languages of politics. To begin with, we shall discuss what writers and commentators are currently saying about women in Europe, and where they are locating women in the space of the EU, within the frameworks of European integration, and through the analysis of member states of the Union, and of the institutions themselves. I shall then suggest the reasons why women in the European Parliament may be in a position to develop potentially new and interesting languages of politics, languages which could contribute to some of the major issues which concern so many of us today: how to make democracy more representative; how to conceptualize citizenship beyond the nation-state; and how to understand the notion of belonging to transnational communities.

THEORIES OF EUROPEAN INTEGRATION

The European Union is one of the few international formal sites of politics. Whilst 'formal' politics has often appeared stubbornly intransigent to women's concerns, entering the world of international relations has traditionally meant participating in a virtually female-free endeavour. As J. Ann Tickener suggested, there has been a long-standing relationship between the realist international relations paradigm and images of masculinity: 'Nowhere in the public realm are these stereotypical gender images more apparent than in the realm of international politics, where the characteristics associated with hegemonic masculinity are projected onto the behavior of states whose success as political actors is measured in terms of their power capabilities and capacity for self-help and autonomy' (Tickener, 1992: 6, 7).

It should be said, however, that, alongside the dominant realist paradigm of international relations, there has also been a liberal-pluralist conception which has understood international relations as a network of transnational linkages with a wide range of political actors and social movements. This view, which effectively challenges the shibboleths of 'high' and 'low' politics, facilitated gender as a global issue entering the field of international relations. Since the end of the UN Decade for Women in 1985, there have indeed been a number of UN-sponsored conferences at the intergovernmental and non-governmental organization (NGO) level which bring groups of women together in a transnational setting to discuss gender.

The EU operates then within this international relations context both of realist paradigm and of transnational network. If we ask the question, 'Where are women located in this transnational site?' we would probably respond with some of Gillian Rose's spatial terms (Rose, 1993) – 'in the blindspots' . . . 'in the interstices' . . . 'in the chinks'. This issue of the ways in which the EU has been theorized is not, I would argue, a matter of incidental concern to those of us with an interest in the politics of power. As Catherine Hoskyns has suggested: 'The dominant discourses and debates in an academic field have a crucial influence on how events are interpreted and what issues are given prominence' (Hoskyns, 1996: 17). In a very real way, the theorizing around European integration, for example, has set the agenda for research and played a considerable role in shaping people's perceptions and, more importantly, their shared understanding of what is permissible to be said in the ongoing debate on the shape of Europe.

Since the inception of the European project, American, British and other European academics have been engaged in trying to provide frameworks to help us understand a phenomenon which was firstly unique in its structures, and secondly burdened by a heavy weight of aspirations and anticipated outcomes. These expectations have inevitably influenced some of the theoretical speculation, with desired inevitabilism mixing with the language of analysis, so that descriptions of the Union at any one time are set within a context of expected (and hoped for) change, or seen against an end result which is implicit, if often unstated. In looking at theory in this area, then, we might note with Clive Church that 'integration theory oscillates uneasily between the analytic and the normative. . . . What is classified as theory, in fact, is often less an explanation of what is happening than a plea that Europe should follow a particular course of action, or a strategy by which given ends may best be served' (Church, 1996: 8).

The theories themselves are often expressed in the vocabulary of movement and change, as academics seek to frame a process that they believe to be (and want to be) developing. Paul Taylor, explaining the nature of David Mitrany's functionalist theory, which was a powerful early explanation of Europe, argued that 'functionalism sees the solution of a problem, not in the obtaining of specific, unchanging conditions . . . but in the DYNAMIC "PROCESS" elements between one condition and the next' (Taylor and Groom, 1978: 268).

Eugen Haas, in his neo-functionalist reworking of this theory, stressed the process elements of integration, maintaining that 'political integration is the PROCESS whereby political actors in several distinct national settings are persuaded to SHIFT their loyalties, expectations and political activities towards a new centre' (Haas, 1968: 16). Federalists like Dusan Sidjanski, although envisaging a very different sort of community from that of the functionalists and the neo-functionalists, also depicted a community which was moving and creating new synergies (Sidjanski, 1992: 440). Policy analysts like William Wallace assumed that there was a dynamic of integration in which the perceived movement to integration in Europe has been accompanied by a similar burgeoning of academic theories (Wallace, 1990a: ix). For some writers, like Wolfgang Wessels, it is possible to see these alternative types of dynamic represented in a diagrammatic form: the linear growth of neo-federal and neo-functionalist theorists, the cyclical up and down of governance theorists, and the decline (to nation-state) curve of the realists (Wessels, 1997: 268).

What is perhaps intriguing about all these theories of dynamic movement is their general failure to engage with the corpus of feminist theory which, as we have already seen in the previous chapter, has been itself in a considerable state of flux and change. Clive Church, for example, in his review of European integration theory in the 1990s, noted the problematic theoretical contribution of postmodernism and globalization in 'changing the focus' of integration theories (Church, 1996: 35), but made no mention whatsoever of feminism.

The invisibility of women in many of the integration theory debates on the EU is a particular loss in view of what some would feel with Rosi Braidotti is 'the empty rhetoric' of the European Union (Braidotti, 1992: 8). If the EU is to be configured as a shared and inclusive cultural space, it is arguably of some importance that the insights of feminism should be seen to contribute to these dynamic analytico-normative debates of European theory. To put it at its most stark, how can we begin to build an inclusive European space when one of the main British journals devoted to EU studies (the *Journal of Common Market Studies*) can boast only two articles on women throughout a 25-year span? If the EU is to be framed in such a way that its development concerns all the population, there are strong arguments for re-visioning the frameworks of EU integration theory in a context which recognizes the importance and potential contribution of feminist engagements with politics and theory.

FRAMEWORKS OF ANALYSIS: THE NATION-STATE

Women are not, however, completely absent from discourses on the EU. If they have failed to influence integration theories, they have still entered the academic debates on Europe, firstly (and perhaps ironically) via the nation-state itself. Here a framework of analysis is used which is basically comparative, with women's situations across the individual nation-states of Europe being compared and contrasted. These nation-state based frameworks have often proved productive in increasing our knowledge about women in the space of Europe, and it is worth examining these frameworks in some detail.

There are four major strategies which characterize the current analysis of gender in Europe through the prism of the nation-state. Each one, as we shall see, uses the framework of the nation-state, but locates women in slightly different positions in the space of Europe. The first is what we might describe as the mosaic approach. The mosaic approach assumes that there is a diversity of women's experience across Europe, but it posits the possibility of what we might term contingent commonality, that women might have common interests built around common causes. This framework has proved particularly fruitful in shedding light on the economic and social status of women in Europe. The collection by Maria Dolors García-Ramon and Janice Monk, *Women of the European Union: The politics of work and daily life* (García-Ramon and Monk, 1996), is an excellent example of this sort of analysis, bringing together as it does case studies on France, Germany, Portugal, Holland, Denmark and Spain, within a comparative context. The contributors to the collection are trying to construct a 'mosaic' of women's work and daily life in the European Union, using a mixture of national, regional and local data, and examining both spatial and temporal scales. The editors of the book acknowledge the difficulties inherent in the comparative cross-national method, and insist on the need to combine transnational, cross-national, regional and local data with qualitative as well as quantitative research. The balance that they seek to strike is that of research in which the comparative context helps us both to understand diversity, and to establish common cause among women across boundaries. The methodology is cross-national comparison – the prioritizing of diverse national contexts – and the result is a mosaic understanding which enables readers to see for themselves common patterns of women's experience in the EU; common ways, within the diversity, in which women are being constructed in the space of Europe. Women are thus placed within the space of Europe in a mosaic of nation-state experiences, with some possible but contingent common interests.

Secondly, the cross-national comparative method has been used to place women politically in the space of Europe. As in the trail-blazing work of Joni Lovenduski (Lovenduski, 1986), this has usually been accomplished by taking traditional political science indicators – patterns of political behaviour, of interest group representation, and of political representation – and comparing them by gender across the nation-states. The approach has been increasingly supported by the production of cross-national comparative gender data on women's representation at local, regional and national level, supplied either on an EU basis (by such networks as 'Women in Decision-Making'), or across the (currently) 40 members of the Council of Europe in specially commissioned reports (Council of Europe, 1998).

On the whole, the result of this work has been less a mosaic of women's diverse economic and social presence in Europe, and rather more a portrayal of women as absent, invisible in the space of Europe, or certainly less visible in some countries than in others. Comparative data of this type is indeed often reused at a national level as ammunition in an ongoing polemic on political equality in specific countries and national situations. The 'parité' movement in France, for example, has made telling use of the comparisons between female political representation in France and in France's 14 EU neighbours (Guéraiche, 1999; Bataille and Gaspard, 1999). As Mariette Sineau has argued, 'Comparison with the other countries of the EU makes the record in France seem even blacker' (Sineau, 1997: 92; my translation). With this work, women are located in the space of Europe again through the nation-state, and very largely this time in terms of their relative absences.

The third strategy is what we might term the convergence/impact approach. This uses nation-state comparisons but sets them more squarely in the context of potentially joint policy developments, judging them in terms of their convergence to a common ideal, or in terms of the impact which EU measures may have had upon national policy-making. Some of the contributions to the stimulating 'Women, Power and Public Policy' special issue of the *Journal of European Public Policy* (*Journal of European Public Policy*, 2000) exemplify the strength of these approaches. Thus, for example, Vicky Randall looks at childcare policy in the nation-states of the EU, notes the historic differences between the rates and range of provision in different countries, and asks to what extent there has been a coming together, a convergence, of childcare policies in Europe over the past ten to fifteen years. In this type of analysis, public policy in the separate nation-states is compared against a convergence model, where the results will be a judgement on the extent (limited in this particular case) to which childcare policies come together. Rather than the implicit assumption of women in Europe as diverse, with common causes only incidentally thrown up (the 'mosaic' assumption), the convergence framework places them within the nation-states, but implies a common (and implicitly better) overarching standard to which we might all subscribe.

The fourth strategy is what we might call the reverse of this framework. It takes the framework of the nation-states, but employs an exclusion thesis rather than one of convergence. This research implicitly accepts the construction of a cross-national European space, but concerns itself largely with the exclusions which operate from this space, usually via the intermediary policies of the nation-states. In these studies, gender is often a particular category within such exclusions. Elenore Kofman and Rosemary Sales, for example, have argued cogently that the treatment of migrant women by the countries of the EU indicates a strongly gendered construction of the excluded 'other' (Kofman and Sales, 1998). Here, convergence of the nation-states within the space of Europe is represented as convergence to exclude, a convergence which has markedly deleterious effects for women as a doubly excluded category.

FRAMEWORKS OF ANALYSIS: THE EU

Women also enter the discursive space of the EU in ways quite separate from the nation-state, and comparisons between nation-state situations. More recent analyses seek to place women centrally within the ongoing dynamic narratives of the EU, arguing that the Union itself, as a developing entity, is a framework within which issues of gender can and should be considered. This research has placed women in the space of Europe in relation to two, often related, debates. The first is that of equality, of equal opportunities. The second relates to definitions of citizenship.

Some of the major work on women in Europe has concerned the equality agenda of the EU, with scholars suggesting that the nature of the EU – a legal structure of integration – has been a particularly propitious site for the development of women's rights and for the production of legal texts on equal rights/treatment for women. Catherine Hoskyns, in her careful assessment of the EU's policies for women, argues the 'swings and roundabouts' of the legal efficacy of the Union as far as equality legislation is concerned: 'The strength of the EU legal system from the point of view of women lies in the binding nature of the rules which are set, and in the possibilities which arise from the interaction of different systems of law; its weakness lies in the fact that the rules are hard to apply and disappointingly limited when matched to the substantive needs of particular groups of women' (Hoskyns, 1996: 13). Hoskyns traces the development of a policy on women's rights at European level from the presence of the famous Article 119 on equal pay in the Treaty of Rome. She notes that the original debate around the Article had never taken the needs of women into account, but that the work of activist women in the EU context ensured that an equality discourse could grow from it. The story Hoskyns tells is one of legal statutes – European Directives on equal treatment for men and women at work – accompanied by transnational activity, both within the European institutions themselves, and within transnational lobby groups and organisations. Thus the Ad Hoc Committee on Women's Rights was set up in the European Parliament after the first direct elections in 1979. The Committee, in its very existence, its open meetings, and its reports, undoubtedly established a space in which the issues of equal treatment for women and men at work could be widened and extended to questions of female choice and autonomy across the social, economic and political spheres. In 1984, the Committee became a permanent standing committee of the Parliament. Hoskyns goes on to examine the parallel activities of transnational lobby groups – the Centre for Research on European Women, the European Network of Women, the European Women's Lobby – and suggests that considerable progress has been made in many areas of direct relevance to women through both the formal and informal mechanisms of the EU.

In essence, Hoskyns' conclusion draws an institution which, because of the very complexity and multiplicity of its political sites, has been a particularly interesting place in which women's rights can develop. This does not mean that women, and feminist analyses, are central to the space of Europe, however. What Hoskyns is suggesting is that the edifice of the EU has 'cracks' which can be exploited, and from which 'seepage' and 'spillage' (Hoskyns, 1996: 210, 209) to related questions can flow. In this interpretation, gender is not actually integrated in the EU so much as having a toehold in a multilevel, multi-sited polity. Women are located at the edges and borders of the EU, working hard at infiltrating their concerns out to the rest of the institutional space.

Following on from this equality-outwards approach, there is a not inconsiderable amount of research into inequalities in various transnational EU groupings, in the public services, for example, or in trade union organizations. The opportunities offered by the multi-site EU enables researchers to examine these issues both in terms of the national/European interface, and through the activities of relevant transnational groups. Jane Pillinger's work (Pillinger, 2000) considers factors emerging from the project on equal opportunities and collective bargaining undertaken by the European Foundation of Living and Working Conditions. In this context, she analyses the activities of one transnational group, the European Federation of Public Service Unions, in the light of gender mainstreaming imperatives. In this type of research, the 'seepage' element of women's concerns in the EU, identified by Hoskyns, is being considered as a key issue in industrial relations at a European level, and women are located in transnational organizations, militating with others for change.

Another area of research in which women have been seen by some scholars to be central to the space of Europe is within the evolving discourses of citizenship. Elizabeth Meehan most notably (Meehan, 1993) has sought to exploit the multilevel diffuse nature of the European space to look again at our different notions of citizenship. Feminist concerns, she claims, are of prime importance in redefining citizenship within the context of Europe. Arguing as she does that the Treaty of Rome, even as extended by committee activity, has enshrined the principle of the citizen-as-worker, she considers whether the transnational networks which have developed, like the European Childcare Network for example, have been able, in practical terms, to expand definitions of citizenship to include issues beyond equality at work. In the end, Meehan seems to come down on the side of qualified optimism, a belief in the permissive qualities of the political space of Europe, and in its potentialities for providing evolving definitions of citizenship, through a combination of Treaty stipulations and activist achievements. Women are seen in this formulation as one of the parties, and one of the key parties, engaged in a continuing and evolving redefinition of citizenship in Europe, and indeed this citizenship theme is one to which we shall be returning in Chapter 4.

WHY THE EUROPEAN PARLIAMENT?

What is interesting about much of the work we have reviewed is its relative failure to position women in the centre of the space of Europe. In most cases, women are seen as interpolating themselves (via equality legislation and parallel activism) in an already existing political space, operating as one of the many groups in the multilevel system of the EU. For those of us interested in the interface between feminism and representative politics, this positioning of women at the edges of the space of Europe is particularly regrettable in relation to discussions of the European Parliament. Richard Corbett's book on the role of the European Parliament in closer EU integration (Corbett, 1998) is a classic example of this omission. Corbett, an MEP himself, reviews the theoretical frameworks which have traditionally explained EU integration – intergovernmentalism, interdependence theories, neo-functionalism, federalism, constituent federalism – and then goes on to test a series of hypotheses associated with these theories, 'starting from the most "pessimistic" from an integration point of view and finishing with more "optimistic" ones, though the progression cannot be strictly linear' (Corbett, 1998: 58). His book has no reference either to women or to feminist theory.

There have, however, been studies which have looked more closely at women in the European Parliament and have suggested that the role of women in the Parliament, if not linked directly to theoretical discussions of integration, could still be of major importance in developing our understanding of women and political representation. As with some of the general frameworks that we have considered above, these studies often use the perspective of the nation-state, and are usually comparative, looking at the situation in one nation-state as compared with that in the European Parliament. Niilo Kauppi, for example, (Kauppi, 1999) compares the position of French women representatives in the European Parliament with their position in the National Assembly in France. His conclusions position the European Parliament as a possible catalyst for political change at the national level: 'The European Parliament creates pressures for augmenting the representation of women in other sectors in the French political field. The significance of the European Parliament in national politics in a unifying Europe might be that it provides a forum for the partial overturning of a multitude of nationally determined political values and hierarchies . . .' (Kauppi, 1999: 339). Here women are seen at the centre of one of the European spaces, the European Parliament, influencing the nation-state.

Catherine Hoskyns and Shirin Rai (Hoskyns and Rai, 1998) take the nation-state/EU comparison a stage further by using a comparison between the Indian Parliament and the European Parliament to examine the relationship between the conceptual categories of gender and class which they claim are normally hidden by the universalizing language of democracy and governance. The authors take a historical perspective to the development of women's position in the European Parliament. They note that women's under-representation in the European Parliament had been recognized as a particular political issue, and treated as such, with advertisements for the 1994 election, for example, asking: 'Why does 81 per cent of Parliament have to shave each morning?' By comparison, the issue of class, they claim, had been effectively swept under the carpet. In this framework, the European Parliament is being described as a site which has seen the recognition of gender as a category of analysis, but one in which recognition is still some way away from redistribution of resources. If gender is currently placed in the 'interstices' of the EU, Hoskyns' implicit argument on the European Parliament seems to be that gender in the European Parliament should expand its spaces by seeking common cause with groups based on other definitions: 'This is important if feminist politics are not to become divorced from the lived realities of the majority of women' (Hoskyns and Rai, 1998: 363).

The most complete study in English of women in the European Parliament is that by Elizabeth Vallance and Elizabeth Davies (Vallance and Davies, 1986). Using data from the 1979 and 1984 elections, the authors examine the political, educational and class background of the women members, and assess the various routes they took to enter the European Parliament. The book is constructed around the implicit hypothesis that women in any Parliament are likely to want to introduce what one might term 'women's concerns' into the political debate. The overall evidence they provide on this is nuanced. Women in the European Parliament are not exclusively or predominantly concerned with women's interests, they claim, but it is, however, clear that a good deal of equality legislation has been supported and helped by women Members of the European Parliament. In this discussion, women are placed centrally in the space of the European Parliament, but within a framework which links them to 'women's concerns' and equality issues.

In a sense, this trail-blazing book, the first which provided a more developed understanding of who the women in the European Parliament were, is posited on the idea that a woman's particular contribution to politics is likely to be in the area of these 'women's interests': 'It is . . . an investigation of whether women make a difference in politics and to what extent they introduce women's concerns into the political arena and press for women's interests in a systematic way' (Vallance and Davies, 1986: viii). Women 'making a difference' is closely identified with 'women's concerns'.

As Vallance and Davies make clear, despite the relative lack of interest on the part of academic commentators, the European Parliament is a very interesting place for the study of women and politics. Firstly, as we have seen from some of the comparisons with nation-states, the overall representation of women in the European Parliament has tended to be higher than that in most of the member states, hence the more optimistic suggestions of possible spillover from the European Parliament back to some of the severely unrepresentative national assemblies. With 25 per cent of its membership female (from the 1994 elections, on which this study is based), the European Parliament has a proportion of women higher than that of many national parliaments in Europe. Comparative figures suggest that of the twelve countries in full membership of the Parliament in 1994, only Denmark (with 33 per cent), Germany (with 26.5 per cent), and the Netherlands (with 31.3 per cent) had a female participation in their national assemblies higher than that of the European Parliament, although the later three members of the Union are at or above this rate: Austria 26.5 per cent, Finland 33.5 per cent, Sweden 40.4 per cent.

Secondly, the European Parliament, particularly after the formation of its Women's Committee in 1984, has had, as we have suggested, a particularly developed reputation for taking seriously issues relating to women voters. The Women's Committee clearly created a space in which women could mark out areas of discussion for and about themselves, and meet other women from transnational groups. Whether the current mainstreaming agenda of the EU will change that space very noticeably is still unclear, but the fact of engendering the public space in this particular way has been a considerable and, compared with many nation-state parliaments, unusual achievement. In both membership and legislative interest, the European Parliament can be said then to be a more 'women-friendly' parliament than that of most of the nation-states within the EU.

It is not only, however, the relatively greater presence and apparent influence of women members which makes the European Parliament a potentially interesting site for the study of women and politics. In the individual member states of the EU, national parliaments tend to be long-established bodies which have developed their traditions and working practices over a relatively long period of time. For women, the difficulties of entering into one of these already established political spaces can be perceived as very considerable. Some of the new women Labour MPs who were elected to the British Parliament in May 1997, for example, seem to have found the experience of working in the Westminster Parliament extremely difficult. Not long after the election they were voicing their disenchantment with the place and the job: 'The House of Commons is a male institution . . . managed by men, for men'; 'I have been desperately unhappy since being elected . . . I hate this place' (Fawcett, 1997).

In comparison with national parliaments, the European Parliament is an institution with a very short history, and one that is largely unencumbered by the long-established traditions of most national assemblies. It is in a sense a new and evolving experiment. As Francis Jacobs suggests: 'The European Parliament is the first, and so far the only experiment in transnational democracy. No other institution in the world brings together under one roof representatives from different states . . . who have been directly elected to that institution. . . . Nowhere is there an equivalent body, eager both to exercise its powers beyond the reach of individual governments and to extend its influence over the decisions that are taken above the national level' (Jacobs et al., 1992: xviii). Unlike the parliaments of the member states, the European Parliament is an experiment, an institution in flux. Rather than traditions to defend, it has new powers and responsibilities which are constantly being added to and developed.

Vallance and Davies indeed suggest in their study that it is precisely these factors – a relatively new parliament, unencumbered by traditions established before women's entry, and one that works in different ways – which have made the European Parliament a potentially propitious environment for women's activity. As Joyce Quin (then an MEP) remarked, the European Parliament is not constructed like the Westminster Parliament as a men's club with places that are ' "holy of holies" where women aren't supposed to go' (Vallance and Davies, 1986: 10). The point about a political space which is new and evolving is an important one from the perspective of women's engagement in politics. Joni Lovenduski and Vicky Randall have argued (Lovenduski and Randall, 1993: 174) that it is actually when the rules of politics are being contested, and when there is an opportunity to change structures, that women are more likely to be able to enter politics on what might be described as rather more their own terms. It is this sense of the European Parliament as a 'new' and changing site of politics which makes it such an attractive place to study potentially new women's languages of politics.

The impression of the European Parliament as an interesting place in which to study women in politics is paradoxically strengthened by its somewhat peculiar position within academic and political discourse. To a large extent, the European Parliament operates within what might be termed a narrative of eccentricity. Although often described as important to the overall development of the EU, its importance is understood in undetermined and vague ways. The European Parliament is placed outside 'normal' political processes. Richard Corbett (Corbett, 1998: 46–52) noted quite recently that the European Parliament has been given very little attention in the abundant integration literature, even in the years following direct elections. Intergovernmentalists were of course deeply suspicious of a directly elected parliament in Europe. Neo-functionalists tended to pay greater attention to the potentially important role of the Commission, as opposed to the Parliament, and even federalist commentators were often divided on the advisability of establishing a parliament within current EU institutional arrangements. The European Parliament, either absent from the literature, or relegated to footnotes within it, was conceived, at the time of direct elections in 1979, as, at best, a journey into unknown territory.

With direct elections, the presentation of the European Parliament has become more visible but arguably no less eccentric. For many, its directly elected status simply reinforced its eccentricity. It was called a parliament, but did not conform to the general national models with which commentators were familiar. Barbara Castle, sitting in the European Parliament after a distinguished career in national politics in Britain, was especially robust in her definition of what the European Parliament was not: 'I continued to sniff round what to me was a parody of a parliament.... There was no government-versus-opposition battle going on ... the lack of cut and thrust in parliamentary debate ...' (Castle, 1993: 519).

This view of the European Parliament as *sui generis*, as operating in an entirely different context, and with very different processes from those of national parliaments, is the one most frequently presented, even by broadly sympathetic contemporary commentators. It is an institution which operates in a space outside 'normal' political discourse, placed within frameworks which are unique, and with a role which is historically different from national parliaments. As Francis Jacobs summarizes it: 'Parliament operates within the broader framework of the European Community whose institutions have no exact counterpart in national political systems.... Moreover, the Parliament has a further role which makes it distinctive from national parliaments, namely that it is interested in system change, i.e. in modifying the nature of the relationships that exist between it and the other Community institutions' (Jacobs et al., 1992: 2).

Arguably, the position of the European Parliament, outside 'normal' political discourse, with little tradition on which to draw and with a role which is at least partly defined as system change, mirrors in many ways the traditional position of women in 'formal' politics – not the norm, outside conventional political traditions, often working differently, and generally interested in changing traditional ways of conducting national politics. In terms of positioning, one might almost say that the Parliament resembles Richard Rorty's 'contingent' community, multifaceted, shifting and viscerally aware of the contingency of its languages of politics (Rorty, 1989: chap. 3): a suitably postmodern political site perhaps in which to examine women, language and politics.

To summarize, then, in answering the question 'Why choose the European Parliament to study the languages of women?' we might say, firstly, that the EU is a unique transnational site of politics, and one that is evolving and developing. Secondly, it seems clear that the academic theories which currently seek to understand it – integration theories – are still largely untouched by the concerns of feminist theory. Thirdly, whilst we might usefully compare the languages of women and politics in separate nation-states, the European Parliament provides us with a formal transnational site which brings together women from across 15 countries in Western Europe in a shared political space. Fourthly, the choice of one of the transnational sites of the European Union enables us to place women centrally in the debate, rather than approaching women's contribution to the EU via spillage and seepage from the equality debate. Fifthly, the European Parliament is a particularly suitable site for this sort of investigation, since it brings women together in a political space which is new and evolving, which has none of the long-established parliamentary traditions of its national counterparts, and which is an institution still developing its working methods. The European Parliament is understood to be *sui generis*, and to have, at least to some extent, a mission of system-change. It seems particularly apposite therefore to consider the potentially 'new' languages of women in politics in a site like this which is operating in a transnational political 'no-man's land', eccentric and evolving.

WOMEN IN THE EUROPEAN PARLIAMENT

The transnational European Parliament – currently with representatives from 15 countries – is a political site which is radically and visibly dependent on language. With eleven working languages (Danish, Dutch, English, Finnish, French, German, Greek, Italian, Portuguese, Spanish, Swedish), the Parliament operates through interpreters in its Plenary sessions and in its committee and group meetings. It translates a vast number of documents in addition to the minutes of Plenary sessions, reports and standing orders, etc. Around a third of the total staff employed by the European Parliament are in fact in its linguistic services. A study of women's language in the European Parliament must therefore start with both the fact of different nationalities of women and the consequent use of different languages and interpretation and translation facilities. In this context, is it actually possible to talk about women's languages across such a nationally varied transnational space? If you like, the subgroup of women we have chosen (Members of the European Parliament) may indeed be heterogeneous, but does the heterogeneity of its mother tongues make it possible to conduct a transnational study of women's languages of politics?

To answer these questions, we shall look at the two types of documen-

Table 2.1

Nationality	Percentage of women MEPs	Percentage in the sample
Belgian	6	7
British	11	15
Danish	5	10
Dutch	7	12
French	19	8
German	24	20
Greek	3	1.5
Irish	3	3
Italian	6	7
Luxembourgeoise	1	1.5
Portuguese	1	3
Spanish	14	12

tation I have used in this study to see both the composition of the category 'women' with which we are dealing, and the ways in which we will approach the linguistic challenges it may represent. To begin with, as we have seen in Chapter 1, the project has involved interviewing women Members of the European Parliament (MEPs) as informants of the culture and political languages of women in the European Parliament. The approach taken to this was firstly to try and interview a group of MEPs which would approximately represent the balance of women representatives in each of the nationalities and political groupings in the European Parliament. As I began the project in 1994, before the then latest acceding countries had had an opportunity to directly elect their representatives, I have limited the group to women from the twelve countries which at that stage had directly elected representatives sitting in the Parliament: Belgium, Denmark, France, Germany, Greece, Holland, Ireland, Italy, Luxembourg, Portugal, Spain and the United Kingdom (and not Austria, Finland and Sweden).

In the end, a total of 60 women MEPs were interviewed, approximately 41 per cent of the directly elected female membership of the European Parliament from the 1994 election. Table 2.1 shows the nationalities from which the women were drawn, the approximate percentage of women MEPs from each nationality in the 1994 female cohort in the European Parliament, compared with the percentage from each nationality in the sample of women interviewed (further details at Appendix 1).

In order to ensure that each woman spoke freely, the interviews were conducted in the first language of the MEP, either by a native speaker of that language or a bilingual. A small research team, incidentally all female, which mirrored the nationalities of the women MEPs, was brought together both to interview the women and to discuss the results. The format used in the interviews was open-ended, with questions asked in the same way, and in the same order for all participants: 'How would you describe the job of an MEP?' 'What is Europe/Where is Europe?' 'How would you describe citizenship in the context of your work in Europe?' 'What is politics for you?' 'How do you feel being a woman influences your behaviour in Parliament?' The members of the research group then transcribed the interviews in the original language. For the purposes of this book, translations into English were then produced by the researchers. In all cases, care was taken to make the translations literal so that the English version kept as closely as possible to the original. This approach of literal translation in order to facilitate transnational comparisons is one which has been used successfully by other researchers (Van Dijk, 1997: 31–64). As a further check in this activity, translations were discussed among different members of the research group.

Members of the European Parliament sit in transnational political groups, formed by broad ideological groupings. These groups bring MEPs from different national political parties together in transnational political blocs. In choosing the women MEPs who were interviewed, therefore, I tried to ensure that there was a political grouping balance which was approximately commensurate with the balance of female representation in different political groups in the European Parliament. Women MEPs interviewed came from the major transnational groupings in the 1994 Parliament: the Group of the European People's Party, the EPP, a broadly right of centre conservative group; the Group of the Party of European Socialists, the PES, a group from European left of centre socialist parties; the Group of the European Liberal, Democratic and Reformist Party, ELDR, in the liberal centre of politics; and the Greens, containing representatives of European Green parties. In addition, a limited number of women were interviewed from four of the smaller transnational groupings in the Parliament: firstly, the European United Left, (EUL), mainly consisting of representatives from Communist or former Communist parties, and the Union for Europe, with members who positioned themselves politically to the right of the EPP. Secondly, a small group of women from the federation of regionalist parties, the ARE, and from a group on the extreme Right, the Europe des Nations, EDN, were also interviewed. Table 2.2 lists the transnational groups from which the women interviewed came, with the approximate percentage of women MEPs contributed by each group to the overall cohort, compared with the approximate percentage of women from each group in the sample.

Table 2.2

Parties	Percentage of women MEPs	Percentage in the sample
EPP	26	28
PES	36	33
ELDR	6	12
Green	7	9
EUL	6	7
Union	6	5
ARE	3	3
EDN	3	3

Note: Women sitting as Independents not included in percentage of women MEPs

Because of the 'waves' of feminist history that we have looked at in Chapter 1, I was concerned to ensure that the women interviewed came, as far as possible, from a mixture of political generations. Table 2.3 sets out the mixture of ages in the group.

Finally, we noted the professional or other backgrounds of the women before they entered the European Parliament. Table 2.4 gives an impression of the range of backgrounds of the women concerned. The high number of these who had had a political career before coming to the European Parliament (defined as having been a representative/in office at national or regional or local level) incidentally reflects the observation of many commentators that there is a relatively large number of members of the EP with previous political experience in the European Parliament (see, for example, Jacobs *et al.*, 1992: 47).

At the end of the day, the group of women MEPs who were interviewed contains a mixture of nationalities and ideological/political affili-

Table 2.3

Age	Number of women
Under 25	0
25–35	2
36–45	13
46–54	23
55–65	19
Over 65	3

Table 2.4

Professional background	Number of women
Political	25
Civil servant	7
Education	6
Communication industries	5
Business	5
Caring professions	5
Interpreters/translators	2
Liberal professions	2
Trade Union	1
Culture	1
Church	1

ations which can be said to be broadly representative of those of the 1994 elected cohort of women MEPs. It is the words of these women which will form a major part of our study of women's languages of politics in Europe.

The second source for the project is a corpus of written material which was designed to complement the interviews, and to provide a broader picture of the languages used by both women and men in the European Parliament – namely, the speeches of MEPs in the Plenary sessions of the European Parliament, which normally take place once a month throughout the year. The verbatim report of the proceedings of each parliamentary session is produced on a daily basis during the week of the sittings. This report, known as the 'Rainbow', contains the members' speeches in the original languages in which they were given. The Rainbow is subsequently translated into all the official languages of the EU, and published as an annex to the *Official Journal of the European Communities*. With this material, then, it is possible to have a complete translation in English of all the speeches and, at the same time, to have easy access to the originals, so that similarity of structures, stylistic closeness of translation and so on can be cross-checked where necessary.

Speeches in the European Parliament are slightly different in format from those in many of the national parliaments. The rules and practice of the European Parliament mean, for example, that the time for individual MEPs to speak is strictly controlled and the scope for spontaneity and the cut and thrust of argument is limited. For these reasons, the tendency is for MEPs to write out their speeches and read them into the record. From the point of view of this project, of course, the lack of spontaneity and the careful crafting of the speeches in question make them of more, rather than less, interest in a discussion of the languages of politics.

With a potentially very large body of material of this sort, a decision has to be made on the choice and number of the Plenary sessions to be studied. At the outset, I examined the verbatim record of seven Plenary sessions: 14–18 November 1994; and then the complete run of sessions from January to April 1995. The total number of speeches or interventions in this run of Plenaries was 3295. After this initial analysis, I selected three Plenary sessions as case studies. The concerns in selection were firstly to ensure that one of the case studies came from early on in the life of this particular parliamentary cohort, when some MEPs at least would be new to the institution. Secondly, the selection sought to examine in greater detail records from full sessions (held in Strasbourg), rather than part sessions (held in Brussels). Thirdly, and most importantly of all, the sessions selected as case studies needed to provide a good cross-section of the range of issues with which the European Parliament customarily deals – institutional, national, economic, foreign, social, cultural, human rights, budgetary, agricultural and so on.

Using these three criteria, the case study Plenary sessions selected were: 14–18 November 1994; 14–17 March 1995; and 3–7 April 1995. The contents of each session are given below to give an idea of the range of issues covered in the speeches.

14–18 November 1994
Resumption of session; order of business; verification of credentials; road vehicles over 3.5 tonnes; approval of the minutes; decision on Urgency; annual report of Court of Auditors; draft supplementary and amending budget; translation centre; Thermie II; votes; Thermie II; safety at sea; additives; excavating machine noise emissions; Europe against AIDS; approval of the minutes; topical and urgent debates; cooperation with the Mediterranean basin and Mercosur; situation in Bosnia-Herzegovina; votes; EEA agreements; carriage of dangerous goods by road; emissions of pollutants; ozone layer; dangerous chemical products; incineration of hazardous waste; trans-European data networks; GATT agreement; question time.

14–17 March 1995
Opening of annual session; approval of the minutes; decision on Urgency; carriage of dangerous goods by road; railway licensing and infrastructure capacity; equal opportunities; stability pact; Copenhagen summit; votes; multilateral surveillance; situation in Croatia; Customs Union with Turkey; question time; approval of the minutes; Commission work programme; protection of financial interests; votes; attack by

the Canadian navy; lifelong learning; competition report; agenda; tele-communications; approval of the minutes; monetary turbulence; Mochovce Nuclear Power Station; topical and urgent debate; tobacco; cooperatives and mutual societies; seeds and plants; financial regulation; macrofinancial assistance to Belarus.

3–7 April 1995
Order of business; shipment of waste; conservation of Mediterranean fishery resources; approval of the minutes; partnership agreements with the NIS; stability pact; right to vote for citizens of the EU in municipal elections; Nuclear Non-Proliferation Treaty; budget; question time; topical and urgent debate; 1992 discharge; accession of Central and Eastern European countries; market in wine; sugar products in chemical industry; support for peace in N. Ireland; Thermie II; ship-building; broad economic policy guidelines; two or three wheel vehi-cles; cableway passenger transport; telecommunications and cable TV; aid to Madeira.

In total, these case studies provided some 1208 speeches by both men and women MEPs from the twelve countries (Belgium, Denmark, France, Germany, Greece, Holland, Ireland, Italy, Luxembourg, Portugal, Spain and the UK) which had directly elected members in the 1994 cohort of MEPs. Such a corpus of material should complement the interviews with women, and enable us to put our findings in a broader and comparative context, where languages of women can be compared with those of men.

STUDYING THE LANGUAGES OF WOMEN

The approach I have adopted to studying the languages of women is to focus on four of the key questions in the debates about women and politics. Firstly, is there a women's language of politics in the European Parliament which can help us to understand in different ways the space of politics, the roles of representation and the process of democracy? How can we engender democracy? (Chapter 3). Secondly, do languages of women contribute to our fast-changing discussions on the nature of citizen-ship? What are the relationships between women, language and citizenship? (Chapter 4). Thirdly, what do women's languages of politics offer to our understanding of how we belong to the transnational community, to our understanding of European identity? (Chapter 5). Finally, does the study of the transnational speech community of women MEPs suggest that this pragmatic category of 'woman' can be a useful term of analysis? To what extent do nationality, political grouping and age nuance the languages of politics we will have heard? (Chapter 6).

Women are at the centre of these discussions (see Appendix 2 for examples of the interview material) and so we shall start off each of these debates by listening to the words of the women MEPs interviewed to see what their narratives of representation are in relation to their jobs as MEPs (Chapter 3); to see what grammars of citizenship they are proposing, that is to say where they locate themselves and the citizen (Chapter 4); and to understand how they imagine the community of Europe (Chapter 5). Using the leads given by the women themselves in the interviews, we shall then look at the corpus of Plenary speeches to see whether in each case these narratives, grammars and imaginings appear to be different for men and for women, to see whether in fact there are distinct languages of women in politics in the EU.

In examining the Plenary speeches, we shall often be using a simple counting technique – counting types of metaphor, items of vocabulary and categories of structure. It should be noted that this quantitative addition to a project with such a clearly qualitative design is not intended to provide statistically valid data. Its objective is to offer an insight into what David Silverman calls the 'direction of difference' (Silverman, 1993: 164), the broad ways in which men and women may colour the texture of their languages.

After looking at this 'direction of difference' between male and female languages of politics in the narratives of representation, the grammars of citizenship, and the imaginings of Europe, we shall revisit the argument about the possibility of positing a collective 'woman', and see the extent to which our conclusions on difference are likely to be nuanced by nationality, political ideology and affiliation, and age.

There are of course risks in this sort of enterprise. Whether the risk of concentrating in the next chapters on the languages of women in politics will be proved justified depends a great deal on the conclusions we can make, and in particular on the applicability of these conclusions to the wider debates on women, politics and democracy. The key 'So what? Where does it lead?' questions will be faced in the final chapter, 'Conclusions'.

CHAPTER 3

ENGENDERING DEMOCRACY: NARRATIVES OF REPRESENTATION

This chapter addresses the important question of how democracy is to be 'engendered', to borrow Anne Phillips' expression (Phillips, 1991). Do women in politics represent a group interest, 'women', which can be said to be distinct and different from men? Do women in politics believe that they behave differently from men, and if so, is this self-awareness likely to affect political behaviour in an identifiable way? To answer these questions, we begin by a brief review of the theoretical and empirical contexts in which these issues of gender and democracy are being discussed. We then examine the various 'scripts' of representation that women are given as MEPs, including very specifically the script of gender. I argue in this chapter that gendering representation is not primarily a matter of the sex of the representative, or of the MEP's self-awareness as a woman. Rather, I suggest, the gendering of democracy may take place through the ways in which women narrate the job of representative, and in the distinct languages in which women imagine the political processes in which they are engaged.

WOMEN, DEMOCRACY AND REPRESENTATION

The discussion on 'Engendering Democracy' has become an increasingly lively one. The well-known paradox from which it starts, as we have seen, is the fact that women are both absent from politics, and present in politics – apparently absent from formal politics, apparently present in so-called 'informal' politics. Certainly, the figures on women's continued invisibility in formal politics make stark reading. The Council of Europe reported in March 1998 that only 15 per cent of parliamentary seats over its 40 member states' parliaments (9656 seats) were then held by women. The percentage of women in government at that time varied from 50 per cent in Sweden to zero in Cyprus, Hungary, Moldova, Poland, Romania and Slovenia, with 27 countries having less than 20 per cent female members of government (Council of Europe, 1998).

The traditional explanation for this absence has been that women are not drawn to politics or/and that they are simply not knowledgeable enough to participate in formal political arenas. A British Government Central Statistical Office Report states baldly that 'women are not particularly interested in Politics' (Stephenson, 1996: 15), and Judith Squires has noted the findings of a MORI poll in the UK, accompanying the 75th anniversary of women's rights, which shows that 76 per cent of women are not involved in any form of party political activity (Squires, 2000: 196). On the basis of interview work in France, Janine Mossuz-Lavau and Anne de Kervasdoué suggested that women seemed to have cognitive difficulties in accessing some of the key debates in formal politics – for example women rarely alluded to economic questions in their discussions, as if this was 'a language to which they did not (yet?) have the key' (Mossuz-Lavau and de Kervasdoué, 1997: 159; my translation). Other writers, whilst agreeing that women do not seem interested in formal politics, argue that their lack of interest is not unrelated to the fact that the agenda common to party politics is one which men have defined and articulated, so that it is little wonder that 'many women are bound to be disconnected from traditional politics' (Wilkinson and Diplock, 1996: 10).

The desire to bridge the gap between women's non-participation in formal politics, and their clear contribution to informal politics, has encouraged new debates on how these representative and participatory strands of politics can be brought together through innovative definitions of 'representation' and 'democracy'. This trend has marked a new engagement by some feminists in the traditional, and formerly often shunned, debates on formal politics. In theoretical terms, the discussion has largely centred on the how and what of female representation in democratic processes. How should women's identities and interests be represented? What sort of representation is acceptable, and what is being represented anyway when we talk about the category 'women'? Anne Phillips suggests that four main reasons are advanced to support the equal participation of women in formal politics (Phillips, 1995, 1998). Firstly, arguments about female role models and arguments about justice. These two approaches both centre on the need to share social resources, with politics seen, in many ways, as a profession, much like any other in which equal opportunities considerations are vital. The other two arguments, however, view the democratic process as being qualitatively different from other professions – politics, according to these debates, is a far more important area for women's engagement than, say, management or the law, or any of the other professions over which equal opportunities campaigners have fought. To begin with, it is claimed, one can describe particular shared women's interests, and these interests would be considerably better represented by women than by men. The basis of this argument, as Virginia

Sapiro suggests (Sapiro, 1998), is not that of the representation of the individual woman, but rather that of the group of women who can be defined as having different and distinct interests from those of men. The problem with this argument, as commentators like Phillips (Phillips, 1998) and Iris Marion Young (Young, 1998) point out, is that, in practice, it is difficult to define such group interests in ways which would ensure sensible representation and effective democratic accountability. Groups are, after all, products of particular social relations, and most people within any given group have multiple and varied identities.

The most appealing, and in many ways radical, of the arguments being advanced for the equal participation of women in politics is based not on the notion of group interest, but rather on the likely group contribution which women would make to the democratic process – their potential as women to revitalize the whole democratic system. Both Young (Young, 1990) and Phillips (Phillips, 1995) believe that women's voices in politics, the rather different ways in which women may engage in the democratic process when they are present in a critical mass, could change the nature of democracy for the better. In this approach then, a politics of presence is combined with a politics of transformative ideas. Both Young and Phillips try to avoid the dangers of essentialism firstly by suggesting that there should be encouragement for these groups to represent a range of needs as well as interests, and secondly by rejecting any too clear correlation between group size and numbers of representatives. To critics like Chantal Mouffe (Mouffe, 1992) who argue that this is nothing more than interest-group pluralism, Young maintains that she is proposing the representation of social groups, based on shared cultural norms, rather than interest groups. What is on offer here in these attempts to synthesize the politics of presence with a politics of ideas is a form of deliberative democracy, with social groups participating in a political dialogue, rather than representing separate interest groups.

The hope, then, in current discussions about women and formal politics is that feminism can in some way contribute to revitalizing democracy. As Mary Dietz puts it: 'Democracy ... awaits its "prime movers" ... one such mover might be feminism' (Dietz, 1998: 394). The major concern attaching to this desire remains what we might term the bind of difference/essentialism: 'We have to find a political language that can recognize heterogeneity and difference, but does not thereby capitulate to an essentialism that defines each of us by one aspect alone' (Phillips, 1991: 168).

In parallel with this theoretical work on feminism as a potential revitalizer of representative democracy, empirical studies both in Europe and the United States have been assessing the current reality 'on the ground' of women's participation in democracy. Broadly speaking, these studies have concerned themselves with two questions. Firstly, and by far and away the more explored of the two: what stops women participating in formal politics? What are the impediments which prevent them from becoming candidates, getting office, etc.? Understandably, these studies tend to deal with the structural and systemic constraints which might militate against female participation in formal politics. Thus, for example, Joni Lovenduski and Pippa Norris have variously examined such issues as political party procedures which help or hinder the selection of women as candidates, and the effect of different voting systems on female representation (Lovenduski and Norris, 1993, 1995, 1996).

In the United States, political scientists have produced models to relate sexual discrimination to elite recruitment procedures (Welch, 1978); looked at specific key potential bottlenecks, like campaign finance (Burrell, 1994, 1998); and sought to gauge the ways in which voters perceive female, as opposed to male, candidates for office (Plutzer and Zip, 1996; Cook, 1998). Inevitably, some of the empirical work has focused on the mediating role of the press and public communication systems, with detailed examination of the comparative images of men and women running for office (Kern and Edley, 1994), and of the types of political advertising used by women as opposed to men (Procter *et al.*, 1994; Williams, 1998).

A generally smaller body of empirical work has been generated by the second key question surrounding women's current participation in formal politics: what do they do when they're there? Is there evidence that women make any difference when elected or holding office? These studies generally concentrate on the extent to which women, once elected, conduct themselves in ways demonstrably different from those of their male colleagues. Do women in fact make a difference to the ways in which we 'do' formal politics? American political scientists, for example, have compared the voting behaviour of women in Congress or in state legislatures (often in a broad historical context to test the 'mass makes a difference' argument) with that of men (Clark, 1998). They have examined the background, aspirations and behaviour of women state legislators (Darcey *et al.*, 1994; Thomas, 1994; Carey *et al.*, 1998), and concentrated on the ways, presumed to be distinctive, in which women occupy key political positions such as those of committee chairs (Whicker, 1998; Rosenthall, 1998).

In many of the studies, an underpinning assumption has been that women are likely to make at least one difference in politics: they will consciously pursue a 'woman's political agenda', variously defined as an agenda of women-friendly policies or equality issues. As we have seen (Chapter 2), Elizabeth Vallance and Elizabeth Davies, for example, argued that, whilst the women they had studied in the European Parliament did not devote themselves exclusively to women's issues, there was evidence that 'their concerted perception of themselves as women, with particular experience and concerns, has greatly affected the emphasis of European politics' (Vallance and Davies, 1986: 132). In these cases, it should be noted, the difference that women in politics can make is being judged in terms of particular outputs, measured by the number of issues raised relating to women (evidenced by written questions), and by the level and extent of equality legislation written and enacted.

Other work has been done testing whether the difference that women may make to politics is connected less to women's equality issues, and more fundamentally to the ways in which political questions in general can be perceived, framed and acted upon – whether in fact women understand political issues in ways different from those of men. These studies, often informed by Carol Gilligan's 'different voices' argument (Gilligan, 1983), have generally focused on a specific political issue, and sought to discover whether women have a different approach from that of men in understanding and resolving the issue concerned. Lyn Kathlene, for example, has used the state legislature of Colorado as a site to examine the different approaches of male and female legislators to the framing of crime policy, arguing, on the basis of a content analysis, and a noun frequency test, that 'the women emphasised the societal link to crime. . . . The view of the world as connected and interacting. . . . Their solutions were contextual, multifaceted and long-term' (Kathlene, 1995: 721). This contrasted, she suggested, with the more strongly instrumental, justice-driven approach of male legislators. Kathlene further claimed that these differences were apparent in the distinctive ways in which women and men approached the gathering of information to inform policy formulation (Kathlene, 1989) and in the speaking behaviour of male and female chairs of committees (Kathlene, 1998).

The approach that this book takes to analysing the 'on the ground' work of women in formal politics is closer in conception to Kathlene's holistic perspective. It views the contribution women are making to politics in a wider optic than 'women's issues' or support for equal opportunities, positing the view that the languages of women in politics may be a distinctive contribution to developing our political processes, to bringing together a politics of presence and a politics of ideas in a new and potentially inclusive democratic dialogue.

Using the case study of women Members of the European Parliament, we shall start to explore the potential for reconfiguring 'representation' and 'democracy' offered by women's languages, both what they say about their role in formal politics, and through the possibly different ways in which they and men may frame the political processes in which they are involved. In the context of current theoretical discussions and empirical work, we shall be asking two questions. Firstly, what do women say about their representative roles? What are the key domains in which they describe their job? What are the stories, the narratives about being a political representative, that they tell? Secondly, is there evidence 'on the ground' that women conceive of the political processes in different ways from those of men? Do they narrate politics in slightly different ways? Are they, as it were, 'speaking' politics differently?

SCRIPTS OF REPRESENTATION

Women MEPs and their male colleagues do not operate in the European Parliament in a vacuum. There are a number of generally held and accepted views of what being a 'representative' means and entails, 'scripts' which are given to MEPs and from which they may read their roles. As we saw in Chapter 2, the European Parliament is unique in parliamentary democracy in its transnational structure, and its international composition. Inevitably, therefore, it brings together a range of these scripts of democratic representation. Firstly, there are a number of national scripts about what is the accepted function and behaviour of representatives in each of the different countries of the EU. Secondly, there are political scripts about how 'socialist', 'conservative', 'liberal', 'green', etc., Members of Parliament are supposed to do their jobs. These scripts pre-position women MEPs as much as their male counterparts, and naturally provide them with basic national and political understandings of their roles as representatives.

To begin with, politically systemic national differences place MEPs from different countries on very different points in the representative/represented relationship. Only two member states (UK and Ireland) had (before the 1999 election) a formal constituency-based system for European elections, although a number of other countries established their lists with locally based candidates. For those from a constituency-based system, there is a pre-existing framework of geographically based political representation ('surgeries', 'newsletters', 'mailbag') which conditions some of their activity, and our expectations of these MEPs. Richard Corbett, in a small case study of UK MEPs (total 18) for example, noted their work as follows:

> all but four held no regular surgeries but meet constituents by appointment, meeting between 6 and 90 people a week, averaging 20;
> all but one circulate a local newsletter on a monthly, quarterly or biannual basis. Circulations varied from 1200 to 40,000 (averaging 5400) targeted at party members, business/trade unions, local authorities, voluntary organizations, libraries, church groups, schools and universi-

ties (with only marginal variation in target groups from one member to another);

their mailbag varied from 200 letters per month to 4000 (excluding junk mail and circulars) (averaging 1090) with the proportion estimated as local ranging from one third (in the case of a committee chairman) to 80 per cent (averaging 54 per cent);

the members averaged 24.6 constituency speaking engagements per month typically with small companies, voluntary organizations, schools and colleges, church groups, etc. (Corbett, 1998: 80)

Clearly, for constituency-based MEPs there is a framework of systems and of expectations which, despite the size of the Euro constituencies, positions them as 'local' representatives, with the associated relationships with constituents. Certainly British and Irish women MEPs use some of the language of constituency-based politics to describe their role. Thus one Irish Green MEP makes the constituency nature of her positioning a distinguishing feature in comparison with that of her continental colleagues: 'We're different from our continental colleagues. We're constituency-based, although the constituents still say, "we never see you",' and a British PES member says that she 'represents half a million people in Birmingham ... the job of a constituency MP'. Even among these two national groups, however, (British and Irish) there is a sense that national definitions of 'constituency' need to be modified to convey the complexity of their activity as representatives in Europe. For both conservative and socialist members, the notion of 'constituency' is hardly appropriate in the European Parliament: '(it's) a misnomer ... it's the equivalent of six Westminster constituencies' (British, EPP); '(it's) a unique role in overviewing an area, four boroughs. It's a mixing role, telling one borough about another' (British, PES).

It would be a mistake, however, to assume that the language of constituency representation is limited only to national groups which (for the 1994 elections) had a constituency-based system. Other women MEPs also position themselves with the traditional language of constituency activity – 'seeing people at home', 'correspondence', and 'feedback'. One German PES member, for example, describes her week in terms very similar to those of British and Irish members: 'a lot of constituency work. ... Of course people must understand that an MEP is not available to the same extent as an MP'; and a Spanish EUL representative describes the job of an MEP as hard, 'because if we want to keep in touch with the citizens, there is the necessity of travelling to Spain every week, and using the weekend for feedback'.

Systemically, though, MEPs from some continental countries are positioned further away from the 'local' citizen because of the operation of a list system which substitutes departing members with the next name on the list. Historically, the most notorious example of the rolling list system was that of the French Gaullist Party's which decided, in the first directly elected parliament, to replace each candidate elected after one year by the next name on the list, and to continue this year on year. In this framework, there is no delineated citizen/representative relationship, and no associated set of citizen expectations.

Rather than the local constituency link, there is a systemic tradition in some countries of positioning the MEP as related directly to national politics, either through the dual mandate system (not permitted in all member states), or through the election of major national political figures, like Rocard, Tindemans or Soares for example, or through the election of well-known regional politicians. In these cases, MEPs are placed in a relationship with national and regional politics by virtue of their present national or regional posts, or past regional or national experience, and the drawing of the elector in this framework is a much less geographically defined portrait.

In some cases, women MEPs express this national positioning in terms of an issue-based representative brief given to them. Thus a Danish EDN member argues that she is representing 'those in Denmark opposed to the EU', whilst, at the opposite end of the political spectrum, her Belgian PES colleague defines the job as one of convincing her compatriots of the benefits of more integration: 'I see myself firstly as an exponent/interpreter of the expectations of the people of Europe ... people need to be informed, convinced of the importance of more Belgian cooperation.'

For others, it is a broader and less defined role which is envisaged. To a Dutch ELDR member, for example, the function of an MEP is both European and national: 'Defending the interests of and responding to queries from European citizens in general and from Dutch people in particular.' More usually, women MEPs describe their representative role in the classic terms of 'those elected', or those who 'represent the interests of' or 'carry the voice of' the citizen: 'you have to make your voice heard, because you shouldn't forget that the EP is the only institution of the EU which is really representative of the citizens, in that we are elected by the people' (French, ARE); '(the job is to) carry the voice of the citizen from the single state into the European ambit' (Italian, EUL); 'In principle it is similar to the job of any MP in any parliament, namely to represent the interests of the citizens within an institution and also the other way round, to represent the interests of an institution, if one considers them right ... towards the citizens' (German, EPP).

Beside the citizen/representative positioning, the expanding network of interest groups and lobbies places MEPs in a series of other potential positions which are broadly issue-related. Some of these are occasional and informal – MEPs are the recipients of lobbying information at a local or European level, in mass briefings (receptions in Strasbourg, for example), or on a one-to-one basis. Others are semi-structured through the intergroups, of which there are currently around 50 in the European Parliament, which bring together MEPs and interest groups to discuss particular themes, ranging from specific issues (animal welfare, family policies), to the defence of activities (cycling, hunting), to the friendship groups for extra-EU countries – Friends of Israel, Baltic States, for example. For all the MEPs, there is the formal membership of European Parliament committees which inevitably focus the MEP's attention on specific sets of issues and associated legislation, and provide a focal point for much lobbying and interest-group activity. MEPs are all full members of at least one specialized committee, and sometimes of a second committee as well. They also act as substitutes on one or more committees. It is on the committees that much of the detailed work of the Parliament is done, and it is here that MEPs engage with issues relating to their committees' areas of concern: Foreign affairs and security; Agriculture and rural development; Budgets; Economic, monetary affairs and industrial policy; Energy, research and technology; External economic relations; Legal affairs and citizens' rights; Social affairs, employment and working environment; Regional policy and relations with local authorities; Transport and tourism; Environment, public health and consumer protection; Culture, youth and media; Development and cooperation; Civil liberties and internal affairs; Budgetary control; Institutional affairs; Fisheries; Rules of procedure, verification of credentials and immunities; Women's rights; Petitions; and Employment.

To some extent this networking with lobbyists and interest groups around particular issues is equally common in national parliaments, although the very open nature of the European Parliament's activities has made the development of this area especially marked. On an EU level, it is certainly true that the European Parliament is the most porous of the institutions as regards interest group links. There are thus scripts about relationships with issues and interest groups which position MEPs and establish ways in which we relate to them.

Attachment to specific issues is an integral part of many of the self-definitions given by women MEPs. Sometimes, this issue interest is expressed as membership of particular parliamentary committees: 'I am a member of the Budget Committee, and substitute member of the Committee for Energy Research and Technology, and for the Women's Committee' (German, PES). In other cases, however, the description suggests interests which have grown in the framework of the European Parliament's own development, as when an Irish EPP member explains her work in the area of abducted children as something that started as a result of the European Parliament's response to the plight of Algerian mothers. Some women MEPs' interests have come with greater specialization within the committee structure: 'I am in the two committees for Development and Cooperation and Culture, Youth and Media. In one field, I am more concerned with clearing of land mines . . . and in the cultural field, I find it important that something of the enthusiasm which we as students have felt will be kept alive in the coming generation' (German, EPP).

The MEP, both male and female, is also positioned on an international stage, firstly in the sense that Plenary sessions are open to visitors from across the Union, who can sit in the public gallery and listen to debates, or wander around the Parliament buildings. Nicole Fontaine gives a useful breakdown of the nationalities visiting the European Parliament during sessions, including those coming on the specially designed youth programme, with overall figures for one year of 150,000 visitors (Fontaine, 1994: 9). Secondly, MEPs are placed within an international framework by media coverage, which has certainly increased – as measured by numbers of TV reports of sessions and numbers of hours of TV coverage. Whilst MEPs may be placed on this international stage, and read from this international script, however, the amount of media attention they might personally expect to receive in their first-language presses, and in those of other countries, is relatively slight. The international stage is perhaps more often related to the 'spectacle' of Strasbourg – an internal international site – than to the global communications system.

As far as the relationship with the national elector is concerned, then, the scripts from which members read in the European Parliament are mixed. Some MEPs are positioned in a slightly attenuated constituency representative role, with the work and expectations that go with this. Others are linked, by experience, or dual mandate, to a national or regional citizenry. Most MEPs are positioned by their scripts within the network of interest groups and lobby organizations, which have proliferated in Strasbourg and Brussels, according to the particular issues which the individual MEP chooses to follow, or the parliamentary committees on which she sits. And finally, the MEP is, to a greater or lesser extent, on an international stage, either, more normally, by virtue of being seen in Plenary sessions by the multi-national visitors, or because their activities are noted and reported on in the national presses.

These scripts for the role of an MEP are also affected by the political positioning of their job. Each MEP belongs to a national political party, and then generally to a transnational party federation or group. National political party expectations of MEPs differ considerably, depending on the distinct national and party traditions. The fact, however, that the business of the European Parliament is largely conducted through transnational groups, who set the parliamentary agenda, choose rapporteurs, and allocate speaking time, has the effect of attenuating the control of individual national party machines over their members' activities in the European Parliament. If one adds to this the relatively weak leadership structures in these transnational political groups, it becomes clear that MEPs can exercise a very considerable measure of political independence, compared with many of their national counterparts. As Francis Jacobs suggests:

> individual members do play a considerable role in the life of the European Parliament, especially compared to their equivalents in national parliaments like the House of Commons where the need to maintain government majorities leads to much tighter whipping systems, and to less freedom of manoeuvre for individual members. . . . Another factor which encourages independence is the relative weakness of leadership structures within the European Parliament as a whole, and also within the Political Groups. (Jacobs *et al.*, 1992: 48, 49)

Interestingly enough, out of the 60 women MEPs interviewed, only 16 (27 per cent) positioned themselves within a political party framework in defining their jobs as MEPs. Certain nationalities predominated in this description – Germans, Dutch and British – and others – French, Luxemborgeoise, Danish and Belgian – made no mention at all of the relevance of political party or transnational grouping. Perhaps unsurprisingly, MEPs belonging to the smaller transnational federations – EUL, ARE, EDN – did not mention belonging either to a national party or to a transnational grouping. On the whole, the party references that are made concern national affiliations. Thus a British PES member, for example: 'I stand as a member of the Labour Party. I represent the manifesto of the Labour Party'; and a Dutch EPP representative, positioning herself with the words: 'I am (1) a member of Parliament, (2) a member of the second largest party (both for men and women), (3) a member of the CDA delegation within the party in the EP.'

Certainly, the structures of the European Parliament provide a political space in which members can have greater freedom from party political scripts than is the case in most national settings.

Overall, then, women MEPs, as much as men, find themselves prepositioned in relation to a variety of national and political scripts which are themselves diversified and redefined in the particular international and transnational site of the European Parliament. It is within this unusual and mixed setting that women MEPs express their narratives of representation.

THE GENDER SCRIPT

One of the scripts which women representatives are often given is that of gender. This can be expressed, for example, as representing women, or representing women's issues, or behaving in politics in demonstrably female ways. Are women in the European Parliament consciously engendering their roles as MEPs? Is there evidence that they perceive a collective 'woman's identity' which influences their scripts of representation? To reverse the output model that we noticed Vallance and Davies using in the last chapter (Vallance and Davies, 1986), can we discern the input of a shared a priori sense of what being a woman means in political representation?

When women MEPs were asked the question: 'How do you think being a woman affects your work in the European Parliament?' 45 of the 60 questioned (i.e. 75 per cent) said they perceived a difference between a man's and a woman's relationship to the political process. We shall be looking at the influence of age, nationality and party on this type of response in Chapter 6, but at this stage we might note that of the 15 (25 per cent) who saw no difference, 60 per cent were in the age groups 55–65 or over 65. The nationalities with the largest numbers of respondents in this category were the Spanish (4 respondents) and the Dutch (4 respondents), and the only political groups with no respondents in this category were: ARE, Europe des Nations, and Union.

If we take first those women who rejected the proposition that gender might be specifically relevant to their job. This group suggested three principal reasons for not engendering the role of representative. Firstly, and perhaps paradoxically, they argued that the European Parliament was more woman-friendly than other political bodies. It presented, they claimed, a special case for women in politics, and one that was largely favourable to them. In this depiction, the European Parliament is a privileged site of political endeavour which makes gendering the role of MEP irrelevant. Thus a Spanish PES member explains:

'In the European Parliament, I think the fact of being a woman has actually very little importance. It's where you notice it least. It is the most equal Parliament, men and women are treated equally, there are no concessions and no special comments. . . . I think this is due to the fact that there are so many cultures and languages that the difference between the sexes is no longer important. The background of the EP is different from the national Parliaments. And then, the language in the EP is much simpler . . . the speeches are not so rhetorical. It is a much easier Parliament than the national ones. The age-old doubts that women have about whether they can express themselves as well as men are simply lost here, or don't occur.'

For a German EPP representative, it is the critical mass of women in the European Parliament which has made gendering the role of an MEP less relevant: 'I feel that there is no distinction in the European Parliament. The reason is perhaps the higher share of women in the EU Parliament. Perhaps it is seen as normal . . .

A second group of MEPs argued that gendering the role of representative was irrelevant because the business of politics transcends gender. In this presentation, the European Parliament is gender blind because the issues it addresses are not gender-defined:

'I have found that it matters little whether there are men or women working in politics . . . many questions transcend the sexes – peace and security for instance – as opposed to day care for children to cite another example.' (Dutch, EPP)

A third group of MEPs, all Dutch, refused to entertain the basis of the question, namely that there was any possibility of gendering political representation. It was impossible, they argued, for an individual to distance herself enough to be able to answer such a question. Gender is an unconscious attribute so that any colouring of the political space by gender has to be equally unconscious. As one of them puts it: 'I don't know. I am a woman, so the behaviour I present is simply that which I present, it could hardly be otherwise' (Dutch, PES).

On the other hand, the majority of the MEPs, three-quarters of the sample (45), did draw something specifically gendered in the relationship of a woman representative to politics, and it is among their responses that we should try to investigate what gendering representation might mean in practice, 'on the ground'. Perhaps unsurprisingly, the nature of this relationship – gender/political representative – and the effect it might have on the behaviour of women as a group in a representative assembly was not unproblematic. The largest number of definitions of identity started from an essentialist conception of how women approach politics, and how they operate within it, based on a variety of a priori female identities, primarily related to what might be called a 'woman's gaze', and a 'woman's voice'.

Firstly, women said they perceived themselves as 'seeing differently' in politics. For some MEPs, this woman's gaze was a matter of essentialist difference – 'glasses', 'seeing', 'view', and 'vision' are categorized as specific to women. One Belgian PES member, for example, interestingly described the gaze of women in politics as focusing on the same issues as men, but seeing them differently: 'I see these (social protection and poverty) through different glasses from my male colleagues', and this sense of a woman's gaze being slightly different from that of a man is a consistent theme across nationalities and political groups: '[women] do see things differently' (German, Green); 'the fact of being a woman makes you see things from another point of view' (Spanish, PES).

In practice, however, the focus of this distinct 'woman's gaze' is less defined. If some women MEPs claim that women do indeed see things differently from men, it is legitimate to ask what exactly constitutes the different vision they feel themselves having, and it is here that there is no real consensus. For some MEPs, women see things in a broad context, a view echoing, for example, the empirical work we have already noted from the United States on policy-making in the Colorado State Legislature (Kathlene, 1995). This broad-sweeping contextualist approach is summed up as being akin to the different ways in which men and women go into a room:

'when men enter a room they steer towards a seat, sit down and look around. It is quite the opposite in the case of women. They enter the room, walk towards the seat, but first look around. And most women also halt a moment . . . there is the moment of glancing around, taking everything in. That is typical female . . . the different approach of women, it is all embracing and it does not neglect the intermittent nuances and the emotional responsibility . . . It is also typical for women, when they enter a room, to ask: "How are you? How is the family?" . . . (men) focus on their goal and have not time to look to the left and to the right.' (German, EPP)

For other women, the female gaze is one which takes in details as much as the broad sweep of issues: 'women also have a better eye for detail than men, often details which men would dismiss but which can be extremely important' (Danish, EDN). It is women's attention to detail rather than broad context which marks them out from men. In a sense, then, whilst there is some consensus that 'women see things differently', it is unclear exactly how, in practice, this different vision, this distinct gaze, is constituted, and what it might therefore imply for political behaviour.

Secondly, some women MEPs identify the male/female difference in politics as being a matter of voice rather than gaze. It is how women contribute to the political process rather than the distinctive ways in which they might see and formulate issues. Again, as with the depiction of a specific female vision, there is no agreement as to what constitutes a 'woman's voice' in politics. For some women, the female voice is simply one which operates in harmony: 'I am less interested in scoring for the sake of it, and more in consensus. Searching for a consensus perhaps is a feminine trait . . .' (Dutch, ELDR); 'a more conciliatory approach' (British, PES); and '[women] don't just bay at each other like men do' (Irish, Green).

For others, the woman's voice is short and sharp, noticeable as much by its brevity or complete silence, as by its harmonious tone. One Belgian EPP member summed it up as: 'women . . . do things/get things done with less words'; 'Women speak less and act more. They have no time to waste on endless bla bla. They want to do things' (Luxembourgeoise, EPP); 'A woman is not so vague and comes quicker to the point and pushes on quicker. Men like to sit and talk for hours. . . . They like to listen to themselves' (German, Green).

Rather than the identity of the woman representative being constructed by an a priori different vision or different voice, some women MEPs, all socialist, argued that what made women representatives different was not their identity but their positioning, their inevitable location as marginal, and as outsiders. In this self-presentation, women are the historically excluded, and hence intrinsically identify with others like themselves: 'women had no presence for centuries, and therefore they can understand people who are not present' (Greek, PES); 'women are aware of social exclusion, of individuals and groups which face problems in achieving their full potential' (British, PES).

This marginality is one which some MEPs embrace as a present working manifesto. Here, women MEPs constitute themselves as outsiders in order to challenge existing political structures and existing ways of 'doing' politics. Being a woman representative means by definition upsetting the existing order: 'we're ready . . . without being encumbered by the diktats of our respective parties' (French, PES); 'the whole way in which I would like to do politics, not to respect simply the inflexible structures which exist. Structures are there, but they . . . need not remain the way they are . . . many men . . . look at laws in a very rigid way, whereas I say, "OK. Laws are there, but we are legislators and can, therefore, change them." . . . Perhaps one could define it in such a way, to have more courage to change things' (German, PES).

Overall, it is evident that a majority of the women interviewed (75 per cent) believed that their identity as women affected their jobs as MEPs. What is less clear is the exact nature of this self-perceived identity and hence its likely effect on political behaviour. For some MEPs, it is a matter of a woman's gaze. Women see things differently, either in a contextualist framework, or a detailed framework, or in both. For others, it is a matter of voice. Women participate in politics differently, either by the voice of reconciliation or by saying very little at all. And for still others, women's identity is bound up with their marginality. Women are the historic and continuing outsiders who challenge a status quo which excluded them.

From the words of these interviewees, it seems that, across nationalities and main political groupings, women MEPs consider gender to be an important category in their self-definitions as political representatives. It is equally clear however that the basis for a shared a priori understanding of what might constitute this 'representative as female' identity is low. The gender script, as it were, is apparently a very mixed one.

NARRATIVES OF REPRESENTATION

Rather than looking at the various scripts which women can be given in order to create the role of an MEP, it may be more useful to examine the languages they use themselves when narrating the role, telling the story, as it were, of what it is to be a representative in the European Parliament. The women MEPs in our sample were asked an open question: 'How would you describe the job of an MEP?' The languages they use to express a narrative frame produce a focus for the job, a style of being an MEP, and it is to these narratives that we shall now turn in some detail.

Women MEPs describe three main narratives of representation – what we might call:

- The narrative of representative as **Political actor**
- The narrative of representative as **Personal traveller**
- The narrative of representative as **Interpreter**

For ease of reference, the numbers, and percentage of the group, constituting each framework of narration are given in Table 3.1.

In Chapter 6 we shall return to some of the possible national and party political nuancing of these narratives. At this stage, we shall examine each of these narratives, by looking in detail at the language used by the women in expressing them. An analytical table (Tables 3.2, 3.3 and 3.4) is provided for each framework, and this sets out the words of each of the women using that framework, within separate columns for nouns, adjectives, verbs and images. After each Table, there is a comment on some of

Table 3.1

Narrative frame	Number of women	Percentage of total
Political actor	14	27
Personal traveller	15	29
Interpreter	23	44
Total	52	100

the conclusions we might draw, and then a full quotation from one of the MEPs concerned, so that we can see the framework as it is being narrated.

The narrative of representative as Political actor (14 respondents: 4 British, 3 Dutch, 3 German, 2 French, 1 Spanish, 1 Luxembourgeoise. Political groups with no respondents – Greens, and ELDR).

Table 3.2

Language of the narrative of representative as Political actor

Noun	Verb	Image	Adjective
Committee, meetings, Plenary			
Constitution, Presidency			
Electors, citizens, national parliaments, (legislative) control, Policies	Represent		Legislative
Committees, delegations, Party meetings Agenda, meetings	Attend, stance is prepared		
Intermediary, representative, legislation			
Interests, Directives, national policies, standards, laws	Represent, pass (laws), written down, put them into practice, manoeuvre		Valid
(Legislative) activities, committee, constituency	See (people)		Legislative
Influence, alliances, (common) goals, constituencies, correspondence, committees, socialist group			
Parliament, Commission, Vice/President, cohesion, correspondence, electorate, industry associations, committee, Party meetings			

Table 3.2   (*Continued*)

Language of the narrative of representative as Political actor

Noun	Verb	Image	Adjective
Vice Chair, Party, enquiries			Busy
Votes, committees, Rapporteurs, Party, delegation	Represent, ensure		
(Political) control, executive, (legislative) role, elaboration of texts			Political, legislative
Budget, scrutiny, powers	Represent		Legislative

In the examples in Table 3.2, the narrative of representative as **Political actor** is constituted by the overwhelming use of nouns, drawn from the traditional registers of formal politics, of representative democracy, governance, and political parties: 'votes', 'electorate', 'party'; 'parliaments', 'legislative control', 'executive'; 'agenda', 'meetings', 'delegations'. The job of an MEP is constituted as a primarily noun-based function. With the exception of 'is' or 'consists of', verbs are sparsely used, and those the MEPs do employ are the common currency of parliamentary process: 'represent', 'elected'; or of legislative procedure, 'pass (laws)'. Adjectives seldom appear, and are mainly restricted to the same register: 'legislative', 'political'. Only one adjective, 'busy', appears to offer some sort of value-judgement. Linguistically, the framework is composed of institutional sites or political 'instances', with the MEP present within the structure, but with little focus on the actual contribution she personally makes. The emphasis throughout is on the political and representative system, with an involvement by the MEP which is itself drawn as part of the mechanics of the system.

A closer examination of one of the responses in this group from a German EPP member will illustrate the way in which the narrative voice prioritizes the political system. The text of the response is given first.

'in the same way as with all other MPs, to represent the interests of the individual region in the parliament for which one has been elected. What is perhaps different in the European Union is the area for which one works, the whole European Union and there have, of course, to be laws passed. . . . In the end the Parliament passes laws as well, which are, of course, valid. The Directives will be put into practice, but in the end they are valid for a very large area. Therefore there are two elements which are in my view specific. As the area is so heterogeneous one has to make sure that the directives passed are wide enough, so that there is enough room for national parliaments to put them into practice with relevance to their specific conditions ... one must ensure that in the country in which one lives, the government can manoeuvre within them, in other words, one must know the interests, the situation, the conditions of life of the people by whom one is elected. ... An example. The same environmental standards everywhere. We had the case of solar energy. ... I remember that a Finnish MP said at that time: "but in our country the time of daylight between May and October is only ... hours." This cannot be written down in such a way.'

This answer to the question 'How would you describe the job of an MEP?' takes as its starting point a comparison with the work of a national MP, so that a framework of existing political representation is immediately set. The MEP then builds up a series of nouns associated with the system of governance in the EP: 'laws', 'directives', 'national parliaments', 'interests/ situation/conditions', 'standards'. Verbs are mainly those relevant to the procedures: 'pass (laws)', 'put into practice', 'manoeuvre', 'written down'. Adjectives are not much in evidence, with the exception of 'valid', and 'large' and 'heterogeneous', the latter two linked to the difficulty of legislating for such a wide area as the EU. There are no images, but the MEP finishes by providing an anecdote, with a direct quotation from one of the political actors. The fact that the story is prefaced by 'example. The same environmental standards everywhere', and rounded off with 'This cannot be written down in such a way', ensures that the anecdote is made subsidiary to the depiction of the system of governance itself. It is presented as a symptom of the difficulties with which the EP as a political system has to deal.

What is given in this response is less the personal narrative of an MEP, and more a description of the actual processes of the European Parliament. The MEP has written a narrative of representation which focuses on the processes and those bodies contributing to the processes, with the precise role of the individual MEP drawn only in relation to the system itself: 'one must ensure that in the country in which one lives, the government can manoeuvre within them'. The MEP has established a model of representation which integrates an MEP into an already established political and representative system. In this narrative, the system (representative democracy, political party organization, legislative process) is constituted with nouns, and the MEP's own precise activity is drawn lightly and with little personal involvement.

The narrative of representative as Personal traveller: This narrative was proposed by virtually the same proportion of women as the framework of Political actor (15 respondents: 4 Danish, 3 Spanish, 3 German, 1 Dutch, 1 Danish, 1 Portuguese, 1 Belgian, 1 Italian. Political groups with no respondents: EUL and Union).

Table 3.3

Language of narrative of representative as Personal traveller

Noun	Verb	Image	Adjective
A site; your own space; a site which fits your profile	Find		Interesting, difficult; creative
Horizon	Work; travel; pack; produce papers	Machine for papers	Diverse; wide (horizon); hard
	Shape, plan; create, change		
(Continuous) movement			Continuous
	(Newly) shaped		Creative
Stage of learning		Sowing seeds	Difficult
(Beyond) borders	Pass (beyond); look (beyond)	Look beyond the rim of the plate	
			Hard
		Planet Zorb	Impossible; consensual
	Travel; waste time		Stressful; difficult
Variety	Learns (so much)		Absorbing
	Travel		Hard, interesting; tiring, stressful
Visions; ideas; distance	Travel; create		
			Exciting; hard
Visions; ideas	Create; travel		

In this narrative framework, women MEPs are using more verbs than in the **Political actor** narrative, and these are verbs of movement – physical movement: 'travel', 'pack', 'pass (beyond)', or mental movement: 'create', 'change', 'shape', 'plan'. Unlike the **Political actor** narrative, MEPs in this framework constitute their activity at the centre of the definition, hence the very high number of adjectives which describe their work in personal-value terms: 'interesting', 'difficult', 'hard', 'creative'. The verbs of movement are complemented by the choice of nouns which either create an impression of physical travelling: 'horizon', 'distance', 'borders', 'stage'; or of mental movement: 'ideas', 'visions'. Some of the MEPs offer images which (with the exception of the 'machine for papers') suggest development and change, from the 'sowing the seeds', to the 'look beyond the rim of the plate'. The description of the world of the EP resembling 'Planet Zorb' for a first-time MEP is particularly suggestive of a frame of reference which looks beyond the system that is apparently there. If we look in detail at one of the responses in this group, from a Spanish EPP member, we shall see how she narrates her job as an MEP.

'I think that the first thing to say is that it is extremely interesting, but difficult work. The first thing an MEP has to do is find a site, given the large number of platforms which exist. It's a matter of finding a site which fits your profile, and that of the region you represent. It's a matter of creating your own space within the Parliament, in the committees which allow you to bring your region to the Parliament. The MEPs are representatives of their countries. The work in the Parliament has a creative ingredient which is creating your own space.'

In this reply, the woman places herself at the centre of the MEP's activities, and in effect remakes the parliamentary space to suit herself. The verbs 'find' (repeated), 'create', 'bring ... to' suggest that she is engaged in a personal journey, an impression reinforced by the nouns, 'site' (repeated), and 'space'. The adjectives she employs – 'interesting', 'difficult' – are value-judgements which echo her introduction of the personal in the 'a site which fits your profile'. Finally, she sums up her description of the MEP's job with the words: 'The work in the Parliament has a creative ingredient which is creating your own space.' Creativity and individual activity are prioritized and the legislative and governmental systems are played down or not recognized. The MEP is in the centre of the narrative, changing and developing what may already be there.

The narrative of representative as Interpreter: This narrative frame is constituted by the largest number of respondents, across the widest range of nationalities (23 respondents: 5 British, 4 German, 3 Spanish, 3 Dutch, 2 French, 2 Italian, 2 Belgian, 1 Danish, 1 Irish. Political group not represented: EDN).

Table 3.4

Language of the narrative of representative as Interpreter

Noun	Verb	Image	Adjective
People at home	Convince; Push through		New
Outside world; supporters; public opinion; media; points of view	Communicating		
Interests (of people)	Stand for democracy; introduce (interests to individual institutions)		
People; voice	Make (the voice) heard; contribute to getting (the voice) heard		
Interpreter; citizens; (own) electorate			Consultative
Contact; interest groups; exchange programmes	Bring what seems to happen far away closer to home; looking for		
		Ambassador	
	Push forward (idea)		
Interests; citizens; queries	Defend (interests of); respond to (queries from)		
Voice; citizen	Carry the voice		
Citizens; concerns; associations; NGOs	Integrate (concerns); transfer (concerns); keep contact	Chain transmitter	
Influence			
PR job	(Young) talk to (young)		
People who send me	Represent and represent back to (people); participate		
Feedback; citizens; mission	Keep in touch		

Table 3.4 *(Continued)*

Language of the narrative of representative as Interpreter

Noun	*Verb*	*Image*	*Adjective*
Spokesman; citizens; intermediaries		Bridge (between national . . .)	
Citizens; those of your country; those concerned	Bring close to (the European committees); attend to (the questions); inform; defend		
Diversity	Negotiate; work across; talk across		
Interpreter; exponent; expectations (of people); persuasiveness; people	Get (Commission) on our side; learn (from each other); (need) to be convinced; try to convince		
Synthesis; citizens; interface	Take a step in the direction (of the other)		
Liaison	Telling	Ambassador	Mixing (role)
Collaboration; compromise; coalition			

Unlike the narrative of **Personal traveller**, the narrative of **Interpreter** uses very few adjectives, and the descriptions of the job are not coloured with value-judgements. In comparison with the narrative frame of **Poltical actor**, the emphasis of MEPs here is on the verbs as much as the nouns which constitute their role. The verbs used are normally transitive: 'convince (someone)', 'introduce (something)', 'bring (something)', and the nouns establish the subjects and objects of these verbs. The noun vocabulary is either made up of synonyms of the givers of/receivers of information: 'people', 'outside world', 'citizens', 'interest groups', or describes the processes by which information is transmitted: 'media', 'voice', 'interpreter', 'exchange programmes', 'persuasiveness' and so on. Verbs are largely taken from the register of communication: 'convince', 'make (the voice) heard', 'inform', and usually imply, as we have said, that there is an object, something that is being communicated, or someone who is being convinced. Interestingly enough, one of the images MEPs in this group use is 'ambassador' (a person who goes from one country to another to communicate that country's policies). Communication between people ('bridge') and advocacy ('the voice') is key to the construction of this narrative.

If we examine one of these responses in detail, the way the narrative is constructed may become clearer. The words are those of a Belgian PES member.

> 'I see myself firstly as an exponent/interpreter of the expectations of the people of Europe among whom the lack of genuine sensibility/awareness ... of the EP is a problem – I am referring to the Parliament's lack of power. ... At the EP, we work with many different nationalities, none of which monopolizes power. We are lucky enough to be able to learn from each other in such a situation. What we try to do is to work together with women's organizations as well as with employers' associations, with women's lobbies and with groups representing migrant women, but also upwards with national institutions. The aim is to try and get the Commission on our side in order to convince the Council of Ministers. Persuasiveness should be directed downwards – not only upwards, to the ministers – people need to be informed, convinced of the importance of more Belgian EU cooperation. Within my own group of colleagues as well, I try to convince them of the need for systematic equality between men and women within the EU.'

Here, the MEP proposes a narrative frame which rests on the iteration of a series of verbs – 'work with', 'try to get ... on our side', 'convince', 'inform', 'convince', 'convince' – with their objects, either people to be convinced – 'women's organizations', 'employers' associations', 'groups representing migrant women', 'Commission', 'Council of Ministers' – or issues to be advocated – 'importance of more Belgian EU cooperation', 'need for systematic equality'. She describes herself at the beginning of the response as 'an exponent/interpreter', and positions herself in a model of advocacy which goes 'downwards – not only upwards'. The emphasis in the narrative framework the MEP creates is on the voicing of views to and between different groups, with the MEP as a channel – 'interpreter', 'downwards' and 'upwards' – of this voicing.

What is particularly interesting about these three narrative frames is the relative unpopularity of the narrative of representative as **Political actor**: 73 per cent of the women interviewed constituted an entirely different framework for their job. Of the two alternatives, by far and away the more popular was that of the representative as **Interpreter**, and this is also the narrative shared by the widest number of nationalities (9) and political groups, excluding only one of the latter. Given the different national and political scripts of representation which provide the context for Members of the European Parliament, the rejection of the **Political actor** narrative, and the relatively large number of women narrating their role as **Interpreters**, is of some interest. Rather than describing a role of representation centred on what is being represented (individuals, geographical areas, specific issues, or groups) or the political sites in which the representative may operate as a political actor, this narrative frame tells a story of 'representation' as a process of communication, as ambassadors and interpreters – a communication between individuals, and between groups, and a communication which is situated at a variety of different levels.

IMAGINING THE POLITICAL PROCESS

Having looked at the narratives that women MEPs give for their roles as representatives, we will now look at some of the ways in which they understand their participation in the political process. The site of politics is an essentially imagined space, and the manner in which we imagine it, the images, as it were, through which we call it into existence, is a key elements in our narration of the political process and thus of the ways in which we 'speak' politics. As well as narrating stories of representation, MEPs are also framing the 'business' of politics, and some of this framing is achieved through metaphors. By identifying the often abstract processes of politics with fields that are more concrete, MEPs frame what they understand politics to be in particularly significant ways.

Cognitive linguists have argued for some time, of course, that we use metaphors as conceptual systems in which we understand and experience one thing in terms of another. George Lakoff and Mark Johnson for example, maintain that metaphors in effect 'structure how we perceive, how we think, and what we do' (Lakoff and Johnson, 1980: 4). More recently, Paul Chilton (Chilton, 1996), drawing together the insights of discourse analysis and cognitive-semantic analysis, has explored the centrality of metaphor in specific political discourse. In this perspective, the metaphors we use may be said to define situations, apportion roles to participants and structure our understanding of outcomes and results.

Looking at the political space of the European Parliament as an 'imagined community' (Anderson, 1991) focuses our attention on the ways in which MEPs are helping to construct this imagined political site through their speeches in the Plenary sessions. How do they constitute political processes (are they, for example, sports, wars, buildings being constructed?) as they discuss the many and varied issues with which, as we have seen from the case study Plenary sessions (Chapter 2), they have to deal? Most importantly, from our point of view, do men and women constitute this political space through metaphor in any different ways?

To begin to address these questions, we can look at speeches (411 in total) selected from the case study Plenaries, in which MEPs are using metaphors, and in so doing are imagining the political processes in particular ways. There were 771 occurrences of metaphors in these speeches, which can be allocated to 25 very broad conceptual domains: 'politics is war', 'politics is sport' and so on. The focus here is not on how particular individual policies are being conceived, but rather on how roles are being assigned to participants through the political speeches, and hence how a political space is being imagined at any time. As we have argued in Chapter 2, the exercise of analysing these domains does not aim to produce rigorous quantitative results. What it seeks to do is to provide some qualitative indications of the ways in which the discourses of men and women are nuanced and coloured by metaphors in the European Parliament, and what such colourings can tell us about the ways in which men and women conceive the political world in which they operate.

Table 3.5 sets out the major domains in which metaphors occur, gives the number of examples of metaphors in each domain, and shows the approximate proportion of each domain in relation to the others (given in percentages).

To begin with, it seems clear from the sample that MEPs are imagining the space of politics in the European Parliament in a richly varied way. When we look at the distribution of metaphors in relation to the gender of the speaker, we also find some interesting similarities and differences. The twelve domains of metaphor most frequently used by women and by men are given in Table 3.6, with an indication of the approximate proportion of each domain.

The four most frequently used domains for men and women constitute approximately 40 per cent of the metaphors for each of them (38 per cent for women, 41 per cent for men), and contain three identical domains – 'fighting', 'culture' and 'medical' – and one domain specific to each: 'parts of the body' for women and 'borders' for men. To begin with, we shall explore the nature of the two domains which are specific to each sex, 'parts of the body' for women, and 'borders' for men, before moving on to look at the domains shared by both sexes.

In the domain 'parts of the body', women provide 47 per cent of all the metaphors in this category. By using metaphors from the body to imagine the political process, women are imagining two main political relationships. Firstly, parts of the body metaphors describe politics as conflict, but conflict of a specific sort, as the examples suggest (Table 3.7). In these examples, a conflict is being imagined in terms reminiscent of a

Table 3.5

Domain	Number	Percentage
Fighting	107	14
Sport	35	5
Science	4	0.5
Machines	43	0.6
Parts of the body	49	6
Lacuna	8	1
House and environs	14	2
Water	19	2
Medical	67	0
Movement	33	4
Commerce	20	3
Culture	61	8
Animals/birds	27	4
Borders	64	8
Fragments of a piece	10	1
Clothes	4	0.5
Written text	29	4
Spoken word	10	1
Building	37	5
Religion	47	6
Family	19	2
Law	21	3
Housecraft	9	1
Natural world	31	4
Crossing bridges	3	0.4
Total	771	100.4 (percentage rounded up)

playground scrap, of a conflict which is presented as close up and personal, face to face – 'noses', 'face', etc. Secondly, the body is used by women to imagine a political process which is not operating entirely efficiently, where there are problems (Table 3.8). Again, the effect of this is to personalize the inefficiency and bring it close up to the speaker: policies and processes, like conflicts above, are intimately connected to those speaking. The body, and hence the person, is engaged in the conflict and in whatever is going wrong: political adversaries slap us, a

Table 3.6

Women	
Domain	*Percentage in women's discourse*
Fighting	13
Parts of the body	10
Culture	8
Medical	7
Natural world	5
Water	5
Machines	4
Fragments of a piece	4
Borders	4
Movement	4
Religion	4
Sport	4

Men	
Domain	*Percentage in men's discourse*
Fighting	15
Medical	9
Borders	9
Culture	8
Religion	7
Machines	6
Parts of the body	5
Sport	5
Natural world	4
Building	4
Written text	4
Movement	4

failure to act in a given situation is described as 'twiddling thumbs' and so on.

For men, one of their main usages of metaphor, which is only slightly shared by women, is a domain we have called 'borders'. We mean by this

Table 3.7

Americans are giving us a firm kick
Thumbing its noses at
We've had a slap in the face
Pointing the finger at

Table 3.8

Closing our eyes to
Turning a blind eye to
Left hand does not know what the right is doing
Twiddling their thumbs

Table 3.9

Elasticity of the forms
Reports with sharp outlines
No fixed contours
In the mould of
Symmetrical

that politics is being imagined as a process drawn within contours and boundaries (Table 3.9). In this domain, some of the business of politics is being imagined as activities which should be capable of being shaped and constituted within given boundaries. The suggestion of shapes given to the activities – 'outlines', 'contours', 'mould' – argues for an imagining of political issues as malleable, or as being judged for their potential malleability.

Apart from the 'parts of the body' and 'borders' domains, men and women have the most frequent domains in common. In two of these types of imagining, however – fighting and medical – there are some slight differences in the ways that men and women use the metaphors. If we take the first, 'politics is a fight', we are entering the domain which is the most popular form of imagining for both men and women. In a sense, this is no great surprise. Lakoff and Johnson pointed out some time ago (Lakoff and Johnson, 1980: 4) that the conceptual metaphor **Argument is war** is reflected in much of our everyday language. More recently, Deborah Tannen has claimed that the battle metaphor is a particular characteristic of Western culture: 'It is the Western tendency to view

Table 3.10

Fight against fraud
Combat fraud
Fight revisionist theories of the Holocaust
Strike a blow for democracy
Fight for equal opportunities

everything through the template of a battle metaphor, and to glorify conflict and aggression' (Tannen, 1998: 4). Carolyn Straehle and her colleagues (Straehle *et al.*, 1999) have explored the way in which the notion of 'Struggle as metaphor' is used in the context of EU discourses on unemployment.

It is not especially surprising that men and women should use the battle metaphor. What is interesting for the purposes of engendering democracy is the evidence that they use this metaphor rather differently; that the fight they are imagining is constructed in different terms.

As presented by MEPs in these speeches, there are three distinct types of fight being constituted. Firstly, a fight which is against an undisputed evil, or for an undisputed good (Table 3.10). In this form of the fight metaphor, the emphasis is on the abstract enemy against which we are fighting (fraud), or the abstract good for which we are acting (democracy). In both cases, the nature of the fight is not detailed, and there is no notion of opposing sides drawn up in battle for war.

In contrast, the second form of the metaphor, which we might call 'politics is an army war', suggests physical combat, with battle plans, and army manoeuvres. The enemy, if not specified, is implicitly present, either retaliating, or potentially seeking to frustrate the plans of the army (Table 3.11). Vocabulary here is taken from the register of military wars – 'vanguard', 'rallied to the position', 'flanking measures', etc. – with the

Table 3.11

In the vanguard
Issues as hostages
Sharpshooting majority
Rallied to the position
Under assault on two fronts
Flanking measures
Parading under discriminatory colours

Table 3.12

Protect people's health
Take refuge in
Defending identity

'business' of politics being imagined as a military encounter between two appropriately armed foes.

Finally, the fighting domain provides examples of 'politics as a defensive fight', where what is being imagined is indeed a fight, but one in which the emphasis is not on the enemy in conflict, or on an abstract good or evil for which we are fighting, but rather on what needs to be protected, looked after and saved (Table 3.12).

What is particularly interesting about these three forms of the 'politics is fighting' domain is the rather different distribution of each form between men and women (Table 3.13). Politics is clearly imagined by both male and female MEPs as being a fight, and this, as we have suggested, is neither surprising nor unexpected. What is more unexpected, however, is the rather different ways in which the fight is more typically imagined by each sex. From this evidence, men clearly imagine politics more frequently than women (74 per cent of the fight metaphors for men, as opposed to 55 per cent for women) as a fight is akin to an army war, with an identifiable set of enemies, battle plans drawn up, and manoeuvres made. Women, on the other hand, imagine the fight more frequently than men (31 per cent for women in contrast to 14 per cent for men) as being a defensive struggle, where what is at issue is primarily the good to be

Table 3.13

	Women	Women	Men	Men
	Number	Percentage of women's fight metaphors	Number	Percentage of men's fight metaphors
Versus evil	4	14	9	12
Army war	16	55	58	74
Defensive	9	31	11	14
Total	29	100	78	100

Table 3.14

Coronary disease affecting transport
Cancerous growth
Impotence
Probing the wound of one's country
Psychosis
Manic

defended, rather than the enemy that threatens or the nature of the battle itself.

The second domain shared by men and women which appears to be nuanced differently by each sex is the medical one: 'politics is a medical matter'. For men, the site of politics tends to be imagined in this domain as being a site which is diseased – diseases which might be physical or mental, but which are in most cases extreme (Table 3.14). Coronary disease, cancerous growth and mania, for example, indicate a political space which is chronically diseased, with problems which are likely to be very difficult to solve.

In comparison, women use the domain of medicine to imagine a site of healing ('palliative', 'antidote') and, at worst, a site of relatively minor physical disturbance ('bug') (Table 3.15).

The two spaces of politics being imagined here, and the two approaches to them, are clearly different in tone. For men, politics is being imagined as a site of very major problems, where the problem itself and its disabling/addictive nature is what is important. For women, politics is being seen as a site of solutions, with the emphasis on the viability of the solution, rather than the gravity and intractability of the problem.

Finally, apart from the 'parts of the body' and the 'borders' domains, the only other domains which occur in one sex and not the other in the top twelve domains are 'water' and 'fragments of a piece' for women, and

Table 3.15

Best palliative
Holistic approach
Antidotes
Sick and tired
Bug

Table 3.16

Flounder about in this area
Choppy waters
Pouring cold water on
Small stones dropping into a pool

'written text' for men, and it may be useful to review these different domains.

Women provide 58 per cent of the examples of metaphor from this sample in the 'politics is water' domain. What is interesting about this is not only the greater frequency of usage, but also the rather different form of politics men and women imagine when they use this domain. For women, once again, the metaphor constitutes an imagined site of politics which is close and within their personal ambit – water is poured, stones are dropped into pools (Table 3.16). In comparison, for men, water seems to be providing an imagined site of politics which is large and potentially quite threatening, with oceans and rising tides (Table 3.17). Water, then, generally creates a political process for women which is close to them, within reach and largely controllable. For men, it appears to describe a universe which is large and often very problematic.

Besides the 'water' domain, women also have the domain we have called 'fragments of a piece', as an imagining of politics which is little shared by men – 80 per cent of the occurrences in this domain are provided by women. Here, the political process is being imagined as an integrated whole into which individual elements fit – mosaics, fabrics – with issues being meshed and woven together (Table 3.18). The site of politics being constituted here is one in which interconnectedness is of very major importance: interconnectedness of issues, of economies and of cultures.

For male speakers, the only domain they use (in the top twelve domains) which is not used by women is what we have termed the 'written text'. Here the political process is a written textualized one.

Table 3.17

Ocean of malnutrition
Rising tide of nationalism
Wave of refugees

Table 3.18

One piece of the mosaic
Meshing of the national economies
Weaving culture into every strand
Fabric of regions

Men are implicitly imagining a site which is in some senses regulated by and judged against something written down on paper or in lists (Table 3.19).

Table 3.19

Struck off the list
Ink was hardly dry
Not worth the paper it's written on

From the evidence of metaphors we have looked at, it seems as if men and women are imagining slightly different sites of politics. The political site imagined by women is one in which conflict is more attenuated, with less emphasis on metaphorical armed warfare, and more on defensive struggle and protection. The conflicts are more likely to be close up and personal, rather than conflicts with more far-away blocs and groups. The political processes imagined by women are ones where solutions and possible remedies are likely to be prioritized over the diagnosis of large and extremely difficult problems. Issues are more often imagined by women than men as being interconnected, as being linked together into a whole, rather than being contained and managed within particular borders.

CONCLUSIONS

We started off this chapter by noting that much theoretical debate at the moment concerns ways in which a politics of presence and a politics of ideas can be synthesized, possibly through an understanding of feminism as a potential revitalizer of democracy, as one of the means by which our notions of representation and democracy may be nuanced. Some of the current empirical work, we noted, is trying to see whether women already participating in formal politics actually make a difference, and if so, what these differences might be.

Any representatives in a democratic system are given a number of potential scripts from which they can read their roles in parliament. Gender, the script that positions women representatives as specifically representing women, is one of these possible scripts. Here, via a politics of presence, women are being presumed to represent women's issues, or women's interests. Our discussions with women in the European Parliament, however, indicate that, whereas the majority of those we talked with believed that being a woman influenced their political activity, there was no consensus on how this influence translated itself into the behaviour of the representative. Women talked about differences of gaze and of voice, and of the more traditional position of the marginalized outsider. In practice, though, they seemed to have a variety of views about what this meant: for some, for example, the gaze of women was broad and far-reaching; for others, it was closely focused and detailed. In effect, the collective identity 'women' that the gender script implies is as difficult for women MEPs to accept and operationalize as it is for feminist theorists to constitute today.

Instead of looking at engendering democracy by a politics of presence based on the female identity of representatives, the evidence of this chapter is that we may be better advised to give greater attention to some of the languages of politics that women MEPs are actually already speaking, and see these languages of politics – ways of framing the job of a representative and of engaging in the political process – as languages which might be of use to other people participating in democracy.

The voices of women MEPs have suggested to us that they tell different narratives of what their role of MEP is, but that one of the most popular of these is the narrative of representative as interpreter, ambassador and communicator. As we looked at the languages through which men and women were constituting the site of politics, it became clear that, whilst men and women share common notions of engaging in politics as a fight, and viewing politics as the seat of problems, the ways in which they construct these descriptions are slightly different. Women imagine a less confrontational and more personal and defensive fight. They engage with politics as in a site of cure rather than a site of problems, and they tend to emphasize the connectedness of issues in preference to their containment within parameters.

If these are languages that women tend to talk slightly more than men, they are not of course languages that cannot be learned by others, both men and women. A contribution towards engendering democracy might then be to suggest that these ways of narrating the roles of representatives and of understanding their engagement in the imagined site of politics could usefully be extended to others. We might envisage a script of representation which calls on our representatives to see themselves as interpreters, as communicators between individuals, between groups and between sections. We might begin to ask our representatives to narrate the 'business' of politics in rather different ways, borrowing from some of the imaginings of female MEPs, and eschewing other formulations. Above all, we might assert with Phillips that 'Details matter' (Phillips, 1991: 159), and that some of the key details in revivifying democracy may lie precisely in the languages in which we choose to narrate our roles in the political process.

CHAPTER 4

GRAMMARS OF CITIZENSHIP

An important locus of interest for those keen to revitalize democracy is the redefinition and development of the concept of citizenship, a concept which has been under considerable pressure over the past few years. In this chapter, we are going to look at the languages in which citizenship has traditionally been expressed, and review the various critiques which feminist commentators have made of them. Then, we consider how the official institutional EU text of citizenship fits into these languages. I am going to argue in this chapter that a useful contribution to the discussion of citizenship could be provided by taking a grammatical approach, examining citizenship in a more specifically linguistic context. In this perspective, the grammars of citizenship used by MEPs, I will argue, point to distinct differences between the ways men and women 'say citizenship' in the European Parliament.

LANGUAGES OF CITIZENSHIP

For feminists, the language of citizenship has been at one and the same time deeply problematic and a potentially promising area for feminist involvement. Defining 'citizenship' necessarily involves a mapping of identities and relationships, and this is of central concern to people interested in the place of women in politics and society. The traditional ways of thinking about these issues, the liberal democratic and republican traditions of thought, have both argued that there is a core distinction between the public space and the private space. For liberals, the private is equated with individual freedom, and represents a sphere which has to be guarded jealously against interference from the state. For republicans, the private is linked to specific areas like bodily needs, and these should be hidden from view. For them, freedom is associated with the notion of being able to act together with others to promote the public good. As Joan B. Landes points out, the well-known feminist slogan, 'The personal is political', challenges both these traditions by describing a feminist movement which 'moves in two directions, placing the gendered organisation of both public and private space at centre stage' (Landes, 1998: 1).

At the root of much of feminism's critique of the first tradition, liberal democracy, has been a suspicion of liberal democracy's discourse of neutral ungendered universalism. The liberal model of citizenship is derived in essence from T. H. Marshall's classic formulation of rights granted to the individual by the state – civil rights, political rights and social rights (Marshall, 1950). Marshall's model, strongly influenced by post-war discourses on the welfare state, continues to serve as a starting point for liberal debate on citizenship. Essentially, the model imagines a pluralistic society in which pluralisms are respected by the articulation of entitlements held in common, in practice generally political entitlements and rights. The liberal model of citizenship necessarily posits an unproblematic common humanity to whom the same political rights can be given unproblematically, and a humanity that is largely passive – a citizenry to whom rights are accorded and entitlements given.

The second tradition, usually termed the civic republican model, imagines a very different citizenry. It operates in effect on the basis of a homogeneous group of people who hold a similar shared cultural framework. Whereas the liberal model primarily assumes a political identity, the civic republican model positions its citizens as social subjects, and replaces the language of rights accorded with that of responsibilities discharged. The passive individual citizen of the liberal model becomes the collective participating citizenry of the civic republican imagination.

The broad lines of the debate – rights as against responsibilities, passive possession or active participation, the individual or the community – have tended to be set within the implicit (if not explicit) framework of the traditional nation-state which characterized Marshall's early formulation. More recently, however, challenges to the integrity of national borders, the development of transnational organizations like the European Community, and popular beliefs on the likely effects of globalization, have begun to call into question the territorial imperative of citizenship. Ruth Lister (Lister, 1997), for example, has argued that citizenship must now be placed in a context which transcends the nation-state, and one in which elements that the two models of citizenship see as essential are transcribed into a transnational setting. In practice, transcribing the two traditions of citizenship transnationally would argue in the liberal model for a structure of government which could accord individual (at the least) political rights outside the framework of the nation-state. For the civic republican approach, it would suggest the creation of a civic public sphere in which citizens could participate, and one which would be wider than, and outside, the nation-state.

Even without the added dimension of territorial challenge, the two dominant models of citizenship have posed problems to feminist commentators and theorizers. To put it at a very basic level, the liberal model assumes, for many feminists, a specious universalism in which a norm of humanity, and one which has been historically constructed as masculine, is taken as the starting point for the granting of rights. This model has no time at all for the notion that identities are socially and economically constructed; that identity is in a sense socially embedded. The civic republican model, on the other hand, holds a strongly assimilatory view, imagining a form of cultural conformity which necessarily has the potential to exclude those who do not conform naturally or by choice to the dominant culture. Both traditional models of citizenship, then, present some difficulties for those of us particularly interested in the place of women.

Feminist attempts to deal with this by reconceptualizing citizenship have taken three main forms – the maternalist redefinition, the recuperation of the civic republican model, and what we might describe as rejections of binary thinking through relocation. To take the maternalist redefinitions first: Jean Elshtain (Elshtain, 1981, 1982, 1998), in a number of influential contributions, has argued that the liberal model, with its assumption of the primacy of the individual, is fundamentally flawed. In contrast to this, a maternalist version of citizenship, she claims, would provide for the values of the private sphere as the basis for a new model of citizenship. Strongly influenced by the ethic of care arguments, maternalist citizenship takes what it perceives as the values of motherhood – 'attentive love' (Elshtain, 1998) for example – and sets them as a potentially wider social imperative. Those who have rejected such maternalist redefinitions of citizenship, most notably Mary Dietz (Dietz, 1998), have been concerned at both its essentialist ahistoricism (all women are the same everywhere and at every time) and the failure, as they see it, to articulate a viable political expression for maternalist thinking which might challenge the key sites of power. Dietz (Dietz, 1998), and Carole Pateman (Pateman, 1992), although from slightly different perspectives, have both sought to recuperate the civic republican model, by arguing that women should be engaged as women in participatory and democratic politics, and that the maternalist critique of the exclusion of women from political rights has failed to take account of the historic inclusion of women as mothers, with motherhood as a political status. Rather than the moral contribution of women proposed by Elshtain, Dietz and Pateman argue for feminists to become active within a civic republican tradition which prioritizes participation, collective action and the translation of collective identities into political practice.

In between these two approaches – redefine citizenship with maternalism, and recuperate the civic republican tradition as a means of bringing the private and public spheres together – there have been a number of writers who propose what we might call a relocation strategy, a strategy which rejects both maternalism and civic republicanism. Chantal Mouffe (Mouffe, 1992), most notably, has argued that the vision of civic republicanism is not, as Dietz would have it, likely to provide fertile soil for women's engagement. It actually implies, she claims, a type of social obligation which poses a highly restrictive notion of the public good, and which is as ultimately universal and potentially tyrannical in its effects as the universalist discourse of the liberal model. For Mouffe, what is vital is an understanding that there is a plurality of communities and hence a variety of overlapping engagements within them. Her proposal for a relocation of citizenship is based on differentiating clearly between social and political communities. Political communities would be bound not by identities (being women, for example) but rather by their common interpretation of a set of ethico-political values. In a sense, this approach displaces the identity politics of feminism to a past which arguably has been socially constructed, and says that we can relocate the issues, that we have it in our power to produce different discourses of citizenship in which gender is no longer relevant. In this optic, the desire to develop a radical democratic politics which could fuse the two models takes precedence over a specifically feminist theory of citizenship.

At this stage of the ongoing discussion, we might say that the languages of citizenship are still marked by the discourses of both the liberal and civic republican traditions, but that the debate is moving into areas in which notions of fluid territoriality, and multiple and overlapping communities of identity or of belief and practice, are becoming more commonly seen as the basis on which citizenship could be considered. In a sense, the private/public spheres dichotomy which marked much early feminist debate on citizenship is being displaced into a more fluid notion of what actually constitutes the space of citizenship, and the vocabulary of commentators – 'multi-layered' (Lister, 1997: 196), 'multiple' (Meehan, 1993: 1), 'dynamic contested resource' (Yuval-Davis, 1997: 23) – reflects as much as anything else the siting of citizenship within a space whose contours are neither fixed nor sure.

LANGUAGES OF CITIZENSHIP IN THE EU

Some commentators have argued (Behnke, 1997) that the European Union represents a particularly interesting site for the development of these post nation-state languages of citizenship. The EU, after all, both presumes a national citizenship, constituted by the nation-state, and produces a new context for citizenship from which the nation-state itself is absent. In this sense, it may provide a space in which the two received traditions can be challenged, and in which the geographies of public and private space which are so central to feminist inquiry can be reinterpreted.

Before we examine the ways in which women MEPs construct citizenship in the European context, it may be helpful to look at the institutional context in which they are constructing citizenship. To do this, we shall examine the 'official' language of citizenship in the European Parliament to see how one of the major institutions of the EU represents this concept of a citizenship outside the nation-state. The text quoted below comes from the European Parliament Fact Sheet on 'Citizens of the Union and their rights' (European Parliament, 1999), one of a series of Fact Sheets addressed to the general public, with the purpose of explaining the workings of the Community to them. The text is long, but is worth reproducing in much of its detail.

2.2.0. Citizens of the Union and their rights
Legal Basis
Articles 17–22 (8–8e) of the EC Treaty
Objectives
Inspired by the freedom of movement for persons envisaged in the Treaties, the introduction of a European citizenship with precisely defined rights and duties was considered as long ago as the 1960s. Following preparatory work which began in the mid-1970s, in 1990 this project was placed in the context of the European Union. As a result of the Treaty on European Union, Article B of which (now Article 2) refers to 'citizenship of the Union' as an objective, this became part of the EC Treaty (Articles 17–22 (8–8e) ECT).

Imitating the concept of national citizenship, citizenship of the Union is intended to describe a binding relationship between the citizen and the European Union which is defined by the former's rights, duties and political participation. This is intended to bridge the gap between the increasing impact of Community action on citizens of the Community, on the one hand, and the almost exclusively national safeguarding of rights and duties and participation in democratic processes, on the other. The identification of citizens with the EU is to be enhanced, and a European political consciousness and a European identity are to be furthered.

Moreover, protection of the rights and interests of nationals of the Member States is to be strengthened (Article 2 (B), third indent EUT). In addition, citizenship of the Union can also act as a source of legitimacy for the EU.
Achievements to date
According to Article 17 (8) ECT, every person holding one nationality

of a Member State is a citizen of the Union. Nationality is defined according to the national laws of that State. Citizenship of the Union is complementary to national citizenship and comprises a number of rights and duties in addition to those stemming from citizenship of a Member State.

For all citizens of the Union, citizenship implies:
- the right to move and reside freely within the territory of the Member States;
- the right to vote, and to stand as a candidate in elections to the European Parliament and in municipal elections in the Member State in which they reside under the same conditions as nationals of that State;
- the right to diplomatic protection in the territory of a third country (non-EU State) by the diplomatic or consular authorities of another Member State, if their own country does not have diplomatic representation there, to the same extent as that provided for nationals of that Member State;
- the right to petition the European Parliament and the right to apply to the Ombudsman appointed by the European Parliament concerning instances of maladministration in the activities of the Community institutions or bodies, with the exception of the Court of Justice and the Court of First Instance. These procedures are governed by Articles 194 and 195 (138d and 138e) ECT.

With the exception of electoral rights, the substance of Union citizenship achieved to date is to a considerable extent simply a systematisation of existing rights (particularly as regards freedom of movement, the right of residence and the right of petition), which have now been enshrined in primary law on the basis of a political idea.

By contrast with the constitutional understanding in European States since the French Declaration of Human and Civil Rights of 1789, no specific guarantees of fundamental rights are associated with citizenship of the Union. Admittedly, Article 6 (2) (F (2)) EUT states that the 'Union' will 'respect' fundamental rights in accordance with the European Convention on Human Rights and the 'constitutional traditions common to the Member States', but it does not make any reference to the legal status of Union citizenship . . .

Union citizenship does not as yet entail any duties for citizens of the Union, despite the wording to that effect in Article 17 (2) (8 (2)) ECT, which constitutes a major difference between it and citizenship of the Member States.

The second paragraph of Article 22 (8e) ECT and Article 48 (N) EUT provide opportunities gradually to develop citizenship of the Union and thus provide citizens of the Union with an enhanced legal status at European level . . .

Role of the European Parliament

In its political initiatives and resolutions Parliament has always drawn the attention of the Council, the Commission and the Member States to the need to develop a policy which would involve European citizens in building up a living Community capable of fulfilling the aspirations of the European people.

In the elections to the European Parliament under Articles 19 (2) (8b (2)) and 190 (138) ECT, Union citizens are exercising one of the essential rights of their Union citizenship, that of democratic participation in the European political decision-making process.

Parliament has always wanted to endow the institution of Union citizenship with comprehensive rights. It advocated the determination of Union citizenship on an autonomous Community basis, so as to give citizens of the Union an independent status. In addition, from the start it advocated the incorporation of fundamental and human rights into primary law and called for citizens of the Union to be entitled to bring proceedings before the Court when those rights were violated by Union institutions or a Member State (resolution of 21 November 1991).

During the process of drafting the Treaty of Amsterdam Parliament again called for the rights associated with Union citizenship to be extended, and it subsequently criticised the fact that the Treaty had still not shown sufficient progress on the content of Union citizenship, either in the case of individual or collective rights. One of Parliament's outstanding demands is for the adoption of measures by a qualified majority to implement the principle of equal treatment and ban discrimination (resolution of 11 June 1997).

The language of this institutional text of European citizenship is of interest for two main reasons. Firstly, it sets out current formulations of citizenship within a vocabulary derived from both major traditions, and then it judges these formulations as being currently deficient in the EU. Secondly, it describes citizenship in the EU as one of the means through which a European public space and a European identity will be constructed. We shall look at how both of these themes are worked out in the text above.

The Fact Sheet argues that citizenship in the EU is analogous to citizenship in the nation-state – 'IMITATING the concept of national citizenship' – in that it is intended to describe 'a binding relationship between the citizen and the European Union which is defined by the former's RIGHTS, DUTIES and political PARTICIPATION'. Citizenship is therefore set out in terms of 'rights': 'the RIGHT to move freely', 'the RIGHT to vote', 'the RIGHT to diplomatic protection', 'the RIGHT to petition'. The objective which the European Parliament sees from the outset with the creation of European citizenship is to establish 'precisely defined RIGHTS and DUTIES' which would be 'COMPLEMENTARY to national citizenship and (would comprise) a number of RIGHTS and DUTIES IN ADDITION TO those stemming from citizenship of a Member State'. European citizenship is thus positioned as a citizenship parallel to that of the nation-state. In both its ambitions and its terminology in this text, the European Parliament is placing European citizenship within a framework which is instantly recognizable in both the liberal democratic and civic republican traditions.

As the Fact Sheet acknowledges, however, the problem with this framework is that it clearly shows that current formulations of European citizenship are grossly deficient. It seems as if a language of disappointment and thwarted ambitions threads its way through this text, constituting European citizenship as a category which is deficient, and positioning the European Parliament itself as the champion of a different 'real' European citizenship. Negative collocations – 'it does NOT make any reference to the legal status of Union citizenship'; 'union citizenship does NOT AS YET entail any duties for citizens of the Union, despite the wording to that effect' – represent the lacunae in the present legal understanding of citizenship. The European Parliament's self-presentation as an increasingly disappointed onlooker in the development of European citizenship is suggested by the insistent use of adverbs – 'Parliament has ALWAYS drawn the attention of the Council, the Commission and the Member States to'; 'Parliament has ALWAYS wanted to endow the institution of Union citizenship with comprehensive rights'; 'During the process of drafting the Treaty of Amsterdam Parliament AGAIN called for the rights associated with Union citizenship to be extended' – and the past tense polemical verbs – 'It ADVOCATED the incorporation of Union citizenship on an autonomous Community basis'; 'in addition, from the start, it ADVOCATED the incorporation of fundamental and human rights'; 'During the process of drafting the Treaty of Amsterdam Parliament again CALLED FOR the rights associated with Union citizenship to be extended, and it subsequently CRITICISED the fact that'.

By the standards of the traditional languages of citizenship with which the Fact Sheet is describing European citizenship, it is evident that the Parliament both finds what exists to be deficient, and places itself in the position of the frustrated onlooker whose ambitions to develop a 'real' citizenship have been thwarted over a significant period of time.

Whilst there is a mixture of vocabulary in this formulation from both the rights and participative responsibilities traditions, future ambitions for European citizenship seem to centre on the creation of a European public space, with citizenship as one means through which a European public opinion can be developed: 'the need to develop a policy which would INVOLVE European citizens in BUILDING UP a LIVING

Community capable of fulfilling the aspirations of the European people'. The discourse of rights and responsibilities shifts with this focus to that of 'identification', 'consciousness' and 'identity'. What is particularly interesting about this change of focus is the singularity of the vision that is presented. Indefinite articles – 'A European public opinion', 'A European political consciousness' and 'A European identity' – suggest the construction of a unified and homogeneous space which will become 'A living Community'. Indeed the possibility of plurality within this European space is implicitly denied by the use of the singular 'European PEOPLE'.

In a sense, this text shows with striking clarity the limitations of both the liberal democratic and civic republican traditions when engaging with definitions of citizenship outside the nation-state context. A discourse of European citizenship rights would argue for some form of central authority independent of the governments of member states. As the Fact Sheet suggests, what would be needed would be 'an AUTONOMOUS Community basis, so as to give citizens of the Union an INDEPENDENT status'. A discourse of European citizenship participation, on the other hand, would require the creation of a European public space which would itself provide 'a source of LEGITIMACY for the EU'. In this case, the space is seen as necessarily other than, and outside, the public spaces of political participation in the nation-states, hence perhaps the constitution of a unified homogeneous site composed of one (in the singular) 'European people'.

WOMEN'S LANGUAGES OF CITIZENSHIP

The fact that the transnational site of the EU currently represents one of the few post nation-state formal political spaces and that its own citizenship languages are, as we have just seen, in some state of flux, makes it an interesting place, 'on the ground', in which to explore the contribution of gender to citizenship discussions. We might ask, for example, whether women MEPs use the frameworks of liberal democracy and civic republicanism when they talk about European citizenship. Whether they have a sense of a European public space of the sort that the Parliament's own Fact Sheet is seeking to establish. Whether there are particular ways in which women MEPs are imagining European citizenship and the spaces in which it operates, and whether such spaces might help us to reinterpret the public/private dichotomies that have been the subject of so much feminist debate.

To begin to answer these questions, we will consider the responses of the 60 women MEPs to the question: 'What is citizenship in the context of the EU?' Again, in a later chapter (Chapter 6), we will examine the extent to which nationality, political grouping and age appear to nuance their replies. At this stage, however, we will try to see what languages of citizenship women are using in relation to the traditions we have already explored.

The first conclusion in analysing these answers is that women MEPs do not generally constitute citizenship within either of the two traditions: either the liberal democratic or civic republican traditions. Of the 59 women who spoke about citizenship, only 17 (29 per cent) used vocabulary taken from these languages. Those who did use these broad frameworks mostly describe citizenship in terms of the liberal democratic emphasis on rights accorded to the individual, within a context of defined legal and political status: 'It's about the fundamental RIGHTS people have – classical human RIGHTS – free speech, not to be discriminated against in all areas. These are the bedrock of citizenship . . . It's a citizen who has access to fundamental RIGHTS and to democracy' (British, PES).

For some women here, the vocabulary of the liberal democratic model is used to constitute an EU citizenship which is deficient, as in the European Parliament's Fact Sheet above: 'European citizenship is still a minority, DEFICIENT concept. We should give European citizenship a PROPER status, within a common legal framework of RIGHTS and DUTIES. . . . The new Treaty should recognize the political character of citizenship' (Spanish, EUL). Indeed, once the vocabulary of liberal democratic citizenship is employed, women on the Left and the Right can unite in this 'deficiency' view of European citizenship. For the Left, this is a matter of disappointment: 'a very MEAGRE definition' (Dutch, Green); 'a meagre citizenship . . . in which people do not recognize themselves' (Belgian, PES). For those on the Right, who are wary of weakening nation-state citizenship, the weaknesses of current notions of European citizenship are to be applauded: 'I see NO POINT in EU citizenship . . . we should retain ONLY NATIONAL citizenship' (Danish, EDN).

Some women reuse this language of liberal democratic citizenship in a possibly more hopeful political context – European citizenship is not deficient, so much as different. What is on offer in the European context, they argue, is indeed an attribution of rights, but an attribution of rights accorded in the framework of nation-state reciprocity, rather than within individual nation-states, or parallel to nation-states: 'The advantages of an EU citizen are the facilities which the EU states have developed over time against each other in a MUTUAL legal system which are, of course, valid for all who have citizenship of one of the 15 member states' (German, EPP).

Only one of the women uses a vocabulary which fits more closely with that of the civic republican tradition, arguing that the EU constitutes a new political space for its citizens which is participative: 'Far beyond the concept of citizens described in the Treaty – "the rights to participate actively or passively in local elections, the right to turn to the European Ombudsman, the right to diplomatic protection from any of the member states" – there is a citizenship created through the application of progress together, the exchange of people, the recognition of degrees, the achievements towards freedom to circulate . . . the access to documents required, the Ombudsman, the presence of citizens' associations in the Parliament, and so on' (Spanish, PES).

The majority of women interviewed (42/59, or 71 per cent), however, use vocabulary which is derived from neither the liberal democratic nor civic republican traditions, and it is within the texture of their responses that some of the key issues of gendering a post-national citizenship may be raised. For most of this group of women, the language of citizenship they are speaking is intimately related to that of identity. Four of the MEPs indeed suggest that their own plural identities are specifically emblematic of European citizenship: 'European citizenship . . . is something I feel very close to me as an individual. I was born in Germany, educated in Sweden, and am an MEP for Spain' (Spanish, PES). What is being constituted here is not the notion of 'A' European identity, but rather of a plural identity which is the basis of 'being European'. European citizenship is not having rights or responsibilities, so much as having a particular identity or, in this case, an overlapping set of different identities.

Even for those women who do not situate themselves personally within a plural identity, citizenship is constituted as something which is by definition linked to feelings of plurality, either in the sense of an awareness of a quality added to what you are already – 'an added value' (Dutch, ELDR) – or as a perception of being part of an essentially plural grouping – 'the feeling of belonging to a community which transcends national frontiers' (Italian, EPP); 'You have a feeling towards all the others' (Greek, PES). In this context, European citizenship is a matter of an evolving cultural identity: 'Identity cannot be prescribed. It has to be found by itself' (German, PES).

In these replies, European citizenship is being represented in terms which relate to personal identity, but to an identity which is radically dependent on an ever-expanding and changing imaginative space. At the most basic level, the definition of citizenship depends on the changing locations through which the citizen moves, with identity imagined as moving pluralities. As one Danish PES member puts it: 'Culturally, when I am outside Europe, I am European. When I am inside Europe, I am a Dane. When I am in Denmark, I am from Zealand; when I am in Zealand, I am from Hillerod.'

The key in this formulation is the notion of moving across frontiers of identity, either physically and mentally: 'European citizenship is giving people the means to travel, to meet, to get to know each other, to live in another country, to exchange understanding, to discover different cultures' (French, EUL); or imaginatively: 'It's a question of opening new horizons' (Spanish, EPP). Intimately connected with this definition of citizenship as an evolving identity is the tendency to draw citizenship in terms of its changing and frontierless space. One Portuguese PES member, for example, describes European citizenship as a space around which you move: 'it is a civilized space which we like and in which we feel comfortable . . . we can travel across Europe . . . we feel at home wherever we go. We don't even need to show our identity card. If we compare this present situation to the dramas that used to be in the past when we crossed frontiers this is wonderful.' Here, citizenship is being described with the vocabulary of location, as a crossing of frontiers in a space which is in a permanent state of evolution: 'citizenship doesn't exist yet. Citizenship is in the process of being made. Frontiers don't mean anything any more. It's being constructed. The feeling of belonging . . . free movement' (Luxembourgeoise, EPP).

It seems then that for the majority of women MEPs in this sample, citizenship within the post-national space of the EU is understood in language very different from either the liberal democratic or civic republican traditions. What is prioritized is the naming of plural and overlapping identities which move over personal frontiers. The space in which these movements take place is by no means the potentially unified public space which the European Parliament's Fact Sheet proposed. It is in essence a space which is in constant flux and change. Citizenship is not expressed in the language of rights or responsibilities. Rather it is represented as an understanding of plurality, with overlapping identity as the key defining perspective. The space in which this citizenship operates is one which is moving and changing and one therefore which is extremely difficult to define. Both physically and metaphorically, 'Frontiers don't mean anything any more'.

CITIZENSHIP AND TRANSITIVITY

In order to try to give greater definition to these conceptualizations of citizenship, I want to argue that we need to get beyond the choice of vocabulary, whether taken from the liberal democratic and civic republican traditions, or from that of identities and plurality. Citizenship, I shall be arguing in this section of the chapter, is fundamentally a matter of grammar. Citizenship is in essence a relational category: a citizen relates to the state, to institutions, to other citizens and so on. Paul Close (Close,

1995: 1), seeking to establish a framework for modern European citizenship, trawls through a range of definitions to produce a set of common conceptual features:

(a) citizenship is a status and a set of rights;

(b) citizenship is a RELATIONSHIP;

(c) citizenship is, first of all, a RELATIONSHIP with the STATE;

(d) citizenship is basically a LEGAL RELATIONSHIP;

(e) citizenship as a legal RELATIONSHIP provides capacities which may not be readily, fully and equally realised owing to interference from prevailing societal inequalities of condition and opportunity;

(f) citizenship is a MULTI-STRANDED RELATIONSHIP, being not just legal, but also political, economic, and otherwise social;

(g) citizenship, being a RELATIONSHIP with the state, brings people into CITIZENSHIP RELATIONS with each other;

(h) CITIZENSHIP RELATIONS are power relations;

(i) CITIZENSHIP RELATIONS are characterised by process and change;

(j) CITIZENSHIP RELATIONS occur to some extent BETWEEN PEOPLE within and through COLLECTIVITIES (and thereby between collectivities), but citizenship per se is always an INDIVIDUAL RELATIONSHIP;

(k) essentially, citizenship is an INTERNALLY ORIENTED RELATIONSHIP which people as individuals have with the nation-state of which they have full membership by virtue of their enjoyment of the full range of citizenship rights granted, guaranteed or enforced by the state.

With the exception of the first feature (a), Close is defining citizenship within a series of relationships: relationships with the state, within the law, between other people, within and between collectivities, between individuals. The idea of a network of relationships within which citizenship is set is arguably close to a notion derived from linguistics: the notion of transitivity. Transitivity concerns the linguistic manifestations of the roles of participants and the ways in which they relate to each other. It thus focuses inevitably on agency – who does what to whom? In a sense, the linguistic nexus subject–verb–object (or who/what doing to what/ whom) is the establishment, as Halliday would express it (Halliday, 1971), of a world view, of a view of the ways in which relationships are drawn. A discussion of grammar necessarily explores how actions are represented: What kind of actions are being constituted? Who is the subject, who does them? Who is the object, to whom are they being done? In schematic form, the Hallidayian model divides verbs into categories, depending on the activity to which they refer, and to the participants' role in the activity – whether they are performing the activity (the subject/ agent), or having it done to them (the object/ the acted upon). Sara Mills

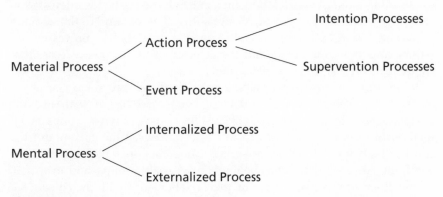

Figure 4.1

(Mills, 1995: 144) provides a helpful diagrammatic representation of some of the range of process-participant roles (Figure 4.1). In this diagram, 'material process' produces actions by people ('A does something to B' (transitive), or 'A does something' (intransitive)), or events ('The computer broke down'). Action processes are either of 'intention' (i.e. A intended to do something to B' – transitive; or 'A intended to do something' – intransitive) or of 'supervention' (unintentional events – 'I left the book on the train'). The other half of the diagram, 'mental processes', describes, as the name suggests, processes related to the mind, or to perceptions, or feelings. Such processes may be 'internalized' ('I like him', 'he's thinking about that'), or 'externalized' (i.e. giving the results of the mental process – 'She said that. . .'). The 'internalized process' could further be divided (although Mills does not do this in her diagram) into such categories as perception ('seeing', 'hearing'), reaction (i.e. value-judgements – 'liking', 'loathing') or cognition ('thinking', 'wondering').

The root of this type of transitivity analysis is a belief that a range of choices is open to a writer/speaker and that any 'text' could conceivably have been produced in a different way. A study of transitivity is thus an investigation of a world view that is being created. Just as Halliday (Halliday, 1971) used transitivity analysis in a literary text (Golding's novel *The Inheritors*) to show the different world views of literary characters, so transitivity analysis can help us to explore the nature of relationships established in more overtly political texts.

If this type of analysis seems a world away from politics and citizenship, it is as well to remember that any discussion of transitivity inevitably implies a consideration of power, control and agency. Deirdre Burton, in arguing for precisely this sort of process-participant analysis of texts, suggests that transitivity analysis is, almost by definition, one way of establishing what power-relationships exist: 'If the analyst is interested in "making strange" the power-relationships that obtain in the socially constructed world . . . then, crucially, it is the realisation of processes and participants (both the actors and the acted upon) in those processes that should concern us' (Burton, 1982: 200).

In addition to process-participant roles (Is the citizen subject or object of the verb? What sorts of verbs are being used?), we shall use the portmanteau title 'grammars of citizenship' to look at what groups, what relationship categories (to return to Close's analysis) the citizen and the speaker both inhabit. These relational categories, in which, on the one hand, the citizen is defined as belonging to certain groups, and in which, on the other, the speakers describe their relationships with the citizen, are an additional indication of the location of citizenship. In grammatical terms, the question 'How is citizenship said?' becomes not 'What vocabulary of citizenship is the speaker using?' but rather 'Where is the citizen being positioned and in relation to what and to whom?'

GRAMMARS OF CITIZENSHIP

To see how this approach might work in practice, we will take one of the responses from a woman MEP, describing citizenship within the terms of mobile and plural identities, and see whether we can learn more about this particular language of citizenship by applying a transitivity analysis. The example I have chosen is from a socialist Portuguese MEP who sets her response within both the framework of rights and that of plural identities. The text of the response is set out below:

'I feel I am a European citizen. I like the differences which exist from country to country. We have so many different cultures, but we understand them. We are integrated; it is a civilized space which we like and in which we feel comfortable. Sometimes people forget the benefits and advantages we have acquired in the European Union. People forget what life was like before, the problems encountered at the frontiers, resulting in quarrels, delays, all types of aggravation with the police and the customs. Now we can travel across Europe with such facility! We feel at home, wherever we go. We don't even need to show our identity card. If we compare this present situation to the dramas that used to be in the past when we crossed frontiers. . . . This mobility is wonderful! I may be in France one day and Greece the next and I am just in Europe.

And we have the right to vote. People only exist politically speaking when they vote. We still have many immigrants in Europe and it is so important that they are able to vote in the European Parliament's elections. And for a country like Portugal who has so many immigrants, it is extremely important that they are able to vote. They are now appreciated by the candidates. They did not exist before – they were just there. They didn't politically exist because they did not vote. And now they do. They bring out their problems and participate in discussions.'

If we take out the verbs which are relational (i.e. bring two elements together) and concentrate solely on the material and mental process elements, we would get a table much like Table 4.1.

Looking at these 22 examples, there are a number of things that can be said about the process-participant roles which they are constituting. To begin with, over half the verbs here (12/22) have a first person singular or plural as the subject: 'I like the differences'; 'WE understand them'. In this definition of citizenship, then, the MEP is identifying herself closely with the concept of citizenship, and with the citizens of Europe she represents. Of the other ten examples, seven have 'immigrants' (or

Table 4.1

I feel	Mental internalized
I like the differences	Mental internalized
We understand them	Mental internalized
Which we like	Mental internalized
In which we feel comfortable	Mental internalized
People forget the benefits	Mental internalized
(benefits) we have acquired	Mental internalized
People forget what life was like	Mental internalized
The problems (they) encountered	Mental internalized
We can travel across Europe	Material intention
We feel at home	Mental internalized
Wherever we go	Material
We don't need to show our identity card	Material intention
If we compare this situation	Mental internalized
When we crossed frontiers	Material intention
When they vote	Material intention
They are able to vote	Material intention
That they are able to vote	Material intention
Because they did not vote	Material intention
And now they do (vote)	Material intention
They bring out their problems	Mental internalized
(They) participate in discussions	Mental externalized

'they', referring to 'immigrants') as their subject; two have 'people'; and one has 'problems' as the subject of the verb. Evidently, in this construction of citizenship, the citizens themselves (either with the MEP or as a group) are agents; in other words, they are given an active role. In particular it is noteworthy that the MEP places 'immigrants' as a constituent (and in the case of this response, main) part of the description of citizenship.

What sort of activity is attributed to these active citizens of Europe? What does the choice of verbs tell us about the ways in which this MEP is understanding the notion of citizenship in the EU? Twelve of the 22 verbs in this sample are in the mental internalized category. Citizenship is something which is felt – 'I FEEL I am a European citizen'; 'a civilized space ... in which we FEEL comfortable'. It is also something which is related to cognition: citizens UNDERSTAND each other; they sometimes FORGET the benefits and advantages of being citizens; they COMPARE present and past situations, and ENCOUNTER problems.

By comparison, the verbs of material process, describing actions which are observable in the real world and have visible consequences, are relatively fewer in number: 9/22, compared with 13/22 for mental process. These verbs of material process firstly refer to travelling – 'TRAVEL across Europe', 'wherever we GO'. Secondly, five of the verbs describe electoral participation: 'they are able to VOTE in the European Parliament'; 'they did not VOTE' – where the subject is in all cases 'immigrants'. Finally, the remaining two verbs both have direct objects indicating the areas in which the agent (the subject of the verb) is having effect – 'We don't need to SHOW IDENTITY CARDS'; 'when we CROSSED FRONTIERS'.

In a sense, the material process verbs are giving the concept of citizenship an outward manifestation, as opposed to the picture of perception and feeling which emerges from the rest of the response. For this MEP, citizenship materializes as travel across the space of Europe, as crossing frontiers and not showing proof of one particular identity, and as participating in electoral processes, giving political voice as it were. Citizenship is thus a matter of political rights (strongly associated in this formulation with the rights of minorities), and of movement across a space in which frontiers and fixed identities are specifically of no relevance.

Overall, the result of this transitivity analysis of the response of just one of the MEPs has been to develop our initial observations about the vocabulary of citizenship of the 71 per cent of the respondents who did not use the liberal democratic or civic republican frames. Citizenship is a matter of perception and feeling rather than of codified rights and responsibilities. It is something which is strongly linked to personal (and collective) identity, and something with which the MEP herself identifies.

The emphasis is on the people themselves ('I', 'We', 'People', 'Immigrants') rather than the institutions and structures and legal processes. Citizenship is associated with the notion of travelling across boundaries and rejecting fixed frontiers or single fixed identities.

MALE/FEMALE GRAMMARS OF CITIZENSHIP

Is this particular grammar of citizenship one which is peculiar to women MEPs? Do they locate citizens in different ways from men? In comparing male and female grammars of citizenship as expressed in speeches in the Plenary sessions of Parliament, we shall be asking some very specific questions. What are the roles that MEPs give to the citizen, and are these assigned roles influenced by the gender of the speaker? In what relational categories do MEPs place the citizen, and is there a tendency for men and women to emphasize certain categories as opposed to others? How do the MEPs say that they relate to the citizen, and is the location in which they place themselves relative to the citizen influenced at all by the gender of the speaker?

Within the case study Plenaries, speeches were selected for this analysis against the following criteria: speeches where MEPs used the words 'citizen' or 'people'; speeches in which they alluded to groups of people or categories of people – 'fishermen', 'consumers', 'business people' and so on; speeches in which MEPs named individuals within the space of the European Parliament. In this way, we can study a small corpus of speeches (368) in which the citizens of Europe, in some guise, make a formal entrance into the discursive site of the European Parliament. Once again, the aim of this analysis is to see whether there are signs of difference in the grammars of men and women, and what these 'directions of difference' might be.

Using a simple type of transitivity analysis on these speeches, we can gain an idea of the ways in which citizens are being located within the space of Europe: are they the agents (the subjects of the verbs), or are they being acted on (the objects of the verbs)? Are they being placed in particular groups, and if so, which ones? A simple counting of the numbers of examples in each of these categories (agent, acted on, groups) produces some 664 examples, distributed between the three categories as in Table 4.2.

If we now map the occurrence of these examples against the sex of the speaker, we find a number of interesting differences (Table 4.3). To begin with, it should be said that, in making such a selection of speeches in which citizens were appearing, were 'named' as it were, we have deliber-ately operated 'gender-blind', selecting speeches for analysis solely on the

Table 4.2

Category	Number of examples	Percentage
Agent	140	21
Acted on	239	36
Groups	285	43
Total	664	100

Table 4.3

	Male	Male	Female	Female
Category	Number	Percentage of male examples	Number	Percentage of female examples
Agent	57	17	83	25
Acted on	133	41	106	31
Groups	135	42	150	44
Total	325	100	339	100

Table 4.4

Plenary session	Percentage of female contributions
14–18 November 1994*	25.5
16–20 January 1995	25
13 February 1995	28
28 February–2 March 1995	27
14–17 March 1995*	25
3–7 April 1995*	24.3
25–27 April 1995	19

basis of the above criteria. What is particularly striking about the results, as set out in Table 4.3, is the very high proportion of examples in the naming of citizenship which have come from women speakers: 339 examples, as opposed to 325 for men. This is even more surprising in view of the fact that women's average participation in Plenary sessions (as judged by our original seven Plenary sessions) stands at about 24.8 per cent, or approximately at the same level as their membership of the directly elected cohort to the 1994 Parliament. As a check on this, Table 4.4 gives the percentages of women speakers in each of the Plenary sessions we originally looked at, with the case study Plenaries from which the selection of speeches was made asterisked for easy reference.

With this comparison between women's participation in the Plenaries of the European Parliament (around 25 per cent) and their naming of citizens in these sample speeches (51 per cent of the total examples), we might argue that women appear to be bringing the people of Europe into the discursive space of the Parliament with somewhat greater frequency than their male colleagues. By this reckoning, women may be said to tend towards 'humanizing' the citizen in the space of the European Parliament, giving the citizen a bodily rather than abstract form, by naming 'citizens', 'people' or individuals or groups of citizens. The evidence is by no means conclusive, but when it is set beside our earlier observations about the ways in which women MEPs construct citizenship – relating it closely to identity, and involving themselves in the description – it is highly sugges-tive of a rather different approach to the definition of citizenship 'on the ground'.

Secondly, the mapping of examples against the sex of the speaker suggests that whilst both men and women position the citizen more strongly as acted upon, rather than acting, women MEPs may have a slightly greater tendency to name the citizen as agent. For both, the most frequent naming of the citizen is as a part of a group, within specific relational categories. We shall now look at these categories to try to gain an idea of the ways in which the citizen is being defined.

For both men and women, this categorization of citizens, the naming of people as part of groups, is a key component of the grammar of citizen-ship. The groups in which we choose to position people provide a particular role for them in relation to others, and in relation to processes and structures. This categorization, this naming of people in groups, is an important part of the grammar of citizenship, of the ways in which we define the subject or object participant. As an example of this, we will look in more detail at five of the key positionings to see how members of the European Parliament are using this particular aspect of the grammar of citizenship. Table 4.5 gives details of these groups, with an indication of the proportions of examples in each group given by men and by women.

In the first two groups (consumers/producers and sectorial) the pro-portions of male/female references are approximately 60–70 per cent from men, as against 40–30 per cent from women. In the last three groups (minorities, women and artists) the proportions are very different, with examples from women speakers either equalling or outnumbering those from men.

We shall take the groups where the proportions are approximately

Table 4.5

Group	Male percentage share	Female percentage share
Consumers/producers	67	33
Sectorial groups	62	38
Minorities	50	50
Women	16	84
Artists/cultural workers	12	88

60/40 first, starting with the consumers/producers. Whereas in a national parliament it would not be unusual to see citizens categorized as 'taxpayers', there were only two such descriptions (one by a male, and one by a female MEP) in this corpus of speeches. In comparison, a frequent positioning of the citizen is, perhaps unsurprisingly, as part of a consumer/producer relationship. Here, the citizen is drawn in an essentially commercial framework which implies a set of relationships based on production and consumption. The citizen is described in the classic terms of citizens who are customers of a particular business or industrial sector. Thus, for example, in a debate on telecommunications and cable television, an MEP introduces the citizen as consumers who may find that the service they are being offered is deficient, and who will therefore need well-established means of customer redress:

> 'The second point from Mr Hendrick's report, which has come up in every telecommunications report before this Parliament, is the need for clarity and certainty about universal service, about the principles on which it should be based, how it should be financed and in particular what redress CONSUMERS should have if universal service is not available.' (Read PSE British (F), 5.4.95, 4–461/160)

'Consumers' can also be used in a more generic way where what is being proposed is less a citizen in a specific supplier relationship, but rather the citizen as a consumer who may be endangered by the failure of institutional safeguards. The latter is most typically seen in relation to an issue like the contamination of beef:

> 'The second criticism relates to the limits on weekly and yearly livestock units: we are opposed to any further increase in maximum production limits for small-capacity establishments. . . . An excessive increase in such limits could jeopardize the hygiene quality of the final product and thus CONSUMER health which, as we are all aware, is the principle which must be at the forefront of the Community legislator's mind.' (Azzolini Italian FE (M), 7.4.95, 4–461/234)

Not surprisingly, our second category, the citizen as member of a particular sectorial grouping (farmer, fisherman, professional) is frequently used, as issues relating to each sector are raised in specific debates, or as the concerns of relevant interest groups arise. The farmers are of course a classic EU example, with regular debates on aspects of the agricultural market, which may well position different types of farmers in opposition to each other. In a debate on the market in wine, for example, one MEP explained:

'we are pleased that it has been possible to find some basis for agreement despite a conflict of interest between North and South, and between countries that produce a surplus and those that do not. It is obviously difficult to explain to a Portuguese FARMER – who would be arrested and sent to prison if he made wine enriched with sucrose – that this is normal practice in the North.' (Rosado Fernandes Portuguese EDA (M), 5.4.95, 4–461/117)

None of this – the absence of the taxpayer description, and the depiction of citizens within a commercial relationship, or as members of a professional group – is especially surprising. What does, however, stand out in this sample is the number of references (20 per cent of the total) to the citizen as an actual or potential minority, references which are shared equally by male and female speakers. Minorities enter the discursive space of the European Parliament in two major frameworks, that of rights, and that of integration in/exclusion from the European space. The discourse of rights – rights for minorities to vote, fundamental freedoms for minority groups – is often situated on ground which is clearly moving and changing. So, for example, in a debate on Croatia, MEPs describe minority rights within a comparative context which challenges easy assumptions in any of the member states:

'we are constantly referring to MINORITY and ethnic rights in Croatia. These are exemplary when compared with MINORITY rights in many Member States of the European Union, and I should like in particular to refute what the representative of Forza Italia has just said. Italians in Croatia enjoy rights far beyond the rights of many ethnic groups in Italy, such as those of the Slovenes in the Friuli region.' (Posselt German EPP (M), 16.3.95, 4–460/186)

References to minorities within the integration in/exclusion from the EU framework are often polarized, with those not on the extreme right generally positioning the minority member as a potentially assimilable element in the space of Europe, and those on the extreme right positioning the minority as beyond a particular legally defined space. One might, for example, compare the locations offered to the minority in speeches firstly by a socialist, and then by an extreme right wing MEP:

> 'We do not demand the repatriation of TURKISH workers, who are legally resident and employed in Europe. . . . We demand the integration of these workers and their treatment on an equal footing with workers in the EU.' (Sakellariou German PES (M), 14.3.95, 4–460/43)

> 'This measure gives rise to several concerns, notably on account of the disparities in the legislation of the various Member States concerned. It will allow illegal IMMIGRANTS and traffickers of all kinds to enter the Schengen area at its weakest point and subsequently spread throughout the other states.' (Berthu French EDN (M), 6.4.95, 4–461/204)

The emphatic positioning of minorities within the discourse of the European Parliament is a particularly interesting aspect of the grammar of citizenship in the EU. Even more interestingly from our point of view, the fact that half of the references in the sample come from women suggests that, despite their lower level of participation in the Parliament, women may be naming minorities in the space of European politics with particular insistence. In this case, the simple counting technique that we have used is serving to complement some of the evidence we found in the transitivity analysis of one MEP's interview response. Women's grammar of citizenship in the European Parliament seems to reserve a particular place for the naming of minorities.

There are two other distinct ways in which women position the citizen. Firstly, women MEPs identify the citizen as gendered far more frequently than men do – in our analysis above, 84 per cent of the examples of naming citizens as women came from female speakers. There are four major frameworks in which the citizen as woman is proposed. Firstly, women are often constructed in the role of the historically exploited. In a debate on generalized tariff preferences, for example, one woman MEP argues that the traditional position of women as an exploited group is integral to any discussion of a system of tariff preferences:

> 'we take the view that products manufactured using child labour or where there is unequal treatment of men and WOMEN, especially involving WOMEN being paid very low wages, should not be covered by the GSP. In fact, I can tell the House that these two factors are connected. When WOMEN are very badly paid, they are forced to send their children out to work as well. Then you have child labour alongside these WOMEN's work. It is a story that we are familiar with in Europe from the last century. This is now happening in the developing countries, and it is a good reason for not rewarding such practices in any way by granting further preference.' (Maij-Weggen Dutch EPP (F), 17.11.94, 4–453/192)

Secondly, women MEPs position women as citizens who have special needs and require particularly targeted measures. In the field of education and training, for example, MEPs argue that women must be given specific incentives and encouragement:

'This European Year will also provide an opportunity to open up a wider range of vocational opportunities to young WOMEN and girls, putting an end to traditional notions of suitable careers for WOMEN. This is the absolutely essential condition if we are to bring about true equality of opportunity between men and WOMEN.' (André-Léonard Belgian ELDR (F), 15.3.95, 4–460/127)

For some women MEPs, women are located as citizens who cut across customary definitions of public and private spaces, challenging traditional notions and categories. In this construction, equal opportunities need to be implemented in both so-called 'separate' spheres:

'I regret that so few proposals for legislation have been made in the area of equal opportunities. Why are there still no binding provisions on, say, parental leave, the reversal of the burden of proof or the reconciliation of family life and working life? WOMEN have been waiting a long time for these measures to be introduced and all they get are repeated apologies.

I think the following points need to be given consideration: WOMEN should not be marginalized at the workplace; WOMEN should have a better position in the family and in society; WOMEN should count as workers in family businesses, and there should be no discrimination against WOMEN in matters of social security and tax law.' (Reding Luxembourgeoise EPP (F), 16.3.95, 4–460/162)

Finally, it is women MEPs who tend to give a presence to those women outside the European Union, in the wider international arena, who are in specific difficulties, or suffering particular problems. They may be suffering as groups because of their gender, as in some of the carnage in Algeria, for example (Muscardini Italian Ind. (F), 6.4.95, 4–461/190), or, as in the case of the Kurdish MP, Mrs Zana, they may be suffering imprisonment or persecution as individuals (Fouque French PES (F), 17.11.94, 4–453/180).

Given that it is women MEPs who are making a proportionately larger contribution to the naming of the citizen as female, one might argue that, without their contribution, the grammar of citizenship would be very little marked by gender. From this evidence, it seems clear that it is mainly through the voices of women MEPs that an understanding of EU citizenship as female is expressed.

The second distinct group in which the citizen is placed by women, as opposed to men, is within what we might call an artistic or cultural framing: the citizen as artist, writer, cultural worker, etc.; 88 per cent of the references to people in this category come in the speeches of women MEPs. Whilst the overall number of examples is not large, the suggestion that it tends to be women rather than men who create artistic frameworks for the citizen is reinforced when we see the apparently greater eagerness with which women participate in debates on cultural issues. Thus, for example, in the debate on the (cultural) Kaleidoscope programme (6.4.95, 4–461/211–216) six of the twelve MEP speakers in the debate were women, a rate of participation, as we have seen, twice the norm for women overall in Plenary debates. That this level of female participation was noticeably higher than usual is further underlined by the comment of one of the participants:

'I see, moreover, that almost all the speakers in this evening's debate are women, which leads me to wonder if this subject is their exclusive preserve.' (Guinebertière French EPP, 6.4.95, 4–461/213)

In answer to the question 'Who are the citizens?' we can say from this evidence that the citizen is given a variety of roles in the discursive space of the European Parliament. Some of these are highly predictable: consumer/producer, sectorial member, for example. Others are more surprising, as for example the emphatic drawing of minorities found in a 'rights for minorities' framework, and in an 'integration/exclusion' context.

From the point of view of a putative women's grammar of citizenship, we saw firstly that women had a tendency to name the citizen more frequently than men, to introduce the bodily presence of the citizen into discussions in the European Parliament. Secondly, we noted that women contributed to the naming of minorities more frequently than men. Thirdly, we saw that in the case of two particular categories – women and artists/cultural workers – women had major responsibility for introducing these groups into the discursive space represented by the European Parliament. The citizen imagined by the members of the European Parliament is in a number of relationships: commercial, sectorial, as a member of a minority. Arguably, without the contribution of women in the Parliament, the citizen would appear less frequently as a minority, and would make hardly any appearance as a woman or as an artist/cultural worker.

Using a transitivity analysis, we shall now explore what citizens are said to be doing within the space of Europe, and what power positions are represented to them. Within the grammars of citizenship revealed by this selection of speeches, a process-participant analysis suggests that the citizen is largely represented as being acted upon, rather than as the actor/agent. As we see in Table 4.2, taken from the earlier analysis of the three categories, citizens are more likely to be described as

Table 4.6

	Men	Women
	Percentage of citizen as subject verbs	*Percentage of citizen as subject verbs*
Mental	89	85
Material	11	15

being the objects of the activities of others, acted upon, rather than as being the subjects of actions themselves, the agents. Whilst there is some indication that women may nuance this presentation by placing the citizen slightly more frequently in the subject position than men do, the overall impression created is of a citizen named as the object of action by others.

As in the interviews with women MEPs we analysed earlier in this chapter, the process-participant roles proposed for the citizens as subjects of the verbs are overwhelmingly mental rather than material action – perceiving and understanding, rather than operating visibly in the external world. The proportions of mental/material processes for men and women are approximately the same (Table 4.67).

For both men and women, mental processes include those of perception, of recognition and of cognition. Thus, for example, with mental action relating to perception, MEPs use such verbs as 'felt' and 'see':

'it would not be surprising if many European citizens FELT that (there was fraud).' (Elles British EPP (M), 4.4.95, 4–460/42)

'How on earth do we expect that citizens of the EU can understand . . . when year in year out they SEE that the protection of the financial interests of the European Communities means absolutely nothing.' (Dillen Belgian Ind. (M), 15.3.95, 4–460/114)

Secondly, in mental processes relating to reaction, MEPs position the citizen as acting in response to a stimulus – 'find incomprehensible', 'react', 'accept', 'expect', 'are ashamed of', 'are affected':

'The citizens of the Union FIND this INCOMPREHENSIBLE.' (Blak Danish PES (M), 18.11.94, 4–453/220)

'When the peoples of Europe ACCEPT that certain powers should be exercised at Community level it is because they believe that this will be the best way of ensuring that their interests are defended.' (Souchet French EDN (M), 15.3.95, 4–460/119)

'The citizens of Europe EXPECT us to act, not to comment.' (Green British PES (F), 16.11.94, 4–453/72)

'The people of Europe are directly AFFECTED, so their concern is all the greater.' (Mosiek-Urbahn German EPP (F), 4.4.95, 4–461/32)

Finally, mental processes related to cognition locate the European citizen as thinking about and judging Europe rather than acting in it – 'wondering about', 'cannot understand':

'many citizens of the EU are WONDERING about the significance of the changes in exchange rates.' (Von Habsburg German EPP (M), 15.3.95, 4–460/92)

'the people HAVE NO UNDERSTANDING of this at all.' (Salisch German PES (F), 15.3.95, 4–460/95)

Where material, as opposed to mental, process is indicated – and there are few examples of this – verbs are generally describing activity related to traditional citizenship rights and responsibilities (voting, paying taxes) in the case of male MEPs:

'the roads, for which the citizens have already PAID their taxes.' (Piecyk German PES (M), 14.11.94, 4–453/10)

'During the eighteenth, nineteenth and twentieth centuries people from Sir Leon Brittan's party and people in other countries represented in this House FOUGHT FOR democratic control over those matters which affected the citizens.' (Falconer British PES (M), 16.11.94, 4–453/110)

and activity related to movement and crossing frontiers in the case of women MEPs:

'Men and women are unable to CROSS the frontiers.' (Pailler French EUL (F), 6.4.95, 4–461/203)

'a lot of people are RUNNING AROUND with idealistic notions of a truly integrated Europe.' (Peijs Dutch EPP (F), 16.11.94, 4–453/102)

The answer to the question 'What is the citizen doing?' is thus in brief: generally being done to rather than doing. Citizens within the discursive space of the European Parliament are normally placed as the object of others' activity, being looked after, being given services, being provided with information, and so on. When the citizens are the subjects of the verb, the agents, they are normally positioned by both male and female MEPs as engaging in mental rather than material action. Citizens perceive, react and think in the space of Europe.

Table 4.7

	Men	Men	Women	Women
	Number	Percentage of total	Number	Percentage of total
Rights	27	60	18	40
Dialogic	26	39	41	61
Total	53		59	

As a final part of this grammatical exploration of citizenship, we shall look at how the MEPs situate themselves in relation to the citizen, and what sort of relationship, MEP to citizen, is proposed by their grammars. Earlier in this chapter, we were particularly concerned to see the extent to which women MEPs described citizenship in the traditional vocabulary of the liberal democratic and civic republican traditions. We noted that the majority of them do not use this vocabulary, and tend instead to imagine a citizenship in which personal identity, and very often their own personal identity, is implicated. We will now review the case study sample of Plenary speeches to see the positions in which MEPs place themselves in relation to the citizens, and in particular to see whether there is evidence of positionings related to the two main frameworks we have discussed: the traditional liberal or civic republican framework, and the personal identity framework.

One of the indications of members' relationships with the citizen is their self-positioning in relation to the citizen, the geography of the MEP's presence. A discourse of rights and responsibilities, for example, might place the MEP at one end of a relationship based on a legal structure ('elected by citizens'), with notions of accountability ('judged by citizens'), choices ('choices made by citizens'), and defence of rights and interests ('rights of citizens', 'interests of citizens'). A discourse of personal identity might place the MEP in a dialogic relationship with the citizen, with notions of an MEP engaged in listening ('consulted by the citizen', 'views shared by the citizen'), in being physically closer to the citizen ('give access to the citizen', 'open up to the citizen'), and in receiving a response from the citizen ('thanks from the citizen', 'celebrated by the citizen').

These two categories of relationships – rights relationships and dialogic relationships – are broad, so that any simple counting of the incidence of references to them will necessarily be of indicative interest rather than of statistical validity. Nonetheless, the results are suggestive of slightly different ways of imagining a citizen relationship in the European Parliament. Table 4.7 sets out the numbers of examples of each framework found in the sample speeches, with the proportions in each spoken by men and by women.

From this evidence, men and women MEPs position themselves in both the rights and dialogic relationships with citizens. The proportions in which they express these relationships, however, appear to be exactly opposite, with men favouring the rights relationship more than the dialogic, and the female MEPs placing themselves more frequently in a dialogic relationship with the citizen.

CONCLUSIONS

At the beginning of this chapter we looked at the ways in which the traditional frameworks of citizenship – liberal democracy and civic republicanism – have been under increasing pressure. The pressure has come from three groups. Firstly, from those who argue that citizenship must now be reconstituted in contexts which are wider than the nation-state; contexts which correspond more evidently to a world in which the old certainties of territorial integrity and inviolability are being challenged by globalization, international communications networks, and transnational political structures. Secondly, pressure has come from those who suggest that democracy can only be revitalized and radicalized if we begin to understand citizenship and democratic participation in different ways. Finally, the pressure has come from feminists who, in arguing the well-known 'the personal is political', have called into question the bases of both of the traditional frameworks of citizenship – liberal democratic and civic republican. These commentators have sought both to critique the traditional frameworks, and to relocate the arguments in entirely different frameworks.

The European Parliament has presented us with an opportunity to look at the ways in which citizenship is being currently understood within one particular transnational space, where the challenges to overtly territorial definitions of citizenship are clearly being made. We noted that one of the official institutional scripts of citizenship, provided by the European Parliament itself, draws together the languages of liberal democracy and civic republicanism and argues that, on these bases, present conceptions of citizenship in Europe are grossly deficient. Implicitly, this text proposes a single homogeneous community which would act as a vehicle for the expression of a public will.

Within this context, our attention in this chapter has focused on the languages of citizenship spoken by Members of the European Parliament. In effect, we have been looking at the positions in which MEPs place the citizen within the space of Europe. Overall, the citizen in Europe is firstly positioned as passive, as a citizen who is being done to, rather than doing. When this citizen does become active, and is imagined as the subject or agent of the activity, the actions involved are mainly those in the mind, rather than physically in the political space. Citizen participation in this particular transnational site is understood in terms of perceiving, seeing, understanding and reacting. Secondly, the citizen of Europe enters into the discursive space of Europe in a number of different roles – consumer, producer, professional, etc. Importantly, a key role for the European citizen is that of minority, either as a minority member who is assimilable or as a minority member who should be excluded.

Within this shared grammar, however, it seems that women are using a language of citizenship which is distinctive, and in some ways slightly different from that of men. The majority of MEPs interviewed use a vocabulary which is taken not from the register of rights (liberal democracy) or from that of responsibilities (civic republicanism), but rather from a register of personal identity. The framework proposed argues for a citizen who has a plurality of identities, and accepts a perspective in which identity is both plural and mobile, crossing frontiers metaphorically as well as physically.

In the Plenary sessions of the European Parliament, the speeches of women name citizens more frequently than those of men. In a sense, we might argue that women seem more likely to 'embody' the citizen, to bring him or her into the discursive space of the Parliament, and to give a physical presence to the citizen in Europe. Again, it is women who more frequently name the citizen as a minority, and above all it is women who gender the citizen and provide an artistic/cultural framing. The relationship between the representative in the European Parliament and the citizen is more frequently presented by women MEPs as a dialogic one, rather than as one based on rights and responsibilities. To summarize, then, what women seem to be distinctively contributing to the grammar of citizenship is a prioritizing of plural identities, an embodying of the citizens (including their engendering), and an emphasis on a relationship of dialogue rather than one of rights and responsibilities.

In comparison with the institutional script of citizenship presented in the Parliament's Fact Sheet, the grammars of citizenship we have heard 'on the ground', as it were, in the European Parliament, are somewhat different from that of the deficiency/homogeneous community model proposed by the institution. Rather than the top-down creation of a single imagined community which might fit into one or both of the traditional frameworks of citizenship, the MEPs themselves are operating in a space in which citizenship is articulated as a matter of perception and feeling, of plural roles and identities rather than of unified homogeneity. The contribution of women in personalizing and embodying this plurality, and in emphasizing the primordial role of dialogue within the moving discursive space of the EU, is a highly distinctive one.

It is certainly true that writers have recently focused a great deal more on the expressions of citizenship, and the ways in which citizenship is framed and understood. A special issue of *Critical Social Policy*, for example, has been devoted to 'Vocabularies of citizenship and gender in Northern Europe' (*Critical Social Policy*, 1998). In this chapter, I have been arguing that we might profitably turn our attention away from vocabulary, and turn it instead towards grammars of citizenship in order to see whether an approach which explores the nature of relationships within the citizenship concept might be of more immediate conceptual use in understanding and locating citizenship today. The key relational questions which grammar poses – Who is the citizen? What is the citizen doing? What is the relationship of the representative with the citizen? – are ones which may well help us to keep the citizen at the centre of our concerns, no matter how expanding and global the context in which we all live.

CHAPTER 5

IMAGINING EUROPE

Europe is, as we have seen, a complex site in which to situate issues of citizenship. Andreas Behnke has memorably called the EU 'the first postmodern form of political space . . . different from the traditional forms of political space founded on the pure presence of blood or soil' (Behnke, 1997: 262). If the physical boundaries of 'Europe' are highly disputable, its emotional geographies – the emotional territory on which it is situated – are indeed even more problematic. Without the sort of traditional emotional markers that we associate with the nation-state, blood or soil in Behnke's terms, it is not always easy to see how the affective identity of the EU is going to be constructed. Behnke himself, for example, concludes by characterizing citizenship in the EU as a 'temporary place of those absent from their "native" places' (Behnke, 1997: 262). One would have to say that the identification of the EU as a sort of 'elsewhere' for people temporarily absent from their own native homes, a receptacle as it were for generic absences, is unlikely to stimulate strong citizen affectivity.

In this chapter, we shall examine some of the ways in which a European identity is presently being constructed and see how MEPs (both male and female) are contributing to this marking of the emotional contours of Europe. As the chapter progresses, I shall be arguing that, rather than a space of absence, the EU is actually being constructed as an identity in process, and one which processes or moves within slightly different frameworks for men and for women.

EUROPEAN IDENTITY

The last ten years have seen two apparently paradoxical tendencies among commentators on the European Union. On the one hand, the Union, or often a wider and less differentiated 'Europe', has been a site in which to debate once more the infinitely complex question of community and identity, a discussion given added and often bloody intensity by wars and disputes within the geographical area of wider Europe. Terms like 'nation-state', 'ethnicity' and 'community' traditionally provide the building blocks in the debate, with writers arguing variously that one or other term is dead, irrelevant or dangerous. Definitions of Europe have often been at the centre of these arguments over the validity and relevance of the terms we use to understand complex identities in a changing world.

As far as pessimists are concerned, contemporary Europe gives a striking picture of the break-up and fragmentation of human values in late twentieth-century society. Eric Hobsbawn, for example, has painted a picture of infinite regression into smaller ethnicities as people cope with the complexities of modern society by rooting themselves in familiar landscapes which they defend against outsiders: 'the fear of the unknown, of the darkness into which we may fall when the landmarks which seem to provide an objective, a permanent, a positive delimitation of our belonging together, disappear. And belonging together, preferably in groupings with visible badges of membership and recognition signs, is more important than ever in societies in which everything combines to destroy what binds human beings together into communities' (Hobsbawn, 1992: 4). In this scenario, the ethnic group is the ultimate refuge when society falls apart.

For the optimists, on the other hand, the idea of multiple identities, being played out without fixed notions of what we might share in common (Rutherford, 1990), is an optimistic sign that totalizing and essentialist definitions of 'nation', 'ethnic group' and 'community' are being rejected, and are in a state of flux and renegotiation, a flux of course well suited to the concerns of postmodernism.

At the same time as some writers dispute the key terms of the debate, there has been a continued interest, particularly among anthropologists and popular historians, in the concept of a shared identity in Europe, what this identity might look like, and how it might develop. Victoria Goddard and her colleagues note, for example, that 'the "idea of Europe" as a political ideal and mobilizing metaphor has become increasingly prominent in the latter part of the twentieth century' (Goddard et al., 1994: 26). Politicians have regularly set out their 'vision of Europe' which normally correlates Europe with the actual or potential site of the European Union. In many cases, these types of vision are underpinned by a certain 'idea of Europe', often linked to particular notions of a pluralistic democracy or/and to a social market economy. As Philip Schlesinger expressed it: 'Central to this representation ... are the (social) market economy coupled with various forms of pluralistic democracy and civil society. Whatever the institutional realities, these stand as tokens of a level of civilisation or culture that represents both an aspiration for those who do not have it, and as a normative criterion for the haves with which to judge the credentials of the would-be aspirants' (Schlesinger, 1994: 323).

This vision, of course, can easily become what Jürgen Habermas (Habermas, 1992) calls a form of welfare chauvinism: Europe defines itself by defending the gains of its welfare state against the hostile outsiders, beyond the perceived fringes of this society.

Other writers argue that there are different sorts of markers of a shared European identity besides Europe's present social economy and democratic system. In some senses, Europe shares, they suggest, a broad cultural heritage – the heritage of the Graeco-Roman civilization, Christianity, the Enlightenment, notions of Science, Reason, Progress and Democracy (see, for example, Wallace 1990b). Whichever perspective is taken, however – pessimistic or optimistic (Europe's increasing fragmentation into smaller ethnicities, or Europe's opportunities to allow the productive interplay of different cultures) – visions of shared politico/social structures, or visions of a shared cultural heritage, the ways in which we as Europeans might relate emotionally to it are highly problematic. As John Hutchinson and Anthony Smith suggest, whilst there may be instances of an elite identification with Europe, 'the degree to which a European identity has emerged at the cost of national identities or commands a popular following in most European states remains largely uncharted, as have the meanings which different populations attribute to any such larger identity' (Hutchinson and Smith, 1994: 12). The community of Europe remains one of the great emotional absences today.

The problem is shown in all its acuity by the efforts which the institutions of the EU have made at various times to create what is sometimes called a 'People's Europe'. Quite apart from official, and often bitterly resisted, attempts to develop a legal concept of European citizenship, the Commission has made particular efforts, after the publication of the second Adonnino report in 1985, to address the more explicitly emotional content of European identity. A European passport, a European anthem (taken from the Prelude to the Ode to Joy in Beethoven's Ninth Symphony), and a European flag, were the most obvious symbols of this endeavour to build an affective identity for the EU.

An anthropologist like Cris Shore, however, reviewing the achievements of these attempts at European identity construction, concludes that there is very little 'sense of popular identification and of any real feeling of belonging among its inhabitants' (Shore and Black, 1994: 289). The problem, as Shore sees it, is one of public understanding of the substance behind the symbols (passport, anthem, flag, etc.) with which people are being asked to identify (Shore, 2000). The institutions of the EU are famously very complex – difficult to understand and apparently remote from the day to day lives of most citizens. The emotional distance between the European citizen and the EU is even greater: 'What individual nation-states of Europe hold in common is the existence of symbols, collective representations and political myths. These are born of shared history and experiences which are intimately connected with a sense of belonging' (Shore and Black, 1994: 291). The symbols themselves are not a lot of good unless what they symbolize is a shared emotional foundation.

IMAGINED COMMUNITIES OF EUROPE

Benedict Anderson, in his very influential book on the construction of national identities, famously argued that a nation is essentially a manufactured product, a cultural artefact which is necessarily a matter of shared imagining, rather than of demonstrable fact: '"imagined" because the members of even the smallest nation will never know most of their fellow-members, meet them, or even hear of them. . . . Communities are to be distinguished, not by their falsity/genuineness, but by the style in which they are imagined' (Anderson, 1991: 6). As Anderson argues in his richly allusive text, these imagined communities exist in effect in two temporal zones. Firstly, an imagined time of simultaneous present, represented in one instance by the sharing – and a wholly imagined sharing – of a common communications system like print journalism, where each reader of a morning paper, for example, is 'well aware that the ceremony he performs is being replicated by thousands (or millions) of others of whose existence he is confident, yet of whose identity he has not the slightest notion' (Anderson, 1991: 35).

Secondly, the imagined community is narrated, Anderson claims, in a characteristic 'up time', framed from the present into the past, a past marked by a community of the dead which we imagine beside us: 'World War II begets World War I; out of Sedan comes Austerlitz; the ancestor of the Warsaw Uprising is the state of Israel' (Anderson, 1991: 205).

In the context that Anderson sets here for the imagining of national communities, for the ways in which we develop an emotional identification with a community, a sense of belonging to something beyond our immediate group, the EU clearly has some major problems. To begin with, the imagined community of the simultaneous present is one which is extremely difficult for the citizens of the EU to share. Divided by language, we do not, even in the world of global communications and the internet, actually share a communications medium in the way that a national community may be imagined, broadly speaking, as reading the same newspapers in the morning, or watching the same news programmes in the evening. The simultaneous present, in the way that Anderson describes it, is simply not a time zone that most of us in Europe can be said to imaginatively share.

The second time frame which Anderson identifies as common to the shared imagining of the nation – that of up time, present to past, standing beside the dead of the community – is also one which presents some difficulties for the peoples of Europe. The European community that we might after all be imagining in up time could very well be one marked by quite separate national imaginings, and these are likely to include the dead of internecine conflicts between the different communities of Europe, with dead heroes who are the victims of one or other competing national community. Imagining an affective European identity in this situation is far from easy.

INSTITUTIONAL IMAGININGS

The representations of European identity presented in the official documentation of the EU show clearly the problems inherent in any construction of an emotional community where the past is too potentially divisive to constitute, and the present too blatantly nation-state based to be of much immediate use. In fact much of the official material produced by the EU locates the Community in a sort of temporal ahistorical vacuum. The identity proposed in many of the texts is one which actually separates the EU from the past, either from the past of the individual nation-states or, except in the broadest Manichean terms, from that of Europe as a whole. Rather than 'up time', present to past, we seem to be being placed in an 'other time', where attention is on the process of moving towards a future: travelling, as it were, rather than arriving. This 'other time' is mobile, going to the future and starting from an almost clean sheet of the past, a sort of equivalent of the French Revolutionary Calendar.

Firstly, the origins of the EU are positioned in a historical no-man's land, anchored neither to the separate histories of the member states of which it is composed, nor to the variable circumstances of postwar Europe. A review of recent (1994–8) public information material distributed by the Commission suggests that the beginnings of the EU are best understood as a moral history, of good being brought out of evil. At the root of this presentation is a consistently apocalyptic approach to EU pre-history, whether in the context of the Second World War, or, on occasions, the Cold War. The vocabulary is that of absolutism, with superlatives – 'darkest', 'most creative', 'truly appreciated', 'total collapse', 'completely fresh start'. The nouns are taken from the register of chaos – 'ruins', 'disintegration', 'abyss': 'In Europe's DARKEST hour, amidst the ruins of the Second World War, the MOST creative answer was offered to the question of what was to become of Europe. That answer was integration' (*Europe from A to Z*, 1997: 7); 'Only after Europe had yet again been DEVASTATED by war was the DISASTROUS futility of constant national rivalry TRULY appreciated. Europe's TOTAL collapse and the political and economic DISINTEGRATION of outdated national structures set the stage for a COMPLETELY FRESH start . . .' (*European Integration*, 1995: 5); 'In spring 1950, Europe was on the edge of the ABYSS' (*Seven Key Days*, 1997: 2).

In these texts, Europe has risen out of ruins and devastation as a *tabula rasa* enterprise. It thus has very little precedence from which to draw legitimacy. Where precedence is delineated, it is a quasi-religious precedence of visions and utopian dreams, rather than action and events – 'ideals', 'visionaries', 'dream': 'Until it crystallised into a political concept and became the long-term goal of the Member States of the European Community, the European IDEAL was unknown to all but philosophers and VISIONARIES. The notion of a United States of Europe was part of a humanist-pacifist DREAM which was shattered by the conflicts which brought so much destruction to the European continent in the first half of this century' (*Europe in 10 Points*, 1998: 5).

When precursors are identified, they are either portrayed as martyred by the holocaust to come (Count Coudenhove Kalergi, Aristide Briand), by the 'still dominant tides of nationalism and imperialism' (*European Integration*, 1995: 5), or are refined through the experience of war – 'transcend': 'The vision of a new Europe which would TRANSCEND antagonistic nationalism finally emerged from the resistance movements which had sprung up to resist totalitarianism during the Second World War' (*Europe in 10 Points*, 1998: 5).

The origins of the EU are thus presented in much of the official documentation as divorced from the surrounding historical circumstances, within a profoundly moralistic setting. Where agency – the influence of decisions by individuals or countries – is attributed, the lexis is again that of religious/moral choice – 'better', 'sow the seeds': 'Almost 50 years ago, after the second world war, some of the countries in Europe began to look for ways to make sure that they never went to war against each other again. They decided to work together and build a BETTER future for everyone' (*Your Passport to Europe*, 1995); 'six founder members . . . quite consciously sought to SOW THE SEEDS of greater European integration' (*How Does the EU Work?* 1998: 6).

Key individuals (Monnet, Schuman) associated with the development of Europe are given pantheonic status with the use of epithets like 'founding fathers', 'the father of Europe', and 'early pioneers' (*European Integration, 1995, 9; Seven Key Days*, 1997: 2; *Europe in 10 Points*, 1998: 6).

Whilst it would be fair to acknowledge that public information material inevitably simplifies, there is no doubt that the official presentation of the origins of the EU position Europe as starting postwar from zero, within a context of high moral seriousness. This history of rectitude is a history drawing legitimacy in a Manichean way from disaster and vision, and it is a history, most importantly, which is outside other national histories, in a time zone and context completely separate from the nation-state.

Starting from these origins, the current identity of the EU is characterized in information publications as an identity which is primordially an identity on the move, and one whose chief quality is that of movement and change. From the quotation of Jean Monnet's description of the Community as a 'process of change' (*Citizen's Europe*, 1994: 6), through to the portfolio of information bulletins in the current series entitled 'Europe on the Move', the impression created is one of movement and becoming. Mostly, this movement is described in terms of inevitability, of there having been no choice but to move in particular directions. The Franco-German Friendship treaty, for example, would 'INEVITABLY attract the other Member States in the long term' (*Europe from A to Z*, 1997: 8). The Union today has no other option: 'NO CHOICE but to progress further along the road . . .' (*Europe in 10 Points*, 1998: 8); 'the process of European integration is now IRREVERSIBLE' (*Citizen's Europe*, 1994: 5).

The vocabulary used to depict the development of the Community is most often drawn from the domain of journeys and travelling: 'maps', 'roads', 'ways', and 'paths'. Thus, Winston Churchill in his Zurich speech of 19 September 1946 is described as 'MAPPING out the way forward' (*Europe from A to Z*, 1997: 7), and the Maastricht summit has 'PAVED THE WAY for European foreign and security policy to acquire a new dimension' (*Europe from A to Z*, 1997: 7). Events in the history of the Union are 'ON THE ROAD TOWARDS the European Union' (*European Integration*, 1995: 12), with a 'LINE of treaties' marking the 'ROAD to Maastricht' (*Treaty on European Union*, 1997: Introduction).

Normally progress along this road is a gradual, step by step affair: 'The EU has been created . . . STEP BY STEP over the five decades since the Second World War'; 'postwar STEPS towards European unification'; 'STEP BY STEP, the Union is using its economic power . . .' (*Europe from A to Z*, 1997: 5; *European Integration*, 1995: 6; *Seven Key Days*, 1997: 4). On occasions, however, the journey is seen as considerably more bumpy: '1992 . . . turned out to be a ROLLER COASTER of a year' (*Europe from A to Z*, 1997: 17).

In answer to the question 'Have attempts at European integration always been successful?', one of the more recent official publications replies by seeing the road as a meandering journey – 'U turns' on a 'path': 'European integration has thus grown out of failures, U-TURNS, and projects which were ahead of their time. It basically rests on the political will of the Member States which decide, unanimously, by revising the Treaties, the STEPS to take together on the PATH to European integration' (*How Does the EU Work?*, 1998: 7).

The identity of movement, of becoming, is, however, one which is highly purposeful. Movement is defined as operating within a framework or plan which has been prescribed. The EU is an ongoing project, but it is one which is seen as developing according to a planned design. Sometimes this is expressed in terms of a building, of a structure to be completed on the basis of an architect's designs. There is a 'European Architecture', a 'political architecture', which has been constructed from the 'first STONE in the BUILDING of the European Community' on 9 May 1950 to the Treaty of Amsterdam which 'LAYS THE FOUNDATIONS for Europe's development into the 21st century' (*Treaty on European Union*, 1997: Introduction; *Europe from A to Z*, 1997: 14; *European Integration*, 1995: 9).

The movement of the Community's history is contained within 'frameworks', 'contours' and a 'network' (*Europe from A to Z*, 1997: 7). Patterns and designs are perceived in retrospect to explain the complexity of the process, but they are nonetheless there: 'Viewed as a whole, the postwar steps towards European unification offer a confusing picture that is calculated to baffle anyone but the expert. . . . Looking at their underlying aims, however, a clear PATTERN begins to emerge . . .' (*European Integration*, 1995: 6).

Whilst it is acknowledged that the current context is one of great change, the Union is still presented as a grouping which can and will be organized and designed: 'For some years now Europeans have been living history in quick motion, going through a period full of conflict but without any clear defining pattern – in some respects an era with no name. . . . Europe has to constitute itself, positively and from within. Why should the nations and peoples of Europe BIND themselves together in a common political SYSTEM? And how is that SYSTEM to be organised in such a way that it fulfils its citizens' expectations?' (*Europe from A to Z*, 1997: 7).

There is then the notion of a community which is imagined in a space depositioned from its past and in a time zone which is neither Anderson's shared present, nor his 'up time' (present to past), but rather an 'other time', present to future, where moving, and moving on a route which has a prescribed shape and pattern, is key to the identity being proposed.

There are signs, however, more recently that the considerable and very public difficulties that the Commission experienced at the end of this century have encouraged the new Commission to modify their presentation in some small but potentially quite significant ways. A good example of this is the first speech which the new President of the Commission (coming to office after the resignation of his predecessor, Jacques Santer) made to the European Parliament in February 2000. Romano Prodi's speech provides a particularly interesting slant on the ever present problems of constructing an affective identity for Europe, and so is worth quoting in some detail.

Madame President,
Honourable Members of Parliament:
The start of my Commission's term of office comes at an auspicious time: the dawn of the third millennium. It is the ideal time to look at the challenges and opportunities ahead of us and at what European Integration had achieved so far. The first thing that strikes us is a paradox. On the one hand, European integration has given us a half-century of peace and prosperity unprecedented in the history of our continent. With the launch of the euro, we now have a completely united Single Market, enabling the EU to emerge as a world economic power capable of meeting the challenges of globalization.

On the other hand, Europe's citizens are disenchanted and anxious. They have lost faith in the European institutions. They are losing patience with our slow rate of progress in tackling unemployment. The prospect of enlargement divides public opinion between hope and fear – hope for stability and progress, fear of a Europe without identity or frontiers.

Today's scepticism and anxiety cannot be overcome by harking back to yesterday's successes: ordinary Europeans have to be convinced that Europe's policy-makers and decision-makers are capable of decisive and effective action. That they can modernize Europe and steer it towards a bright future . . .

The European Union has developed, over the years, in a sort of geological succession of layers: first the customs union, then the internal market, most recently the single currency. Policies were developed in parallel, as they became necessary and as each geological layer was established.

Until now, there has been no overall 'master plan' under which policies were designed and coordinated. Our attempts to 'mainstream' certain policies, such as environment policy or equal opportunities, into all other policy areas have not been entirely successful . . .

Our citizens are not happy with the way things are done at European level. It is not just the Commission's recent performance they criticize: they feel remote from all European institutions, and are sceptical that we can deliver the kind of society they want. They are rightly calling for a much greater say in shaping the New Europe.

The challenge is therefore not simply to reform the Commission, important though that is. It is not simply to make all the institutions work more effectively, though that too is essential. The challenge is to radically rethink the way we do Europe. To reshape Europe. To devise a completely new form of governance for the world of tomorrow . . .

I am committed to closing the gap between rhetoric and reality in Europe. . . . We have to create the conditions for a shift from a pro-cedure-oriented to a policy-oriented one. . . . The Commission must become a political driving force to shape the new Europe. . . .

I appeal to Europe's citizens to break the apathy barrier and take a close interest in our progress. . . . Honourable Members, we are living at a time of unprecedented opportunity. The economic outlook is good, and the unique combination of sustained growth, the information society revolution and the expanding European market offers us the 'virtuous circle' we need. If we act boldly and decisively together, we can shape the new Europe our citizens want and that we owe to future generations. . . . Let us work together to make this decade a decade of outstanding achievement and success. A decade history will remember as the decade of Europe. (Prodi, 2000)

In this speech, Romano Prodi locates the European Union as 'new Europe', a project which can and should be 'shaped', and 'steered'. It is, however, 'new', demonstrably different from its immediate, and partially discredited, predecessor. This time also there is a recognition that the Union has not in fact had a 'master plan'. Rather – and the image is interesting – the Union's development has been like a 'geological succession of layers', as 'policies were developed . . . as they became necessary'. The shift from man-made building (the 'architecture' of the previous texts we have looked at) to an image of a natural organic process – 'geological layer' – puts the development of the EU as a more reactive process where overall human agency, and potential blame and dissension, is reduced. Prodi's point here is actually that the time has come to provide a more directive structure, but one which is 'policy-oriented' rather than 'procedure-oriented'.

Movement is still a key descriptor in Prodi's speech – 'ahead of us', 'slow rate of progress', 'steer towards' – but interestingly enough, by bringing citizen–Commission relations into the description, Prodi represents a movement which is not just forward and unambiguously tied to the onward march of progress, but a movement inwards, towards the citizen – 'remote', 'closing the gap', 'break the apathy barrier'. What is being proposed now is not the linear path, albeit winding and with U-turns, but instead a 'virtuous circle' in which progress is not forward, but inwards to embrace a group (albeit an expanding one) of citizens.

The community imagined by Prodi is one still firmly tied to the future: indeed he specifically argues that even the relatively brief shared history of the EU since its inception should be jettisoned – 'harking back'. The proposition is that people will identify with the EU if they can imagine what it will be like in the future – 'steer it towards a bright tomorrow', 'calling for a much greater say in shaping the new Europe', 'radically rethink the way we do Europe', 'reshape Europe', 'the new Europe our citizens want and we owe to future generations'. In this formulation, even history is positioned in the future, looking back to our present: 'A decade history will remember as the decade of Europe'.

Whilst the terms of the imagined community are being slightly modified by Prodi in this speech, the major characteristics of the institutional imagining of European identity may be said to remain intact: movement, and movement towards a future with which we can identify, rather than a past which might divide us. Now, however, we are not progressing towards a particular goal, so much as moving around a circle of identity – 'doing Europe' – performing an identity which will become the NEW Europe.

This notion of a European identity which is imagined as a performative process, rather than as a teleological movement, is (surprisingly perhaps) not that far from the kinds of descriptions which commentators like Homi Bhabha are offering in their writings on national communities. Bhabha suggests that the nation-space is one 'in the process of the articulation of elements where meanings may be partial because they are "in media res"; and history may be half-made because it is in the process of being made; and the image of cultural authority may be ambivalent because it is caught, uncertainly, in the act of "composing" its powerful image' (Bhabha, 1990: 308). To Bhabha, the 'performativity of language' in these narratives of the national community is key.

WOMEN AND EUROPEAN IDENTITY

The question in our investigation now becomes, therefore, not how MEPs imagine Europe, but, rather, how they 'do' Europe. How do they enact this process identity of the EU? For a start, we might feel that an identity which is being imagined in performativity, and as a process, might prove to be significantly more open to the influences of women's languages than affective identities which take their primary legitimacy from the past. As we have been arguing, imaginative constructions of national identity are formed from past cultural values, and one of the major constituent parts of these is kinship. Kinship, the sense of belonging together naturally, by natural ties, is traditionally a highly sexualized and gendered image. The nation is the 'Motherland', often symbolized in a female iconography. Belonging to a nation is being 'at home', and the home is a private realm which (implicitly) may need to be defended and guarded by a man. The past to which we are often called to hold allegiance in the nation-state community is represented as a past of the heroic dead, but heroic dead who were almost always, by definition, male soldiers of the past. Conceivably, the EU's text of 'other time', of present to future as opposed to present to past, of an identity formed in process, could create particular spaces in which women might influence the nature of the imagined community of Europe in rather different ways from those traditional to the imagined community of the nation-state.

To explore this possibility, we shall firstly look at the communities which women MEPs represent when they answer the question: 'What is Europe? Where is Europe?' The double question – 'What? Where?' – was designed to provide as open an area as possible in which women could talk about how they understand Europe.

Over half the MEPs who answered the question (31/59: 52.5 per cent) used terms with which to describe Europe in which movement and change play a key part. There are three major ways in which Europe is represented in this process-movement frame. Firstly, Europe is a community of geographical change. The sense of a physical definition which is moving its contours as we speak is very strong: 'of course geographical Europe is MUCH WIDER and my desire is for it to be WIDER AND WIDER' (French, EUL); 'The EU is an area which is EXPANDING increasingly' (Dutch, PES). At the borders of the definition, as with the geographical continent, there is considerable imprecision: 'Europe is the continent whose BORDERS to the east are NOT SO SPECIFIC' (German, EPP). For some MEPs, the geographical fluidity of the definition makes them want to halt the whole process of movement and change: 'As we enlarge, there's a certain point we shall have to stop. Otherwise we may be IN DANGER OF HAVING NO REAL CENTRE' (Luxembourgeoise, EPP). As another MEP puts it, the geography is fluctuating: 'WHAT DOES Europe stand for . . . WHERE WILL SHE STAND?' (Belgian, Green).

As the contours of Europe's geography change and move, so there is a sense in the representations offered that Europe is a community whose meanings are moving as rapidly as its borders. To understand Europe, these MEPs suggest, you must mix very different types of definitions and change the viewpoint of the watcher at different stages to try to keep up with what is an essentially moving target. Overlapping meanings jostle for recognition. Any definition of Europe 'has to be looked at from VARIOUS POINTS OF VIEW. One has to look at Europe as a continent . . . one could also say it is a way of life . . . movement without barriers within the member states of the Union' (German, EPP).

Finally, much as in the institutional documentation, and indeed the academic narratives of European integration we reviewed in Chapter 2, MEPs identify Europe with a process, a dynamic of movement and change. The outstanding component in these descriptions is movement itself. Europe is an identity in process: 'it is a political project which we are STILL BUILDING, we're NOWHERE NEAR COMPLETING it yet' (Belgian, ELDR). 'Like any other DYNAMIC PROCESS', explained another MEP, 'Europe has a CHANGING scene and content . . . the Europe we are living in now is NOT LIKE THE ONE in 1951 . . . and it will NOT BE THE SAME in a few years' time' (Spanish, PES). A closer analysis of one of these replies (with the text quoted below) gives a flavour of some of the

ways in which Europe is being imagined as a process, and as a process
which draws its validity from the future, rather than from the past, other
time rather than up time.

> 'What is Europe? A brilliant but miscarried idea of a CLAIRVOYANT who
> realized that collaborating with each other is better than to have parties
> waging war against each other. It is a MARVELLOUS IDEA. It may be
> wondered, however, if economic and monetary cooperation automatically
> LEADS TO happiness and to the safeguard of human rights. In other words,
> it is a distorted IDEA, one that has BECOME warped. It is distorted, warped,
> but we may be able to . . . PULL IT BACK INTO POSITION.' (Belgian, PES)

In this extract, the MEP imagines Europe as a process which is moving,
albeit in directions not originally intended: 'leads to', 'pull it back into
position'. The movement is one which is related in no way to the past.
Instead, its links are with a largely unknown mental future: 'clairvoyant',
'marvellous', 'idea'. The impression given here is actually of a process
which may well have a momentum of its own – 'we MAY be able to pull
it back' – rather than of the planned 'architecture' and mapped out
'journey' of the institutional documentation, or even of the less confident
'steering' in a circle presented by Prodi. Europe's identity is imagined as
process, but its movement is not operating within fixed structures or
agreed parameters.

Only a relatively small group of women (7/59: 11.9 per cent) in fact use
terms which suggest that the moving community of Europe is operating
within structures, according to agreed rules, and on a trajectory which is,
in some senses, controllable. One MEP gives as her definition a description
of the structural organization of the Union – 'a supranational organization
which has its own institutions, its own structure, and which produces its
own legislation which has a direct effect on the ordering of the Member
States' (Spanish, EPP) – and other MEPs in this group employ such words
as 'contracts', or 'agreements' or 'rules' to indicate an organized framework which is imagined as enclosing the dynamic of movement and
change. Thus, the community of Europe is said to relate to its neighbours
in a way 'which is fixed by means of contracts or agreements' (German,
PES), and which can only be entered by those who 'are . . . adapting to
the rules of the game' (Spanish, EPP). Overall, however, the process
identity which so many women MEPs describe is not within any framework or pattern.

A larger number of MEPs (21/59: 35.6 per cent) describe Europe in
terms of a plurality, a plurality of countries and regions, a plurality of
cultures, and a plurality of overlapping multiple identities. In this formulation, a process identity is being conceived in terms of breadth, if you
like, rather than as movement in a particular direction. New and overlap-

ping identities propose themselves in what seems like a hectic disorder: 'heterogeneous . . . and for me that's exactly what is interesting at the European level, conjugating . . . all these differences . . . a mosaic of cultures . . . and of specificities' (French, PES). As we have noticed with the grammars of citizenship (Chapter 4), some of these descriptions start from the multiple identities of the MEP herself. Europe is thus understood through the moving and diverse identities of the individual Member of Parliament. One MEP begins her definition of Europe with the words: 'I always felt part of the diaspora. I was born in Ireland. I came to Britain when I was five. I've dual nationality' (British, PES).

A particularly striking example of these imaginings of Europe comes from an Irish Green MEP who contrasts the original (and incidentally male) imagined Europe of the past with her own imagined Europe of the present. Europe today, she argues, is imagined as a movement in diversity:

'We talk about Europe as if it's out there, but it's here. Europe is its regions. . . . What's precious to me is these many different regions. We've heard a lot of talk today about the Treaty of Rome, and the devastation of War. This is all very worthy, but we need to move on from old men in the fifties who see national identity as something negative – Europe instead of national identity. . . . I'm not a nationalist . . . I believe in diversity. The whole is the sum of many different parts. It's probably a generational thing . . .' (Irish, Green)

LANGUAGES OF PROCESS AND MOVEMENT

On the whole, then, it seems as if women MEPs are indeed identifying Europe as process. They are 'doing' Europe, and this identity is performed as a process in diversity and multiplicity more often than as one within structures. If the identity of Europe is essentially performative – if we are imagining Europe by 'doing' Europe – it follows that the vocabulary with which MEPs name the issues of politics in the European Parliament is a constitutive part of this performance. To put it more simply, as MEPs speak in Plenary sessions, the words they use to describe the 'business' of politics is an integral part of 'doing' Europe. A European process identity is being at least partly constituted by the words with which we name politics in the European Parliament.

An identity which is performative and in process is one which is likely to be reflected then in the languages MEPs use, in their vocabularies of process and movement. My contention here is that these vocabularies of movement are not in any way limited to overt discussion of European identity. Rather, MEPs contribute to the representation and performance of identity in speeches which address the many different and varied issues with which Parliament deals. It is not a matter of seeing WHAT MEPs say about European identity now, as much as looking at HOW they 'say' Europe.

In this process/movement identity which we have discerned, the vocabularies of movement are likely to be used in a variety of contexts and ways. To begin with, we shall look at the range of vocabulary which might contribute to this issue-neutral naming of a Europe in movement. Movement might, for example, be described in terms of a journey, using some of the vocabulary we have already noted in relation to the institutional text – 'step', 'distance'. It might be process-related – 'building', 'developing', 'creation'. Movement may simply indicate activity, either directed – 'go forward', 'move out' – or impeded – 'obstructing the flow', 'preventing moving' – in the EU. Movement may connote the crossing over of frontiers, physical – 'inter-state', 'frontier-free' or mental: 'frontiers mean little', 'dismantling of barriers'.

To summarize this for a moment, we might suggest the following categories:

Movement as activity
- Verbs of directed movement; for example: go forward, descend, move away, lead to, level down, move out, forward, move off, work towards, shift, dragging down, spiral.
- Nouns of movement; for example: exodus, impetus, mobility, advance, inflows.
- Adjectives of movement; for example: supersonic, two-speed, multi-speed, dynamic, progressive.
- Verbs of impeded movement for example: preventing moving, obstructing the flow, to stand still is to take a step backwards.

Movement as journey
- Verbs of journeying; for example: step, embark, overtake, lag behind, make up ground, distance oneself, send out a search party, have a long way to go, forge ahead.
- Nouns of journeying; for example: road, distance, step, wayside.

Movement as process
- Verbs of process; for example: construct, process, build, expand, create, establish, promote, enlarge, develop, shape, rebuild, give form/substance to, lay foundations.
- nouns of process; for example: establishment, development, creation, enlargement, expansion.

Movement across frontiers
- Doublets which indicate movement across for example: cross-frontiers, beyond borders, transnational, trans-European, cross-borders, inter-state, frontier-free, inter-regional.
- Phrases which indicate the movement of frontiers themselves; for example: frontier instability, frontiers meaning little, dismantling of barriers.

As an illustration of this in operation – European identity being performed in movement, as it were – I shall take one of the case study Plenary sessions (14–18 November 1994) and suggest how these vocabularies of movement frame a variety of issues, and are used by both men and women. I am not arguing that vocabularies of movement and change are the only ones being employed by MEPs, but I am saying that they constitute an important means through which the performative identity of the EU as movement and change is imagined.

The 14–18 November 1994 session included – as well as the customary order of business, approval of the minutes, and decision on urgency – debates on: internal institutional matters (the annual report of the Court of auditors), economic issues (additives, noise emissions, carriage of dangerous goods by road, GATT agreement, generalized tariff preferences), social problems (Europe against AIDS), and foreign affairs (Bosnia-Herzegovina).

For the sake of brevity, I will take one of these categories, economic issues, and consider the examples in detail. Examples from the other categories (internal EU affairs, social questions, and foreign affairs) are given in Appendix 3.

ECONOMIC ISSUES

In the economic areas debated, MEPs across lines of nationality, party and gender use vocabularies of movement and change of the sort we have indicated above. Movement as activity – 'movement', 'work towards', 'fast transmission', running around', 'complete the internal market', 'started off a vicious circle', 'leading to', 'no obstacles put in the way'; movement as journey – 'a good road to follow', 'further step towards integration'; movement as process – 'enlargement', 'development', 'extend', 'extension'; movement across frontiers – 'cross-border', 'cross-frontier'.

Quotations are given below, first from male MEPs, and then from female, with an indication in brackets beside each quotation of the type of vocabulary of movement being used.

MALE MEPs

'FREE MOVEMENT of healthy goods ACROSS THE INTERNAL BORDERS . . . seen in the context of the ENLARGEMENT of the EU' (Danish, ELDR, 16.11.94, 4–453/83). ('free movement': ACTIVITY; 'across the internal borders': ACROSS FRONTIERS; 'enlargement': PROCESS).

'not just to work towards the future DEVELOPMENT of industrial Europe. . . . I think that is a GOOD ROAD TO FOLLOW' (German, EPP, 16.11.94, 4–453/96). ('development': PROCESS; 'a good road to follow': JOURNEY).

'the right to EXTEND territorial waters . . . is a national issue' (Greek, EUL, 16.11.94, 4–453/116). ('extend': PROCESS).

'CROSS-BORDER bank payments' (Dutch, ELDR, 16.11.94, 4–453/126). ('cross-border': ACROSS FRONTIERS).

(on the Poseima programme) 'wonder whether it should be DEVELOPED and EXTENDED to new areas . . . extended to certain areas' (Portuguese, ELDR, 16.11.94, 4–453/134). ('developed': PROCESS; 'extended': PROCESS).

'preparations for this FURTHER STEP towards integration into the EU . . . logical EXTENSION of the free trade area' (German, EPP, 18.11.94, 4–453/ 206). ('further step': JOURNEY; 'extension': PROCESS).

FEMALE MEPs

'interoperability of applications . . . the exercise of the four freedoms of MOVEMENT can only really be guaranteed with FAST TRANSMISSION of accurate information.' (British, PES, 16.11.94, 4–453/101). ('movement': ACTIVITY; 'fast transmission': ACTIVITY).

'In this Community of ours a lot of people are RUNNING AROUND with idealistic notions' (Dutch, EPP, 16.11.94, 4–453/102). ('running around': ACTIVITY).

'If we want to COMPLETE the internal market we must insist that NO OBSTACLES PUT IN THE WAY . . . in trade with services which involves CROSS-FRONTIER activities' (German, PES, 16.11.94, 4–453/106). ('complete': ACTIVITY; 'no obstacles put in the way': ACTIVITY; 'cross-frontier activities': ACROSS FRONTIERS).

(agricultural set aside) 'we have STARTED OFF a vicious circle LEADING TO the destructuring and even the collapse of European agriculture' (French, EDN, 18.11.94, 4–453/213). ('started off a vicious circle': ACTIVITY; 'leading to': ACTIVITY).

GENDER AND THE LANGUAGES OF EUROPEAN IDENTITY

If both men and women use languages of process and movement in performing the identity of Europe in the European Parliament, we should note that women MEPs were framing this mobile identity in two different ways, when we asked them directly to define European identity. One frame, the less common, was much like that used in the institutional and academic texts we looked at: a trajectory of planned movement within structures, with the emphasis on the type of structures which contained or directed the movement. The other, the more common among the women interviewed, described a movement in breadth, as it were; an identity moving in diversity, where attention was concentrated more on diversity and multiplicity than on the patterns used to direct the movement.

In looking at the speeches in the Plenary sessions, I have selected speeches from our three case study Plenary sessions which contain examples of the process/movement vocabulary we have just been considering, and name a moving identity of Europe. I want now to use the two types of frames we noted with women MEPs – one which I shall call 'rules', moving in organized frameworks, and the other which I shall call 'diversity', moving in plurality – to see whether they are equally common to both sexes. In other words, when MEPs describe Europe in process and movement, as we have discussed above, do they position the trajectory of movement in either of these frames, 'doing' Europe as a moving identity within a structure, and 'doing' Europe as a moving identity in plurality? For both frames, the analysis will be based on broad domains of vocabulary as listed below:

Framework of rules
- Nouns; for example: regulations, standards, norms, infrastructure, rule, structure, procedures, guideline, protocols, order, outline requirements, control, international conventions, basis for own rules.
- Adjectives; for example: structural, quantified, legal bases, framework (conditions), systematic.
- Verbs; for example: regulate, embody in law, shape process, impose sanctions, prescribe/not to prescribe.
- Adverbs; for example: structurally.

Framework of diversity
- Nouns of diversity; for example: diversity, pluralism, imbalance, disparities, differences, multiplicity.
- Adjectives of diversity; for example: mixed (competence) different, diverse, multicultural.

- Verbs of diversity, for example: differ.
- Expressions indicating diversity, for example: does not look the same everywhere, can't allow in Alps what can in Sweden, all the cultures, cultures of the people of Europe, cultures of our neighbours, knowledge of partners' cultural heritage.
- Expressions which indicate a plurality of level/countries, for example: countries of South versus countries of North, transposed in various nation-states, Community/regional/local, south/north/ east/west Europe, Europe of peoples.

In total, I studied 342 examples of vocabulary in the two categories, Rules and Diversity, of which 33 per cent came from speeches by women. Table 5.1 maps the proportion of examples in each category which come from either sex.

Clearly, this exercise is an illustrative one, designed to supplement our qualitative work rather than argue for statistical validity. It is nonetheless interesting in suggesting a slight 'direction of difference' in the frames proposed by women and men. From this evidence, women seem to use a vocabulary of rules less frequently as a frame for enclosing the mobile identity of Europe. In addition, in framing the trajectory of movement, women appear to use a vocabulary of diversity more frequently than men. The evidence is very far from being conclusive, but it does indicate a tendency for women to take a perspective on European identity which prioritizes its moving plurality, rather than its frameworks and rules. For both men and women, we might say that European identity is being imagined as a movement in process, an identity being 'done', and one which has no relationship with the past, or with an imagined (and static) present. The ways in which you 'do' Europe in this moving identity may be slightly different if you are a woman.

As an illustration 'on the ground', as it were, of this apparent rules/ diversity direction of difference between male and female MEPs, we shall look at two contrasting speeches made in one of the case study Plenaries, 14–17 March 1995. I have deliberately chosen an example of a formal set-piece debate (16 March 1995) on a question which is quite technical: the issue of nuclear power stations in Central and Eastern Europe, and in

Table 5.1

Category	Number of examples	Percentage contribution of women to category	Percentage contribution of men to category
Rules	217	29	71
Diversity	125	39	61

particular the EU's approach to the problems posed by the Mochovce nuclear power station in Slovakia. The debate began with a statement from the Commissioner, M. de Silguy, and was followed by speeches from the European Parliament's transnational political groups, the first by the then Chair of the Parliament's Energy, Research and Technology Committee, a male MEP, Claude Desama (Belgian, PES), the second by one of the then three Vice Chairs of the Committee, a female MEP, Godelieve Quisthoudt-Rowohl (German, EPP). The text of both speeches is given in full below.

DESAMA

Mr President, Commissioner, I think I can express the satisfaction of all my colleagues in the PSE Group on hearing your statement. It was clear and precise, and contained firm commitments on the part of the Commission in a number of the areas of concern to Parliament.

The European Parliament has addressed this problem with great maturity. We are aware that any mention of the nuclear issue provokes a whole series of reactions, which are occasionally somewhat heated. I believe that, in its approach to the Mochovce question, the European Parliament has demonstrated that it is able to deal with the nuclear issue with calm and determination: and the compromise resolution which I am sure we shall adopt later today – I hope by a very large majority – will be the proof that this House is able to examine such issues dispassionately.

The Commissioner has pointed out – and we have included this consideration in the compromise resolution – that the Slovak Republic's choice of energy option is above all a matter for that country's government. The Slovak Republic is an independent state – not a banana republic – and we must respect the decision of its government, even if that decision is not necessarily the one a number of us would wish to see.

My second point, and one which the Commissioner also stressed, concerns the conditions which must underlie, so to speak, the Commission's negotiating mandate. The improvement of safety, and notably the application of Western European and Euratom safety standards, are essential preconditions for the granting of the loan, as is the establishment of a binding timetable for the shutdown of the Bohunice units. The Commissioner referred to bloc 1, but bloc 2 should not be forgotten and, in this context, the timetable must be binding. In a sense, this will represent a contribution by the Slovak authorities to the overall improvement of nuclear safety in Europe.

Thirdly, despite the many answers provided during the hearing, or in various statements, a number of questions still remain. Doubts persist, to the extent that not everyone in this House was convinced by the statements from experts. I am glad to hear from the Commissioner in person that the Commission has decided to continue the inquiry, to check for itself that some of the information provided is correct. Similarly, on behalf of my group, I welcome the Commission's readiness to help promote the diversification of energy sources in Central and Eastern Europe. Clearly, there are many possible energy resources other than nuclear power. It is those resources which should be exploited; and, in my view, the Commissioner's immediate support for our proposal for the holding of a high-level regional conference on this issue sends an important message, and one for which I am grateful to him. (4–460/153)

QUISTHOUDT-ROWOHL

Mr President, Commissioner de Silguy, we were very pleased to hear what you had to say in your speech just now, and we would like to thank the Commission and you yourself for the care and attention you are giving this dossier. You put forward all the arguments which we have already discussed on a number of occasions in our group and in the Committee on Research, Technological Development and Energy. You are undoubtedly going to hear a good deal today about the pros and cons of nuclear energy, so I should first like to make a few very basic points.

I would like to call on this House to fulfil its moral duty to support the new democracies in their progress towards a social market economy, including a responsible energy industry. In doing so, we must fully respect Slovakia's sovereignty, and later there will no doubt be other states in the same situation. As politicians we must try to avoid presenting ourselves as yet another group of experts in this debate, but at the same time we must try to be objective. I am very grateful to you, Mr de Silguy, for acknowledging the full implications of this. If we really wish to be objective, then we have to admit that doing nothing means accepting a very unsatisfactory state of affairs, and we cannot afford to do that. The credibility of our whole policy on Central and Eastern Europe is at stake.

In addition to the regional conferences you proposed, Commissioner, I would ask you to consider whether it would not be a good idea, as part of a comprehensive energy policy which includes the improvement of the power plants, to set up a group of experts from the electricity industry with perhaps political representatives from all the main parties. This group would not only have to give its opinion on whether or not to use nuclear power, but would also monitor the situation on an ongoing basis, so that we could avoid ad hoc discussions and perhaps give closer attention to the whole question of alternatives. We must move the debate away from what to do in this particular instance. We need to develop a coherent policy. We must support the new democracies of Central and Eastern Europe in their desire for a completely independent energy industry, which is, after all, no more than we want for ourselves. Thank you for your contribution to this debate, Commissioner. (4–460/153)

In looking at these two speeches, we need to note that the speakers are both operating within the same institutional constraints – that is to say both are timed speeches, representing the views of two of the major political groups, in direct response to an intervention by the Commission. The Commissioner in question is present, and the general custom is to address what she/he has just said and articulate the views of the group in question.

Given this starting point, the speeches of the two MEPs are strikingly different. If we use the rules/diversity grids we have applied to the whole corpus of texts, we find that the male MEP (Desama) mentions vocabulary from the Rules domain seven times – 'resolution' (twice), 'majority', 'mandate', 'application', 'standards', and 'binding timetable'. He has three references to the Diversity domain – 'diversification', 'Central and Eastern Europe', and 'many possible energy resources other than . . .'. In comparison, the female MEP has one reference to the Rules domain – 'monitor', and six to the domain of Diversity – 'new democracies' (twice), 'other states', 'Central and Eastern Europe' (twice), 'all the main parties'.

If we were to do a structural analysis of the development of the two speeches, we would see that these different emphases are reflected in the progression of the themes. If we put the two speeches side by side (Table 5.2), this becomes more apparent. Structurally, in terms of the development of the argument, the Europe which is being represented by the male

Table 5.2

Male MEP (Desama)	Female MEP (Quisthoudt-Rowohl)
Commissioner: statement – clear and precise	Commissioner: care and attention
The EP: maturity. Difficult. Resolution /majority	Discussions in Committee
Resolution: Slovaks' choice	Support new democracies and others
Mandate of Commission. Application of standards. Binding timetable	Must do something. In addition to conference, experts from all parties
Doubts. Continue inquiry	Monitor standards
Diversification. High-level conference	New democracies

MEP is one of a framework and structure for common action, a process by which the issues involved will be addressed. The notion of a diversity of approaches and plurality of actors enters the speech only in the final part.

The Europe represented by the female MEP, on the other hand, is structurally an almost complete mirror image of that of the man. Notions of diversity are introduced at almost every stage of her speech, and the only reference to rules and procedures comes very near the end with the injunction to monitor the situation. The Europe being imagined in this speech is one which engages with a plurality of players and concerns itself relatively little with procedures or rules.

CONCLUSIONS

In relation to the imagined community of Europe, then, there is evidence that both men and women imagine a European identity as a process, a becoming. They position this in an 'other time' mobile frame of reference, a Europe whose prime descriptor is that of movement and change, of becoming in the future. Men and women, however, appear to describe this movement in slightly different ways. For men, there is some indication that the understanding of Europe as moving within structures and patterns is more frequent than that of a Europe moving in diversity and plurality. For women, Europe is imagined less often as moving within a planned framework, and more insistently as changing on a trajectory of diversity, with a plurality of countries, cultures and communities named within the moving identity of Europe.

One of the problems with the EU's current relationship with citizens, as Commissioner Prodi expresses it in the speech we examined earlier in the chapter, is the citizen's emotional remoteness from the EU. Prodi argues, as we saw, that the reason for this emotional isolation is the 'gap between rhetoric and reality in Europe'. When a community is being identified without a shared imaginative present, and outside defined historical contexts, without the images of historical remembrance and dead heroes that are so crucial in the building of national identities, it is evident that a different sort of language, a different 'rhetoric', to use Prodi's terms, is going to be employed. If, furthermore, the community concerned can only be imagined in relation to a future which is, by definition, unknown and therefore difficult to imagine, the task of representing this imagined community is likely to be even more difficult.

What is clear, however, is that MEPs are in effect imagining a community through the ways in which they frame issues and describe the processes of movement to the future. To borrow Prodi's expression, MEPs are 'doing' Europe, performing the identities of Europe, through the languages they are using. Arguably, there is not a gap between rhetoric and reality in imagining a community in Europe. The rhetoric, the language, is itself a creative ingredient, bringing into being a community in process.

From the evidence, women contribute to this creative process by imagining a community which tends to move more in plurality and diversity than with a framework of rules and procedures. Rather than 'shaping a New Europe', women are naming a particular perspective of movement, of a community which is being 'done' in plurality and diversity.

We started off by noting that the community of Europe remains one of the great historical absences of today. It may be that Romano Prodi's concept of 'doing' Europe, of seeing a European identity as one in process, may encourage a more vivid imagining of the EU. It may also be, however, that a perspective of Europe as a community which is changing, but puts an acceptance of plurality and diversity at the forefront of its imagining, may provide a more emotionally charged perspective than one which prioritizes a framework of rules and structures. 'Doing' the imagined community of Europe is above all 'speaking' it in particular ways, and it is through the vocabulary that we use to 'speak' it that we may express a more affective community. As one woman MEP said: 'We talk about Europe as if it's out there, but it's here.'

CHAPTER 6

THE CATEGORY 'WOMEN': WOMEN'S LANGUAGES OF POLITICS

At the beginning of this book (Chapter 1), we discussed the difficulties, in both theoretical and empirical terms, of envisaging a collective 'women'. Two of the current strategies for circumventing this problem – the multiple identities strategy, and the contingent identities strategy – both seemed to present severe limitations, hence our decision to take a pragmatic stance and construct a 'working' category of women, as it were, in relation to a specific site and problem, namely women in the formal politics setting of the European Parliament.

By this stage of the book, however, readers may be arguing that conclusions based on this pragmatic category could well be invalidated by the multiple communities – national, political and generational – of which it is composed. To begin with, we need perhaps to remind ourselves that the two main sources on which this investigation is based are both heterogeneous. The interviews are with 60 women from across twelve nationalities, and this group has been constituted in order to make an approximate balance between the proportions interviewed from each country, and the proportions of women members from each nationality sitting in the European Parliament (Chapter 2, Table 2.1). We have tried to provide a similar balance between the percentage of women interviewed from each transnational group, and the percentage of women MEPs actually sitting in the transnational federations in Parliament (Chapter 2, Table 2.2). At the end of the day, neither balance is perfect. In terms of nationality, the group of women interviewed has a slightly higher percentage of women from the UK, Denmark and Holland than in the overall national representations of female MEPs. In terms of political grouping, our interviewees over-represent the ELDR in relation to the numbers of women actually sitting in the ELDR group. On the whole, however, it has to be said that the group of 60 women who spoke to us approximately represents the group of women in the European Parliament at that particular stage of its elected history.

The second source of documentation in this discussion has principally been the speeches made in three case study Plenary sessions, and these have contained interventions by both men and women, across the twelve nationalities, and all the political groupings with which we have been concerned. The category 'women' has indeed been pragmatically constructed, but I have tried as far as possible to reflect the heterogeneity of European Parliament membership, both female (in the choice of interviewees, and the coverage of the Plenaries), and male (through the same case study Plenary sessions).

In analysing the languages of women, we have tried to be aware of the plurality of approaches women may be taking to the key issues with which this book engages. When we discussed engendering democracy, for example, we noted that the consciousness of a gender script was not held by all the women we talked to, and that those who saw gender as an important part of their role in fact interpreted its effects in a variety of ways. The narratives of representation within which women explained their jobs as MEPs were of three types, and although one, the narrative of Representative as Interpreter, was the most popular of these, the other two – the narrative of Representative as Political actor, and the narrative of Representative as Personal traveller – were both explored in detail. The grammars of citizenship which the majority of women used were outside the two well-known citizenship traditions, but in the same way, we sought to listen to those women who were locating citizenship in terms common to present citizenship debates, as well as to those using less common terms. Finally, whilst the imagining of Europe operated overwhelmingly in the context of change and mobility, we saw that some women framed this mobility in diversity, and a smaller number framed it in rules.

The category of 'women' that we have been dealing with, therefore, has not only been constituted heterogeneously, it has also been listened to as a category which may speak, and does speak, in a variety of ways. There is not then one singular women's language of politics, but several women's languages of politics, much as there are several men's languages too.

In this chapter, I want to explore this proposition in a little more detail. Firstly, we shall look at examples of varieties in the languages women speak in politics, and speculate on why these are being produced. We might helpfully see such varieties as of two types: ones of accenting, that is to say of the stress or emphasis different women may give to particular parts of these languages; and ones of dialect, cases where women may be departing in a discernible way from what seems to be a much more widely held way of speaking about politics. Finally, I want to discuss how my propositions on these women's languages could fit into broader ongoing discussions on essentialism and difference. My argument will be, not that women speak politics 'in a different voice', but that there are some languages of politics which women appear to speak more readily and more often than men.

ACCENTING THE LANGUAGES OF POLITICS

The expression of Europe's mobile identity in diversity, which we looked at in Chapter 5, and the grammatical location of citizens in the space of Europe (Chapter 4), provide good examples of an accenting of languages which seems to be related to national perceptions of Europe, where women may be stressing certain aspects of the languages in response to national public opinion.

A major difference between nation-states in the European Community is of course the level of popular support the EU enjoys in each country. The issue of national public opinion and the EU is one to which the institutions of the EU are understandably very sensitive. The European Commission's Education and Culture Directorate in fact oversees the production of a twice yearly survey of public opinion in the EU in order to gauge views across the 15 member states towards European integration, and towards the development of common policies. These surveys seek to judge the level of confidence national communities have in the EU, its policies and institutions. These standard *Eurobarometer* surveys cover people aged 15 years and over in all the member states, and use a multi-stage, random (probability) design, drawing a number of sampling points with probability proportional to population size and density. The survey completed in April/May 2000 (*Eurobarometer*, 2000) interviewed more than 16,000 people, using the question: 'Generally speaking, do you think that (our country's) membership of the European Union is. . . ? (a good thing/a bad thing/neither good nor bad)'. In terms of national acceptance of and enthusiasm for the development of the EU, *Eurobarometer*'s conclusions in this survey were that 49 per cent of those surveyed take a favourable view of their country's membership, with 14 per cent opposed to membership and 28 per cent regarding it more neutrally as neither a good nor a bad thing. From the data, it is clear, however, that there are certain countries in which public opinion, by this measure, is overwhelmingly favourable to the EU, and other countries in which the EU is viewed with a very much greater margin of suspicion than that of the average. Table 6.1 sets out the hierarchy of those countries thinking that the EU is a good/bad thing. It should be noted that the listing here includes the twelve countries with which this study deals, and not the newest members of the EU (Austria, Finland and Sweden).

From this evidence presented by *Eurobarometer*, it seems then that public opinion in Holland, Ireland and Luxembourg tends to be broadly supportive of EU membership, whilst public opinion in the UK and Denmark perceives EU membership in strikingly negative terms. If we therefore turn our attention now to the ways in which the national

Table 6.1

Countries thinking EU is 'a good thing'

Country	Percentage of respondents answering 'yes'
Ireland	75
Luxembourg	75
Holland	73
Spain	67
Portugal	64
Belgium	62
Greece	61
Italy	60
Denmark	53
France	49
Germany	41
UK	25

Countries thinking EU is 'a bad thing'

Country	Percentage of respondents answering 'yes'
UK	24
Denmark	24
Germany	15
France	14
Belgium	10
Italy	9
Greece	8
Spain	6
Ireland	6
Luxembourg	6
Holland	6
Portugal	5

groups of women (for example Dutch and UK) at the extreme ends of this scale imagine Europe and the location of the citizen within it, we will begin to see examples of the sort of accenting of language that I have talked about.

I argued in the previous chapter that both men and women imagine Europe in an 'other time', a mobile frame of reference. Women, I suggested, appear to imagine Europe less strongly as moving within a planned framework, and more strongly as moving in diversity, naming a plurality of countries, cultures and communities as key elements of the identity of the EU. The diversity framing of process identity is one shared by women in both of these nationalities: 7/9 (78 per cent) of the UK interviewees, and 6/7 (86 per cent) of the Dutch. Nevertheless, there is evidence of a slightly different emphasis between the two in the ways in which this plurality is understood. I quote below the words with which Dutch women from each of the four main political groups in which they sit (EPP, PES, ELDR, Green) describe Europe, followed by those of UK MEPs from the main political groups in which they too sit (EPP, PES, ARE).

Dutch MEPs:

'You are probably referring to the EU. This is a cooperation of a large number of Western European countries. The EU is unique in that it is supranational. The EU differs from other organizations in the world through its three executive bodies. The EP plays the supervisory role in this: since the Treaty of Amsterdam, the EP monitors 80 per cent of the decisions taken by the EU executive bodies. One example which I often mention in lectures: when you make a law in the Netherlands, this is for 15 million people, while the same law will affect 370 million in the EU. And later, after the expansion towards Eastern Europe, it will affect 400 to 500 million. On a global level, the EU is a substantial bloc, both commercially and politically (although the latter is often still a problem). So when you ask me 'Where is Europe?' then I would say that it is very much in the picture. You could call the EU a good second of the world's three main power blocs: US/Canada/Mexico, the AC countries and the EU.' (EPP)

'The EU is an area which is expanding increasingly. If you think of Western Europe, then the EU covers almost the whole of that area. After 2000, countries to the east of this will have joined.' (PES)

'It is a cooperation between countries which are on their way to further political cooperation, but are still halfway there. It started as a commercial union. My ideal is a United States of Europe, but the Treaty of Amsterdam has certainly not brought this any closer. I myself feel you ought to polish this ideal, although I have the impression that it is shared by fewer and fewer people.' (ELDR)

'Geographically, Europe is part of a continent. Politically, it is the EU. This has to be an EU which is focused on expansion. In a political sense, it is a cooperation of 15 countries – we hope for more in the future – set on

providing answers to international issues for which increasingly answers
cannot be found on a national level.' (Green)

UK MEPs:

'I see Europe as an extension of the British personality and adventure, a
new area for us to expand and to work alongside others. Our institutions
will change. That isn't a threat, but a natural evolution. I have a sort of
romantic idea of Europe because one's aware of all the cultural history and
possibly because I'm a musician. . . . I find it fascinating to learn European
languages. . . . Europe is naturally encompassing British identity . . . when
you think of being European, it includes all the Eastern European countries,
up to the Russian frontier, and a long way south.' (EPP)

'The EU is the most significant political development in the continent of
Europe. But the continent is more than the EU. . . . It's based on geography
and working meaningfully together. World citizenship is not impossible in
a global economy. Europe could interface with cultures which are not
necessarily European. Europe is a funny continent. It's fragmented linguistically and politically. That's more difficult to work with internationally.' (PES)

'I've always felt European. Scottish first, then European. I don't feel British
at all. British nationality was done from above. They got England and lost
Europe. Turned away from Europe. Long ago, Scotland had joint citizenship
with France . . .' (ARE)

What is interesting about these descriptions of the imagined community
of Europe is the different emphasis the Dutch and UK MEPs give to both
the movement and the type of diversity imagined. Table 6.2 sets out the
vocabulary used by the two groups in each of the relevant categories we
have been using for analysis: movement and diversity. In a sense, Dutch
women are providing a framing narrative for European identity which
posits a movement more purposeful than that suggested by UK women:
'expansion towards', 'on their way to', 'halfway there'; as opposed to a
notion of movement as 'change', and 'evolution'. Whilst both national
groups prioritize plurality, the Dutch MEPs quoted above position this
plurality as one of volume, with multiple populations, countries, blocs
and political issues. For the UK MEPs quoted, the plurality is more
strongly drawn as something cultural and linguistic, fragmented and less
tangible ('identity') than that of the Dutch imagining. Diversity is
undoubtedly the framework of moving identity for both Dutch and UK
MEPs, but there is a slight difference in the strength with which both the
movement and the diversity are portrayed. Where women's participation
in the European Parliament is based on a generally supportive national
public, women may tend to imagine a community which is both more
purposeful and directed, and more tangible and visible. Where national

Table 6.2

	Dutch	*UK*
Movement	Expansion towards	Extension
	Expanding	Expand
	On their way to	Change
	Halfway there	Evolution
	Expansion	Turn away from
Diversity	Large number of	All the cultural history
	15 million	European languages
	370 million	All Eastern Europe
	Eastern Europe	More than
	Three blocs	Cultures
	Countries to east	Fragmented
	Fewer and fewer	
	Fifteen countries	
	Issues	

public opinion is hostile, the moving identity may be imagined in less purposeful ways, and the diversity drawn in terms which are less tangible and more cultural.

In the same way, some of the grammars of citizenship we have observed are accented by what appear to be national experiences. Women, I argued in Chapter 4, tend to attribute agency to the citizen more frequently than their male colleagues. Table 6.3, based on the interviews with women MEPs, illustrates the proportion of examples in each nationality where the citizen is placed as the agent, the subject of the verb. Again, the more pro-European Dutch are at one end of the table, and the less pro-EU UK MEPs at the other end, although not incidentally at the bottom. Women from Holland, then, appear a little more likely to envisage an active citizen in Europe, a citizen who is the subject of the verb, than do women from the UK. If we compare for a moment the definition of citizenship given by a Dutch MEP and an MEP from the UK, some differences do indeed appear:

Dutch MEP:

'We are involved in a lot of issues which concern citizens directly. Removing obstacles for instance when it comes to recognizing qualifications, being able to take your pension abroad and so on. When the euro comes, citizens will enjoy travelling through Europe with a single currency. We are dealing

Table 6.3

Nationality	Percentage of total examples where the citizen is placed in the active
Dutch	47
French	43
Irish	43
German	42
Portuguese	41
Belgian	40
UK	30
Spanish	28
Danish	27
Italian	20

(Greek and Luxembourgeoise, where only one informant, omitted from this table)

with a number of issues which affect citizens directly: what they can, are allowed to do, rights which can be derived. On the other hand, there will also be situations in which heavier demands will be made and citizens will be required to buy cleaner cars, for instance.'

UK MEP:

'I've just been working on European voluntary service. The point of the programme is to make sense of European citizenship for the young. The relationship, the individual with Europe, is lacking. You can break this for young people. Before, the nation-state was such a powerful entity. It was difficult for people to put themselves in a relationship. Now, because of the global market, there is more sense to European citizenship. It will lead to less xenophobia. But first we need to crack citizenship at a local level, with the erosion of the extended family, and relationships with the immediate community.'

Using the type of transitivity analysis that we applied in Chapter 4 to these two answers, we could produce an analysis as in Table 6.4:. In the Dutch description of citizenship, the citizens are the subjects of three of the verbs ('will enjoy', 'can/are allowed to do', 'will be required'). They are the object of two verbs ('issues concern citizens', 'issues which affect citizens'). In the UK definition, 'citizens' are posed as neither the subject nor the object of the verbs. For both MEPs, citizenship is largely a matter of mental rather than material ascription, but in the case of the Dutch MEP, the citizen is named in the centre of the description, enjoying rights

Table 6.4

Dutch MEP	
We are involved	Mental internalized
Issues concern citizens	Mental internalized
When the euro comes	Material
Citizens will enjoy	Mental internalized
We are dealing with	Mental internalized
Issues which affect citizens	Mental externalized
What citizens can/are allowed to do	Mental externalized
Rights which can be derived	Mental externalized
Demands will be made	Mental externalized
Citizens will be required	Mental externalized

UK MEP	
I've been working on	Material
You can break this	Mental internalized
(citizenship) It will lead to	Mental internalized
We need to crack	Mental internalized

and being affected by issues. In the case of the UK MEP, citizenship is embedded in programmes or levels of operation ('local', etc.) which place the emphasis either on the MEP herself, engaged in the programme ('I', 'we'), or on the concept of 'citizenship', rather than the personalized 'citizen'. When people enter into the description, they do so as indirect objects ('make sense of European citizenship for the young', 'difficult for people to put themselves in a relationship'), which place them at one further remove from the action, neither acting nor being directly acted on. In the Dutch description, the citizen is at the centre of a largely mental internalized understanding of citizenship. In the UK description, the citizen is decentred, and attention focuses on the programmes, concepts and levels of potential citizenship which will ultimately be attributed to the individual citizen.

There is, then, some evidence that popular national perceptions of the EU can vary the languages of politics women are speaking, can accent these languages in particular ways. They may, for example, encourage the imagining of a more or less purposeful identity of 'becoming' for Europe. They may encourage an understanding of diversity in more physical or less physical terms, and they may encourage a positioning of the citizen as more or less actively involved in the creation of citizenship. The basic languages remain the same: Europe imagined as a moving diversity, the citizen named within the space of Europe. The emphasis in each case, the accenting, as it were, given to some elements, is slightly different.

DIALECTS OF ENGENDERING REPRESENTATION

Clearly, though, we have seen examples in this study where a relatively small group of women use a language which is different from what appears to be the commonly spoken form, a sort of dialect in this case. One of these examples comes from the discussion on engendering democracy (Chapter 3), and concerns those women, the minority, who reject the proposition that a gender script is of relevance to their role as representatives. What is particularly interesting about this variation in language is that it seems principally to be a product not of political ideology or party affiliation, but rather of national perceptions, once more, and of the political generation, or ages, of the MEPs concerned.

In Chapter 2, we saw the ways in which some writers used a cross-national framework in order to place women politically in the space of Europe (Lovenduski, 1986) and, in many cases, to point out that the political representation of women in their own countries was grossly deficient by comparison (Sineau, 1997). For some commentators (Kauppi, 1999), there is the hope that the European Parliament's example may indeed, by spillover, prove a positive influence in achieving greater political equality within the individual nation-states.

Whilst, however, the possible spillover, European Parliament to nation-state, has been mentioned several times, there has been less interest in the reverse direction of spillover, nation-state to European Parliament. The experience of female representation at national level, however, can well be of relevance to the ways in which women at the European level conceive of their jobs. Recently, Guy Bédard and Marion Tremblay (Bédard and Tremblay, 2000), for example, studying the case of female local councillors in Quebec, argued that women in councils where there is equal male/female representation, or where female representation is higher than male, appear to see gender as of little relevance at all to their roles, or to the ways in which they work. If we transpose this to the European Parliament, we might wonder whether national experiences of political representation can produce the variations, the dialects, we saw in the languages of engendering democracy. To explore this further, I set out in Table 6.5 the percentage of women in each national group who reject

Table 6.5

Nationality	Percentage of national respondents rejecting gendered role	Percentage of female representation in national parliament
French	0	10.92
Portuguese	0	12.17
Irish	0	12.06
Greek*	0	6.33
Luxembourgeoise*	0	20.00
German	17	26.34
Danish	17	33.71
UK	22	18.43
Italian	25	11.43
Belgian	25	11.33
Spanish	57	24.57
Dutch	57	32.67

* one respondent

the gender script of representation, and next to this, for comparison, the percentage level of female membership in each national assembly (Council of Europe, 1998).

The overall numbers of women interviewed (60) are of course relatively small, so that we cannot argue for a simple correlation between level of female membership in a national parliament and a belief in/rejection of the importance of gendering the role of an MEP. Given Bédard's work, however, to which we have just referred, it is of some interest that national groups where MEPs agree unanimously that being a woman influences their role as representatives come from countries which (with the exception of Luxembourg) have a national female representation in their parliaments below 15 per cent, whilst national groups with higher percentages of women seeing gender as irrelevant come from countries which are fifth (Holland) and ninth (Spain) in the Council of Europe 1998 league table of female representation in national parliaments. There is then a sense here that national experience of female parliamentary representation, either in terms of representation achieved, or of an ongoing national debate on why women should be represented, does inform some of these responses of MEPs to the ways in which representation might, or might not, be engendered.

A Dutch MEP, for example, (with a national female representation of

32.67 per cent) explains why she believes gender is of little importance in terms of political representation by arguing from experience ('I have found'), and from an understanding that gendering representation is less important if there is a reasonably equal representation of both sexes:

'I HAVE FOUND that it matters little whether there are men or women working in politics. I do find that TOO MANY MEN AND TOO FEW WOMEN put the latter at a disadvantage, because men tend to solve those problems which affect them within their own socio-cultural province/sphere. However, many questions transcend the sexes – peace and security for instance – as opposed to day care for children to cite another example. It should not matter at all, but it is good that both groups are represented so that the interests of both are taken care of.'

A French MEP on the other hand (with a national female representation of 10.92 per cent) argues the opposite case. Gendering representation is important, she claims, and the time has indeed come when people need the qualities women can uniquely bring to politics:

'Women and men have different qualities. Women want to see things in immediate concrete terms. We're ENTERING A PERIOD NOW when the way women express things is REALLY NEEDED in politics. IF PEOPLE WANT WOMEN IN POLITICS NOW, it's not because they're women. Rather, they want to see concrete measures taken, and women can contribute to this.'

This use of a slightly different dialect in engendering representation is influenced by age as well as by national perceptions and experiences. As we saw in Chapter 1, since the 1960s there have been 'waves' or generations of feminist writing and theory which have positioned this script in a variety of different contexts. To some extent, our age, our political generation, or the point at which we came upon the scripts, may influence the responses we personally make to them. Certainly, in talking to women about the extent to which they integrate gender within their present role as MEPs, we can see that age may be one of the factors predisposing women to accept or reject a script of gender in politics. Whilst only 25 per cent rejected the idea that gender is important in playing the role of a representative, older women (55–65 and over 65) were more likely to place themselves in this group than younger women, as Table 6.6 suggests.

In this context, a sample comparison between the replies of one of the oldest MEPs (over 65) with that of one of her youngest colleagues is instructive. For the older woman, the question is perceived largely in terms of political structures, equality of representation and equality poli-

Table 6.6

Age	Percentage in age group believing gender not important to role of MEP
36–45	15
46–54	13
55–65	44
Over 65	33

cies, and these are areas which the MEP feels are not closely related to her own self-perception as a representative:

'The fact that I am a woman does not influence my behaviour as an MEP. However, my own opinion and also my PARTY have the necessity of achieving an EQUAL REPRESENTATIVE SYSTEM according to the proportion of women in the community. And, there is a need in Europe for more COMPENSATORY POLICIES that make women EQUAL to men in a lot more social and political fields.'

In comparison, a younger MEP argues from a difference/identity position. Firstly, women have a particular gaze in politics, they see things differently, and secondly, they work differently in politics from male MEPs, finding, for example, that gender can cross ideological boundaries:

'The fact that you are a woman makes you see things from another point of view. For women, the timetable and the style in which politics is lived are more difficult for women than for men. In politics, there's very little respect for privacy. The women who work in the European Parliament are more resilient. It's a lot easier to get agreement between women across the different political parties, like for example the agreements which the Women's Committee produced. And then, the report on mobile phones got through as a result of agreements between women. Women have a point of view which is more closely related to the human dimension.'

For one generation, there may be a greater tendency to see gender as an equality issue, one problem among many which should be addressed by political structures and legislation. For younger women, gender may be integrated into their perception of their own role, seen in a positive particularist light, and constructed as something which affects working practices in a practical way. Interestingly enough, it is younger MEPs too who tend to narrate their role more frequently within the Representative as Interpreter frame (Table 6.7).

Age, political generation then, seems to provide some variety, or dialects, in the languages of engendering democracy that we reviewed in

Table 6.7

Age	Percentage of MEPs in age group using the Interpreter frame
Under 35	50
36–45	46
46–54	43
55–65	28
Over 65	33

Chapter 3. If we compare part of the description of one of the younger MEPs with that of one of the oldest, we can note the very different frameworks of representation created:

> 'There's a massive PR job on Europe to be done . . . it would be patronizing to say that the young can speak to the young . . . there are language barriers . . . you have to learn . . . Committees are dominated by different languages.' (under 35)

> 'here are activities which any MEP carries out. To deal with specialized questions and to bring about decisions. I am in the two committees for Development and Cooperation, and Culture, Youth and Media.' (over 65)

Quite obviously here, the older MEP is positioning her role in the traditional framework of parliamentary representative – 'deal with specialized questions . . . bring about decisions', 'in two committees'. The younger MEP positions herself as an interpreter, from the European Parliament to the outside world – 'massive PR job' – from MEPs to particular population groups – 'young can speak to the young' – and within the European Parliament itself – 'language barriers . . . different languages'.

The very distinct engendering of the role of the representative which we noticed in Chapter 3, and its depiction within a framework of interpreting and communicating between groups, seems to be a language spoken more frequently by a younger generation of MEPs than by an older one.

THE INFLUENCE OF POLITICAL IDEOLOGY

If age and nationality provide some accenting and variation in the languages of politics spoken by women, the influence of political ideology appears to be relatively slight. It is difficult to see anything like a left/

Table 6.8

Party	Percentage of women interviewed using Interpreter framework
EPP	23
PES	45
ELDR	57
Green	60

right divide operating to produce distinct dialects of these languages. When we look at how members of the different transnational political groupings express themselves, the only two accentings that may be related to political affiliation concern the frequency with which the Representative as Interpreter framework is used, and the extent to which women from particular political groupings imagine the moving identity of Europe with a vocabulary of rules as opposed to diversity.

In the four main transnational federations, we interviewed women as follows: 17 women from the EPP, the conservative right grouping; 20 women from the PES, the socialist left group; 7 women from the Liberal centrist ELDR, and 5 women from the environmentalist Greens. Women from all of these political groups narrated their role in the Representative as Interpreter frame. As Table 6.8 suggests, however, women in the conservative EPP federation were markedly less likely to use this framework, in comparison, for example, with women from the Greens.

We might put this observation beside the second apparently political accenting of the languages of politics, which operates in the way in which the mobile community of Europe is imagined. The imagining of this moving identity is, as we have seen in Chapter 5, largely expressed by women MEPs in terms of a diversity and plurality, and much less frequently as a process constituted within patterns and rules. If we return to the sample of speeches we used in Chapter 5 and match the proportion of examples in the Rules (as opposed to Diversity) category given by MEPs from each political grouping, there is a slight sense (Table 6.9), firstly that this accenting may be more likely within the larger federations which dominate the Parliament (the EPP and PES), and secondly that it may be somewhat more frequent within the EPP.

One of the EPP members explains, for example, how she imagines European identity with the words:

'The EU is unique in that it is supranational. The EU differs from other organizations in the world through its three executive bodies. The European Parliament plays the supervisory role in this. Since the Treaty of Amsterdam,

Table 6.9

Political grouping	Percentage of examples in Rules category
EPP	15
PES	6
ELDR	0
Greens	0

> the European Parliament monitors 80 per cent of the decisions taken by the EU executive bodies.'

This sort of imagining contrasts vividly with that of a Green MEP:

> 'One can write a book about "what is Europe?". Europe is the attempt by so many countries, interests, cultures, in some way to unite in a peaceful manner all the opposite interests, culturally, economically. I find it import- ant that we do not have war again, that each country learns from the other strong elements and learns to respect them.'

The languages used in each case suggest very different understandings of what Europe is. For the EPP member quoted above, there is a vocabulary of Rules: 'organization', 'executive', 'supervisory', 'monitors'. For the Green MEP, there is a vocabulary of Diversity: 'so many countries, interests, cultures', 'each country learns from the other'.

If the accenting is evident here, however, we would have to say firstly that the numbers of examples of women using the vocabulary of Rules are not large, and secondly, that the occurrences may have as much to do with the institutionalization of a political grouping in the Parliament (given that the examples are only provided by women in the two larger transnational federations: EPP and PES) as with political ideology.

In the languages of politics that we have been studying in the European Parliament, there are variations of accenting and of dialect, but, interest- ingly enough, these may have more to do with national positions and political generation, than with political ideology or group membership.

WOMEN'S LANGUAGES OF POLITICS

In talking about women's languages of politics, then, I am not suggesting that there is one unified language of politics for women. The category of 'women' with which we have been dealing in this study is, within the terms of this western European debate, a heterogeneous one. It was originally constituted to reflect the heterogeneity of the European Parliament in nationalities and political groupings. In analysing the results, we have been careful to note the sub-groups and mixtures of languages within each of our main themes. Finally, we have noted that any sharing of languages by women is marked by variations, by distinctive examples of accenting, and by more substantial differences, varieties of dialect.

With all these caveats, however, the evidence suggests that there are some languages of politics commonly spoken by women in the European Parliament which are different from the languages men more normally speak. In this part of the chapter, we shall briefly summarize what the main features of these languages appear to be, and then try to situate some of the results in the ongoing debates on essentialism and difference. The results concern each of our main themes: engendering democracy, grammars of citizenship and imaginings of Europe.

To begin with, we noticed in Chapter 3 that women were framing their participation in the political life of the European Parliament in particular ways: they were describing their role, narrating it, as it were, within certain frameworks. A close study of their languages here, what they were actually saying, revealed three main narrative frames for a representative: the Representative as Political actor, the Representative as Personal traveller, and the Representative as Interpreter. Of these three, the last, the Representative as Interpreter, was the most popular among the women we interviewed, and was the narrative frame shared by the largest number of nationalities and political groups. In this framework, women are describing a role of political representation which is centred not on what is being represented in the process – individuals, geographical areas, specific issues or groups – nor on the political sites in which the 'business' of politics may be taking place. Instead, the narrative frame tells the story of representation as a process of communication, of interpretation, between individuals and between groups, within the European Parliament, and outside it. The story that many women are telling about their jobs as MEPs is one that names representatives as ambassadors, bridges, transmitters, and interpreters.

The site of politics in which women representatives perceive themselves to be operating, and the processes of politics in which they are engaging, are, we have seen (Chapter 3), imagined in slightly different ways by men and women. If men and women share common notions of engaging in political activity as in a fight, the fight that women more frequently imagine is one that is less confrontational and more defensive. Men more typically construct conflict in the processes of politics as large and important battles between opposing camps. Women, more frequently, represent it as an intimate, 'up close' encounter. The site of politics in which MEPs operate is also imagined slightly differently by men and by women. For both, it is a site of problems to be faced, and issues to be addressed. More frequently, however, men imagine the site as one of chronic disease with problems that are great and sometimes cataclysmic. Women, more often, describe it as a site of cure, and of problems which can be constructed on a smaller scale: 'coronary disease' as opposed to 'antidote', 'oceans' as opposed to 'pools'. Men more frequently represent politics as an area of activity that can be understood within borders and contours, and written down, textualized and recorded. Women are more likely to see an area which spreads out in some form of linked network, in fabrics or mosaics.

In all this discussion of different male/female ways of imagining what politics is, we have sought to inscribe any differences noted within a language of 'directions of difference', 'slight difference', 'more frequently used', and so on. In looking at difference, then, we are arguing that there are a number of ways in which members of both sexes construct politics, a number of languages used, but that women have a tendency to use the languages we are describing more often than their male colleagues. We will return to the broader implications of this for notions of engendering democracy in the concluding chapter.

When we looked at how citizenship is being understood in the transnational space of the European Parliament, we saw firstly that the majority of women describe it in vocabulary which is borrowed from neither the liberal democratic nor the civic republican traditions. Rather, they use a vocabulary which names plural and overlapping identities, moving over personal frontiers. What is prioritized here is a sense of citizenship as the holding of plural identities within a context of movement and change. Citizenship is a perspective which goes across frontiers, both physical and mental.

The grammars in which both male and female languages of citizenship are constructed place the citizen in the space of Europe as the object of the verb – being done to, as it were, rather than doing. Where the citizen is in the active, the subject of the verbs, the actions involved are those in the mind of the citizen, rather than physically in the political space of Europe. Citizen participation is situated in terms of perceiving, thinking and reacting. In this grammar, the citizen enters into the discursive space of Europe in a variety of roles: as producer, consumer, professional, and so on. For both men and women, the citizen is also understood as a member of minority groups, and positioned squarely as such in the discursive space of the European Parliament.

Within this shared male/female grammar of citizenship, we noted that women tend to name the citizen, to bring the citizen into the space of Europe, a little more frequently than men. This more embodied citizen is gendered, named as female, overwhelmingly more often by women, and it is women too who locate the citizen more frequently as a minority and within an artistic/cultural framework. These grammars of citizenship establish citizen/representative relationships which are expressed by women as dialogic ones – 'being consulted by the citizen', 'opening up to the citizen' – more usually than as relationships based on legal/institutional positionings – 'elected by citizens', 'rights of citizens'. For men, the proportions of this particular grammar are reversed: the legal/institutional relationship is described more frequently than the dialogic relationship. One of the most insistent female grammars of citizenship then appears to personalize and embody citizens, to pluralize their shifting identities, and to stress the key role of dialogue within the moving space of Europe.

The Europe which men and women are imagining, as we saw in Chapter 4, is indeed one which is moving and changing, an identity in process, and one which is situated in an 'other time' mobile frame of reference. The languages with which MEPs are 'doing' this changing identity describe various types of trajectories. There is an identity which is moving primarily within a framework of patterns and rules, to some extent at least contained within understood and planned structures. There is also a trajectory of movement which is one of diversity, where a plurality of countries, cultures and communities is named as the moving identity of Europe. Of these two languages, it is the latter which is more often used by women Members of the European Parliament, with Europe 'being done' in diversity rather than within structures and frameworks.

In the final chapter, I shall try to set these conclusions within the framework of our broader themes: engendering democracy, understanding citizenship, and imagining a European identity. In the last sections of this chapter, however, I want to try to situate these findings on women's languages of politics within the lively ongoing debates in this area on essentialism, difference and women's voices.

THE DIFFERENT VOICE

At the heart of these debates is inevitably the work of Carol Gilligan who, with her book, *In a Different Voice: psychological theory and women's development* (Gilligan, 1983), has in many ways helped to put notions of the 'different voice' of women on the agenda for discussion. Gilligan's work is one of the most cited books in second-wave feminism, and it has become normal to associate the type of concerns which this book raises with her approach, and academic heritage. Indeed, such is her influence that, whilst I was working on this book, I became used to being asked, at least by anglophone scholars, whether I had been a colleague/student/ research associate of Gilligan.

Gilligan's starting point was her dissatisfaction with the general use of exclusively male informants for studies on morality and ethical choice. In the light of her own research, Gilligan argued that any account of moral choice which limits itself exclusively to what might be termed a morality of justice (fairness and so on) was fundamentally flawed. She asserted that there is a different moral voice which is more often heard in the voices of women, and this voice is one which argues for caring and nurture in human relationships as a moral imperative. Thus, an 'ethic of care and relationship' is opposed to an 'ethic of justice and rights'. These ethics were then, Gilligan suggested, closely related to gender: the ethic of justice and rights to men, and the ethic of care and relationships to women.

In a later extension of this work, Nona Plessner Lyons (Lyons, 1988) produced evidence which indicated that these two ethics were related to two quite distinct notions of the self. In a series of empirical studies, Lyons identified a 'separate/objective' self who experiences relationships through reciprocity, rules and roles, and a 'connected' self who experiences relationships as responses to others, an activity of care, and interdependence. Given these two quite different conceptions of the self, Lyons concluded that, whilst there was no strictly causal relationship between these modes of self-definition and Gilligan's typology of ethics of care and justice, there did appear to be some link, on the one hand, between a 'separate/objective' self-perception and an ethics of justice and rights, and, on the other, between a 'connected' self-perception and an ethics of care and relationships. Both were, as Gilligan had implied, gendered relationships, so that it was not unreasonable to see a mapping of the moral domain in gendered terms, with not only two sorts of ethics, but ethics strongly related on the one hand (connected self/care and responsibility) to women, and on the other (separate/objective self/justice and responsibility) to men.

The influence of this body of work has spread, as I suggested earlier, to a very broad range of fields. In the area of training lawyers, for example, Dana Jack and Rand Jack (Jack and Jack, 1988) argued that women were gravely disadvantaged because their distinct ways of understanding ethics and morality were undervalued. They pointed to the open conflict in the Yale Law School in 1984 when women and minority law students had objected publicly to the context in which they were being trained:

> The voice that troubles us is the monolithic, confident voice of 'insiders' who see themselves as the norm and who have (often unconsciously) little tolerance for our interest in diversity and difference. This voice, tone, style is often defended as 'the way lawyers speak' . . . to the extent that this IS the way lawyers speak, WE must conclude that we cannot be lawyers – or that we cannot be ourselves. (Jack and Jack, 1988: 268)

In this sort of argument, of course, Gilligan's work was being trans-posed into a far more political/power-based context than the framework of her original research might have suggested. An even clearer politiciza-tion of Gilligan's approach can be seen in the stimulating work of a political scientist like Lyn Kathlene – 'In a different voice: women and the policy process' (Kathlene, 1998). Kathlene takes the 'different voice' argu-ment into a broader area – the formulation of public policy – to see whether there are gender differences related to the care/justice constructs. Interviewing Colorado state legislators, and using a noun frequency model, Kathlene suggested that women do indeed bring a gendered perspective to the policy process: 'In their pursuit of learning about problems, women saw themselves serving, responding and being con-nected to a wider range of people . . . women emphasized the societal link to crime . . . men emphasized individual responsibility. . . . Women's solu-tions . . . were multifaceted and long term. Men tended to have a more bounded view' (Kathlene, 1998: 201).

In all these 'different voice' formulations, certain points are held in common. Firstly, that there is a distinctive woman's voice. Secondly, that it is a voice which situates itself in and is aware of a multifaceted network of relationships, of connections. Thirdly, that it is a voice of nurturing and care. This is usually implicitly, if not explicitly, compared with the male voice or approach which is also distinct and situates itself in a position of individual autonomy, where rules and the roles assigned to others con-dition relationships with the outside world.

Joan Tronto (Tronto, 1993) has provided one of the most sustained discussions of the validity and implications of the 'different voice' view-points. To begin with, as she points out, there is now some evidence that the differences Gilligan found may also describe differences between working and middle class, and between ethnic minority and whites in relation to ethical and moral choice. In other words, it is possible that the types of difference upon which Gilligan and her colleagues have estab-lished the Different Voice may not be mainly, or exclusively, gendered. Whether empirically well established or not, the gendered view of a Different Voice could be said to have given a kind of scientific grounding to an essentialist vision of men and women as naturally, or through nurture, morally different, and this type of perspective is one which has long been associated with keeping the marginals in any society away from the key levers of power. In political terms, as Tronto points out, it is likely that 'gendered morality helps to preserve the distribution of power and privilege along not only gender lines, but lines of class, race, ethnicity, education and other lines as well' (Tronto, 1993: 91).

Tronto's response to this is to suggest that we need to take some of the insights of the Different Voice, but change the terms of the overall debate on ethical choice and morality, a debate which has traditionally positioned some groups (and not only women) as people who always participate in the debate from the margins. Tronto's focus is less on the nature of different moral choices, but rather on the boundaries that this larger debate has traditionally drawn between moral choices and political life. The way in which we can avoid Different Voice arguments marooning us in a political backwater of separatism, she says, is to use the concept of care, which Gilligan has given us, as a political concept which can effect political change. Care should be seen not as being the specific domain of one of the sexes, but as a core social and political value for us all: 'to recognize the value of care calls into question the structure of values in our society. Care is not a parochial concern of women, a type of secondary moral question, or the work of the least well off in society. Care is a central concern of human life. It is time that we began to change our political and social institutions to reflect this truth' (Tronto, 1993: 180).

In a sense, Tronto is dismembering the Different Voice argument because of its strategic ineffectiveness or political danger, believing that if we continue to champion difference and separation, we will in fact reinforce the status quo and leave the key sites of political power unscathed and intact.

WOMEN'S LANGUAGES OF POLITICS AND THE DIFFERENT VOICE

Several of the aspects of women's languages of politics that we are seeing in this book are not, of course, at all unlike the qualities which the studies on ethics of care and perceptions of the self have drawn to our attention, and which have been used to such interesting effect in the empirical work of Kathlene. We have, for example, noted that women often imagine the political process in terms of interconnections, that they personalize (in the sense of naming) and embody the citizen, and that they embrace the concept of plurality and diversity both in their definitions of citizenship and in the ways in which they describe the moving identity of Europe. Whilst these findings are not by any means the same as Gilligan's ethic of care, there are certainly some suggestive similarities.

Whether or not there are detailed similarities, however, Tronto's substantive concerns about the political implications of a project which identifies gendered voices in the first place is one which this book needs to face squarely. In finding women's languages of politics, are we in danger of marooning ourselves in exactly the same separatist backwater to which Tronto fears Gilligan may have led us? Are the women's languages of politics in the European Parliament the political equivalent of all these marginal groups who stand outside the boundaries of the key debates, being different to their heart's content, without calling into question the structures of power around them?

Throughout this book, I have insisted that we are looking at the languages of women in politics, and this word 'languages' is at the centre of what I see to be some of the main differences between the approach and findings in this book and those of what we might call (as a shorthand) the Different Voice School. There are, after all, differences between 'voice' and 'languages', and these differences are key to an understanding of what I see as the conclusions of this book. 'Voice' implies, I would argue, something which is natural, normally individual, and usually untransferable to others. We may operate together with our voices (singing in a choir for example), but they are basically ours alone. With the exception perhaps of a mimic, voices are seldom learnt or reproduced by others. If there is a 'different voice' for women, then the use of the word 'voice' indicates, I would suggest, a difference which is natural and unlikely to be able to be taught to anyone else. If women do indeed have a different 'voice', then it is not entirely surprising that we find the logical extension of this argument to be that they are essentially different and essentially separate.

'Languages' on the other hand may be said to be culturally produced and developed. Whatever the arguments about the origins of individual languages, 'languages' are situated for most of us in a context which links them to a variety of changing and developing cultures. In the case of such a currently dominant language as English, for example, we normally talk today not about 'English', but about 'Englishes' to mark the fact that any language is or becomes culturally situated (Crystal, 1997). 'Languages', unlike 'voices', are commonly understood to have vocabularies and grammars, and it is indeed these vocabularies and grammars which we study and practise when we try to learn a language which is foreign to us.

If we talked about 'voices in politics', we would therefore be implying, I think, that a variety of different people or groups were participating in politics – indeed the votes that we individually cast are often known as the 'voices' of the people. The term would also imply that we can 'listen' or 'hear' what people are saying in politics. What it would not, however, suggest is that there are ways in which this form of participation, these 'voices', could be transferred or taught to others. The 'voice' of women in politics therefore is one which is not only essentialist, but also untransferable: it belongs to women, and people can hear it or not, as they may choose, but it remains theirs.

The term 'languages of politics', on the other hand, implies firstly that there are several languages of politics, several different ways in which politics can be 'spoken'. Secondly, it suggests that these ways of 'speaking politics' are transferable, that they are the product of a variety of cultural situations. And finally, and perhaps most importantly from our point of view, they have vocabularies and grammars in which they are expressed and structured, and through which they can be learnt by others. 'Languages of politics' can be learnt. 'Voices of politics' cannot.

The women's languages of politics that we have been discussing in this book are some, but by no manner of means all, of the languages of politics within the European Parliament. They are, however, certainly there. Not all women in the European Parliament speak the languages of politics that we have observed, but a large number of them do, and so incidentally, from the evidence of our corpus of Plenary speeches, do some of the male MEPs. Interestingly enough these women's languages of politics cross the boundaries of nationality, political grouping and age in the transnational space of the European Parliament.

Like any language, these languages of politics have identifiable vocabularies and grammars, and what this book has been seeking to do is to try and isolate and understand the vocabularies and grammars with which these languages are constructed. The vocabulary of women's languages of politics narrates their roles as interpreters and provides a differently imagined space for politics and the political processes. The vocabulary performs a European identity which moves in diversity and plurality. The grammars of women's languages of politics draw a series of syntactical relationships for citizens, naming them, embodying them, placing them as subjects of verbs, and establishing dialogical relationships between the representative and the citizen.

In the Preface, I hoped that this project might contribute to the ongoing debate about the presence and activity of women in politics. My contention is that the languages of politics we have identified here are firstly distinctive, and secondly transferable to others – other people, not necessarily female, can learn to speak in these ways. Historically, languages 'exist' for us when they become noticed, when we become aware of the fact that some people are speaking in a different way from ourselves, and when we therefore start to note down the different vocabularies and grammars that go to make up the so-called 'new' language we have found.

Perhaps this book will help us to become aware of these 'new' women's languages of politics, to notice them, and then to start to learn them ourselves.

CHAPTER 7

CONCLUSIONS

There are particular issues which have concerned us in this book: the engendering of democracy, definitions of citizenship in a more complex global environment, and the ways in which we imagine the broader communities, like Europe, to which we might now belong. In this concluding chapter, we shall look at what the contribution of women's languages of politics might be to each of these questions. In other words, what difference does the notion of women's languages in politics make to some of the vital problems and opportunities we face today?

ENGENDERING DEMOCRACY

We discussed earlier in this book (Chapter 3) the very lively debates on how democracy might be engendered: the arguments between a politics of presence and a politics of ideas, the question of whom or what women represent 'as women', and the nature of any transformative difference that their participation in politics might bring. Our study of women in the European Parliament has suggested two specific findings which may be relevant to this debate. Firstly, whilst women themselves seem largely to accept what we might call a gender script for their roles as representatives, arguing that being a woman, their presence as women in a political site, is indeed relevant to being a representative, there is no apparent consensus on how this awareness of a politics of women's presence should actually translate into action. Women talk about differences of gaze and of voice, and of the more traditional position of the marginalized outsider. In practice, though, they have no shared conception of what these so-called male/female differences in political behaviour are. For some women, the gaze of women is broad and far-reaching; for others it is a closely focused gaze, looking at details rather than at the wider context. In effect, the awareness of a collective identity 'women' is as difficult to operationalize politically as it has been to theorize.

Instead of looking at a politics of presence based on the female identity of democratic representatives, and on their awareness of a gender script, the evidence we have found is that it is in the ways that women are currently framing their roles as MEPs, and in the ways that they imagine the political processes, that they can be said to be engendering democracy in practice. Women tell different narratives of what their role as a democratic representative is, but the most popular of these, and the one that most clearly crosses national and political boundaries, is that of the representative as interpreter, ambassador and communicator.

Secondly, women imagine the political processes, the 'business' of politics, rather differently from men. When we looked at the languages through which men and women constitute the site of politics, we saw that, whilst the sexes shared common notions of engaging in politics as in a fight, and viewing politics as a site of problems, the ways in which men and women construct these descriptions are slightly different. Women tend to imagine the conflicts of politics as both less confrontational and more defensive and 'up-close and personal'. They engage with politics more frequently than men as in a site of cure, rather than of chronic problems, and they tend to emphasize the connectedness of issues in preference to their containment within parameters.

These are, as we discussed in the last chapter, languages of politics, rather than the different voice of women. They are also therefore, by definition, languages that can be learnt to some degree by others, by both men and women. In other words, we might envisage a script of representation which prioritizes the need to interpret between different groups and sections, rather than represent particular areas, groups, or interests. We might encourage our representatives to narrate the 'business' of politics in different images, paying greater attention to the ways in which they are thereby constituting what politics is, and possibly borrowing from some of the formulations which seem more likely to be used at the moment by women than by men. Engendering democracy in this perspective would not then be a matter of the sex of the representative and what she or he represents – being there as women to represent 'women's issues', or a variety of women's group interests for example – but of ensuring that more of our representatives (male and female) learn some of the languages of politics which women currently appear to speak more fluently.

The first stage in learning a language is evidently realizing that it exists, that there are, if you like, alternative ways of narrating the role of representative, and of imagining the space of politics. Engendering democracy may be a good deal more radical than simply giving our women representatives particular gender scripts. It may actually be opening out the possibility for all of us to see that there are alternative ways of 'speaking' the democratic process.

DEFINITIONS OF CITIZENSHIP

Definitions of citizenship are of considerable importance to all of us, and particularly so when the sites in which citizenship can be constructed are reaching well beyond the nation-state. For feminists, with concerns about the delineation of public and private space, relocating the concept of citizenship has been a key element in their ongoing critiques of traditional citizenship discourses – liberal democratic and civic republican.

In taking a grammatical perspective to citizenship, concentrating as it were on the relationships between different participants within the concept, we have argued that women in the European Parliament are using distinctive grammars of citizenship. These are largely situated within a context of personal identity, identity which is both plural and changing. In the grammars women use more frequently than men, the citizen is named and embodied within the space of Europe, and described in the positionings of minority and woman. In these grammars, women locate citizens as people who are initiating action, as well as being acted upon, and this is mainly action which is in the mind, of perception, feeling and recognition. Women place themselves at one end of a relationship with the citizen which is more often conceived as dialogic than legal and textual. In these grammars, the perspective taken on citizenship links it closely to the holding of plural identities, identities which can be named and embodied. The representative's relationship with the citizen is placed in a framework of dialogue, rather than a relationship of defined legal responsibilities.

The grammars by which many women in the European Parliament are structuring their expression of citizenship are potentially radical. The long-standing public/private spheres debate is arguably subverted if the context of the grammar is understood as multiplicity and plurality. If citizens in their many relational categories are embodied and engendered in the space of politics, the space itself will undergo a considerable change. Active citizens, with plural identities, engaging in dialogue with their representatives, could provide the perspective of citizenship which Lister calls 'feminist citizenship praxis' (Lister, 1997: 199). It would be a perspective which positions all citizens (male as well as female) primarily as potential agents or actors, and argues that definitions of citizenship which start from the premise of networks of power relationships can be expressed in a variety of different grammars.

It may be argued of course that the transnational context of the European Union is too unique a site for any of the implications we might have drawn from these grammars to be applicable elsewhere. My contention is, however, that the ways in which women are 'putting together' their notions of citizenship in the EU are highly relevant to an understanding of how we might all position our membership of the states and societies to which we belong, when physical borders are of increasingly less use in defining citizenship. There are a variety of ways, a variety of grammars, that might help us to do this, and the women's grammars of citizenship we have seen in the European Parliament are certainly one of these.

IMAGINING EUROPE

Actually identifying with different and larger forms of community is not easy, when the affective roots most of us have in existing national communities are generally related to an imagined shared present, and a past which is a shared realm of the dead heroes of our constructed history. Imagining a shared community of Europe is an especially difficult challenge. Neither systemic visions – a system of democratic pluralism and the social market economy for example – nor cultural ones – a shared cultural/moral heritage – have been able to provide us with an imagined community which engages us emotionally. Without a foundation for this emotional engagement, the attempts of EU institutions to give us so-called symbols of community, largely modelled on those of the nation-state (passports, anthems, flags, etc.), seem almost entirely doomed. Identity-construction in Europe on the traditional model of nation-state loyalties appears unlikely to succeed.

What has been particularly interesting about a study of members of the European Parliament is the sense that they are indeed imagining a community of Europe, but that it is a community which is being imagined by its processes of becoming rather than by its present values, shared culture, or past history.

We found in Chapter 5, indeed, that both men and women in the European Parliament were imagining a European identity as a process, a becoming, a Europe imagined in 'other time', becoming in the future. In effect, MEPs are 'doing' this identity of Europe through the ways in which they frame issues and describe the processes of movement to the future. The identity, in other words, is being performed through the languages they use. In this creative process of European identity, women more frequently imagine a Europe which is moving in plurality and diversity rather than within a framework of rules and procedures. Rather than shaping a 'New Europe', the languages of women name a particular perspective on this movement, a community which is being created in diversity.

An understanding that a community of Europe is in process, and that its key descriptor is diversity and plurality, may seem very different from imagined communities of the nation-states. It may seem unlikely to hold the emotional resonances of a shared imagined present, or a shared imagined past which are common to nation-state loyalties. In fact, imagining a community of Europe as one which is 'becoming', and then encompassing a diversity of cultures, nations and perspectives within this imagining, may arguably provide precisely the sort of space in which people in the twenty-first century can relate to the often unequal and unclear demands of globalization and change.

LANGUAGE AND POLITICS

If there are indeed languages of politics which women speak more frequently than men, with the narratives, grammars and imaginings we have outlined above, we might reasonably ask what the implications of such languages would be in a broader context. After all this, 'So what?' we might say. 'Why does it matter?'

To begin with, we have already suggested how an awareness of the languages of women could contribute to a different sort of engendering of democracy, how it might enable us to see citizenship in another light, and provide other perspectives on the identity of Europe. In all these contributions, what is being suggested is not that languages of women may be better, or that they should replace other languages of politics, but rather that they can offer us alternative ways of 'speaking politics'.

What is being proposed in this book is that we might with profit take a linguistic look at politics and at political questions. We might see, for example, that the ways in which we understand representative democracy are constituted by vocabularies which enable us to narrate stories about representation. We might notice that the political processes in which we engage, the ways in which we 'do politics', and assign roles within it, are imagined through images, through metaphors which position us and the issues in very specific contexts. We might notice that there are grammars which develop power relationships and locations for us all as citizens, representatives and political participants.

Rodney Barker has argued: 'New ways of thinking about politics are both the condition of and a feature of new ways of conducting politics. Thinking "about" politics is to that extent better described as thinking politics' (Barker, 2000: 234). I have been suggesting that these new ways of thinking politics, in Barker's terms, might better be seen as alternative ways of 'speaking politics'.

To speak politics in different ways we need of course to identify alternative languages, to recognize alternative vocabularies, images and grammars. The languages we identify will always seem 'new' when they are first described, when their vocabularies, images and grammars are set down and discussed. Identifying some of the 'new' languages of politics which are currently being used, but which are not always heard and recognized as languages, can give us some real opportunities to see a range of alternative and 'new' ways of speaking and thinking politics.

At the beginning of this project (Chapter 1), we noted a widely held view that language is indeed a vital domain of political life. In a sense, we might argue now that rather than language being a domain of political life, it is politics itself which is composed of a variety of languages. The site of politics is, if you like, a multilingual one, whether it is Trowbridge Town Council, the American House of Representatives or the European Parliament in Strasbourg. There are many possible languages we can use to 'speak' politics, and the awareness of these languages can provide us with alternative ways of 'thinking politics'.

Understanding the multilingualism of politics, and the varieties of vocabularies and grammars that are potentially available to us, will inevitably widen the focus of politics and introduce new emphases, and that, as Barker (2000: 234) puts it, 'is a prospect which is entirely appropriate ... for the beginning of a century in which all options, especially the ones we have not yet observed or described, are likely to be open'.

APPENDIX 1:
LIST OF MEPs INTERVIEWED
(BY NATION)

BELGIUM

Magda Aelvoet
Anne Van Lancker
Annemie Neyts-Uyttebroeck
Marianne Thyssen

DENMARK

Lone Dybkjaer
Eva Kjer Hansen
Kirsten Jensen
Lis Jensen
Karin Riis-Jorgensen
Ulla Sandbaek

FRANCE

Christine Barthet-Mayer
Pervenche Beres
Mireille Elmalan
Armelle Guinebertière
Marie-Thérèse Hermange

GERMANY

Undine Von Blottnitz
Hiltrud Breyer
Evelyne Gebhardt

Anne-Karin Glase
Maren Günther
Jutta Haug
Renate Heinisch
Marlene Lenz
Godelieve Quisthoudt-Rowohl
Christa Randzio-Plath
Ursula Schleicher
Barbara Schmidbauer

GREECE

Irini Lambraki

HOLLAND

Johanna Boogerd-Quaak
Hedy D'Ancona
Nel Van Dijk
Jessica Larive
Hanja Maij-Weggen
Maria Oomen-Ruijten
Elly Plooij-van Gorsel

IRELAND

Nuala Ahern
Mary Banotti

ITALY

Stefania Baldi
Luciana Castellina
Maria Paloa Colombo Svevo
Marilena Marin

LUXEMBOURG

Viviane Reding

PORTUGAL

Helena Torres Marques
Helena Vaz Da Silva

SPAIN

Francisca Bennasar Tous
Barbara Dührkop Dührkop
Laura Elena Esteban Martin
Laura Gonzalez Alvarez
Francisca Sauquillo Perez del Arco
María Sornosa Martinez
Ana Terron i Cusi

UNITED KINGDOM

Christine Crawley
Winifred Ewing
Caroline Jackson
Arlene McCarthy
Eryl McNally
Eluned Morgan
Anita Pollack
Carole Tongue
Sue Waddington

APPENDIX 2: MEP PROFILES

Biographical details are taken from R. Morgan (ed.) (1994) *The Times Guide to the European Parliament 1994*, London: *The Times* Books. Quotations are taken from a selection of interviews conducted by the author and her assistants with women MEPs.

NUALA AHERN

Irish, Green. Elected in 1994. One of the first two Green MEPs from English-speaking countries of the Union. Member of Wicklow County Council. Active in environmental campaigns. Counselling psychologist. Born 1949.

The job of an MEP is an impossible one. We're different from our continental colleagues. We're constituency-based, although the constituents still say, 'We never see you.' When I first got here, I thought I'd been beamed up into Planet Zorb, battleship Galactica. There's no information. It seemed like another planet, far away from the ordinary lives of people. Now I see how the Parliament works, how it affects the laws of member states. There's a lot of thrashing about in committees. You have to be up to speed technically and politically ... that's vital for women.

Women tend to be very practical, focused on change. That gets you so far. But then you have to engage with formal political systems. And that's tedious, because it *is* tedious to sit and hear men talk all day. But you have to put yourself through it. Women are more issue-based than career-based. Women have come into the European Parliament through issues. Men go for power. Europe was a softish place for a long time. There's 30 per cent women now. There's a critical mass. You need a critical mass.

There's a consensual way of conducting politics. It's not just gender. It's a way of dealing with cultural conflict. It's also very European. Westminster is very adversarial. Women are very influential in the European Parliament. They've chaired Parliament. They're vice-chairs, leaders of political groups, very influential chairs of committees. The problem is in the civil service of Europe. If you're looking at the upper level posts, they're mostly male.

When you get used to the system, it's fine. I deal with energy. You need to be up to speed. A lot of reading, and political work back home with the party and the constituency. I also coordinate the ecology working group for the Greens. I'm on two other committees, and a substitute on the regional committee – that's important for member states – and the citizens' rights committee. There aren't enough hours in the day. It's a great life for a woman in her forties.

Politics is great fun. Don't take it too seriously. Politics is a mixture of being passionate about an issue and seeing a way of dealing with it. The English-speaking world takes a different view from the continental. Ireland is at the cusp there. It's been more politicized because of the Independence struggle. And with Green issues: it's clear that you've got to get into politics and win votes, because people take notice of votes. Then while they're dealing with those things, we're knitting a few more things for them to think about.

In English politics, issues are dealt with by NGOs, because there's no PR. It's more adversarial, less friendly to women than PR. NGOs are also the political process. There's a tendency not to think about underlying issues of power . . . a way of depoliticizing issues, and the paradox fails to be addressed. In politics, there's a fun element. The PR system is very interesting. It's like going to the races. The personalities it throws up. Politics in Ireland is great fun. A lot of camaraderie.

When you've made it, men respect you. There's freer communication. It's difficult in the English-speaking world for women to be intellectual and sexual, etc. There's hostility. Group hostility. Politics is very theatrical. Women have to learn this. Women find this hard. You need to see it as theatre, when you're in the arena. Much more fun than if they take things personally. I found it difficult when I first went into politics. I realized it's not personal. I got some admiration when I took it on the chin. It helped, my psychotherapy training. I try to be myself. I don't believe in stereotypes. It's dangerous to assume that women are inherently more peaceful or nicer. There's a lot of evidence, but no proof of what you'd do if there were no constraints.

I want to deal with technical issues. It maddens me in committee if one comes up against male sexist assumptions. In the Energy committee, it's very hostile. It was pro-nuclear. Hard. Tough. There's money. Lobbying. Not a softer committee like Environment. The women in there are amazing. They've changed the whole dynamic. From every political group. They're making a difference. Women across the political spectrum . . . it's the issue. We can be practical about it. We don't just bay at each other like men do.

I've a psychological perspective. Politics is a substitute for aggression. Men eyeball each other. Women focus. They're more practical. No biological imperative. No instinct to eyeball. Women are about protecting children, getting resources. Just different. So we deal with each other more rationally.

The committee changed because of the women. Powerful and effective. Women tend to be powerful because they're effective. The women on the committee meet informally: all women.

EUROPE

We talk about Europe as if it's out there, but it's here. Europe is its regions. One thing I most enjoy in the European Parliament ... there's always some presentation from the regions: you have an uproarious time, enjoying the food, etc. from an Italian region. What's precious to me is these many different regions. We've heard a lot of talk today about the Treaty of Rome, and the devastation of war. This is all very worthy, but we need to move on from old men in the fifties who see national identity as something negative – Europe instead of national identity. It didn't work in Eastern Europe. We don't have to get into that situation. I'm not a nationalist. I'm a Green. I believe in diversity. The whole is the sum of many different parts. It's probably a generational thing. There's conflicts in the Greens, etc. The Italians like federation. The Irish are very much European. The Catholic culture. It's normal in Europe. Unlike the British, we have a very positive experience. But we're cautious. Ireland is a neutral state. That's a very strong part of Irish identity. That's why we wouldn't have a common defence policy. Most Irish are luke-warm there. It's not part of the identity.

CITIZENSHIP IN EUROPE

Citizens ... what I mean is people. We can be wordy. European politics is more formal: words and politesse ... more formal. Less blunt. The Nordics have their own form of rituals. The English-speaking world and the Nordics form a cultural group: short, sweet and very blunt. This has been introduced into the Green group, an end of doctrinal wrangling – a more interactive form of group discussion.

The experience of Northern Ireland is to the point. Women's groups especially, but also community groups. Northern Ireland was ungoverned and ungovernable for 25 years. There were formal layers in a stand-off situation. Westminster does everything because there's no consensus. In this vacuum, community groups have held Ireland together, but they're still excluded from power. The way to deal with this is through Europe. We were helped by a woman Commissioner [Monika Wulf-Mathies, Regional Commissioner, 1995–2000]. She made it her business to see money went to these groups in a structured way. I didn't think she'd do it so well.

Europe is the normalization of political life for these groups. This is where we get stuck with nation-states. It's a matter of how we live together, deal with conflict and human rights. I was born in Belfast. I had direct contact with cross-border committees and local groups.

JOHANNA BOOGERD-QUAAK

Dutch, ELDR. Elected 1994. Former member of the Zeeland regional council. Joint owner of an agricultural company. Born 1944.

Individually, I do not see any difference, in the sense that women are taken as seriously as men. However, there are fewer women. When you look at positions such as that of chairman in the EP, then the percentage is a reasonable reflection, but not half. I would say, though, that the power of women does not lag behind in the EP, far from it.

My main domain is employment and social affairs. I am coordinator for the liberals and democrats, which includes my own party D'66. I am thus the first negotiator and speaker and therefore have some power. Furthermore, I am a member of the commissions for economic and monetary, and for agricultural affairs, and as such deal specifically with questions relating to the internal market. This is also my personal preference.

Politics is transferring a political philosophy of your own, or belonging to a political party or to a group of people, into policies, and creating the right measures, deals, regulations for this.

I have been doing things together with men for a long time. I usually forget that I am a woman, but I thus also forget that men are men. This does not mean that I feel like a man in such an environment. I am simply myself. I don't think it is a question of being a woman, but perhaps more to do with character. I am less interested in scoring for the sake of it, and more in consensus. Searching for a consensus is a feminine trait after all. This probably has to do with women's role as carer in the family. The cause is more important than personal gain.

EUROPE

It is a cooperation between countries which are on their way to further political cooperation, but are still halfway there. It started as a trading union. My ideal is a United States of Europe, but the Treaty of Amsterdam has certainly not brought this any closer. I myself feel you ought to polish up this ideal, although I have the impression that it is shared by fewer and fewer people.

CITIZENSHIP IN EUROPE

A difficult question. We are involved in a lot of issues which concern citizens directly. Removing obstacles for instance when it comes to recognizing qualifications, being able to take your pension abroad and so on. When the euro comes, citizens will enjoy travelling through Europe with a single currency. We are dealing with a number of issues which affect citizens directly: what they can, are allowed to do, rights which can be derived. On the other hand, there will also be situations in which heavier demands will be made and citizens will be required to buy cleaner cars, for instance.

CHRISTINE CRAWLEY

UK, PES. Elected 1984. Chair of Women's Rights Committee pre-1994. Member Didcot Town Council and South Oxfordshire District Council. Teacher. Born 1950.

I haven't sat in the national parliament. I was attracted by the job of an MEP. So much of it is negotiating on complex issues, complex in content (biotechnology/ cloning), but also working across, negotiating, so many political philosophies. Talking to people across language, cultural borders. I find it totally engrossing, challenging. I like the methodology, the diversity. Spanning that diversity to reach decisions not always amounting to legislation, but they form the political platform in Europe. I stand as a member of the Labour Party. I represent the manifesto of the Labour Party. I represent half a million people in Birmingham, with different backgrounds. I'm a constituency MP.

EUROPE

A wide context. I've always felt part of the diaspora. I was born in Ireland. I came to Great Britain when I was five. I've dual nationality. I felt European first rather than Irish or British. It's the common feeling of people from the diaspora. I'm not great in languages. I try with French. That's not a barrier to feeling European. All the countries who make up Europe, beyond the EU. We've all gone through a learning curve on central Europe. Russia is European.

CITIZENSHIP IN EUROPE

It's about fundamental rights that people have, classical human rights, free speech, not to be discriminated against in all areas of our lives. The bedrock of citizenship. From there will grow connection with democratic government at any level. A citizen who has access to fundamental rights and democracy.

ARMELLE GUINEBERTIÈRE

French, Union. Elected 1994. Local councillor and vice-president of Poitou-Charentes regional council. Born 1944.

There are several facets to the job. There's the legislative/representative role: delegations, inter-parliamentary groups, etc. And then there's the intermediary role. In the region: ambassadors of Europe, and pro-grammes/operations on the ground. The art is to manage these initiatives of the leaders in the service of the people, of the peoples.

As far as women are concerned, I'm 100 per cent. I am in Parliament with my physiology ... I'm not at all feminist, but the fact of being a woman has conditioned my brain, my physical reactions, my physical condition. Everything. The balance of women's minds. ... omen want to achieve things. They're extremely serious. They are willing to really take on work. My impression is men are 50 per cent present in their work, women are much more present, much more active. An achievement rate 50 per cent more. Women are much more trenchant. They take up positions. Men are more 'perhaps ... yes/but'. Women are much more certain. That's a motive of their action. The capacity to have clear positions, but not necessarily inflexible.

EUROPE

Europe's a geographical zone, I think. A political will. There's an aspect which is political/geographical. Theoretically it's a continent ... the Atlantic to the Urals, if I can take up General de Gaulle's words. It's a project of union among countries ... a voluntary project: 6, 10, 15, 22, 23 countries which are positioning themselves on the present project. Between the West and the East, but more at the West for the time being.

CITIZENSHIP IN EUROPE

It's a notion of belonging to a land, with a desire to be a citizen. It's at one and the same time recognition, firstly belonging to a land, and being of service to the land. The desire not to exclude any zone in the land ... in human understanding.

ANNE VAN LANCKER

Belgian, PES. Former lecturer and party worker. Elected in 1994. Born 1954.

The role of an MEP? Growing, although still insufficiently. This is fundamentally linked to the lack of power of the EP itself. The male/female ratio is still a problem and something ought to be done about it. Both quantitatively and qualitatively the EP is growing in the sense that more women are joining it. For instance, the chairman of the Budget committee is a woman. What this shows is that women are, to a lesser extent, being pinned down to traditional roles/posts. An increasing number of women are assigned strategic posts. However, 28 per cent is not the same as parity. Although this is more substantial than the 15 per cent representation on a national level, it is still not enough for a real impact on the Parliament's decisions. These specific problems, however, cannot be disassociated from that of the actual impact of the Parliament as a whole.

I see myself firstly as an exponent/interpreter of the expectations of the people of Europe among whom the lack of genuine sensibility/awareness and legitimacy of the European Parliament is a problem – I am referring to the Parliament's lack of power. The following issues ought to be the EU's priorities: social justice for people and employment. At the EP, we work with many different nationalities, none of which monopolizes power. We are lucky enough to be able to learn from each other in such a situation. What we try to do is to work together . . . with women's lobbies and with groups representing migrant women, but also upwards with national institutions. The aim is to try and get the Commission on our side in order to convince the Council of Ministers. Persuasiveness should be directed downwards – not only upwards, to the ministers – people need to be informed, convinced of the importance of more Belgian EU cooperation. Within my own group of colleagues as well, I try to convince them of the need for systematic equality between men and women within the EU. I consider this to be very important – I am part of the Women's committee – in order to ensure that women do the same job as men, to reach a fairer, more proportional balance . . .

Politics is an addiction. I get angry when I see injustice and I cannot help myself to try and change things. Politics is there to realize the 'makeableness' of society. Politics is useful and necessary, and politicians themselves should keep an eye on quality, credibility and legitimacy. There are a number of political scandals in the news at the moment, according to me there is a need for order in our own house. At the end of the day, politicians have to play by the normal rules of the game much more so than the average citizen; they have to be stricter with themselves. The purpose of politics is to attain justice in society through democracy. Politics is translating into action the often diverse wishes of citizens, otherwise all you are is a fat cat.

On being a woman . . . I find this a difficult question, because I cannot abstract/regard the fact that I am a woman. It is not a process I am always aware of. The only thing I can say is: I have been socialized as a woman, therefore I am sensitive to certain issues. One example is the issue of social protection and poverty. I see these through different glasses than my male colleagues. If we broach the subject of careers, then for a man, having his female partner work is convenient and pleasant, although some prefer this not to be the case. These are life choices which are made more evidently by women than by men. But if as a result of these choices women find themselves at a disadvantage because of proportional pensions – in the case of events such as divorce which will affect the lives of these women in a negative way – then I would advocate abolishing proportional pensions, redressing the balance.

The way in which my being a woman affects my work has to do with where I come from: a middle-class family. I have always been able to do what I wanted, no one put a spoke in my wheel. I used to think that men and women had different styles when it came to politics. However, I have gradually discovered that this has nothing to do with it. There are as many individualistic and aggressive men as there are individualistic and aggressive women. I worked for the Flemish Ministry of Employment and Social Affairs. I headed a group of 20 to 25 employees. Of the two leadership styles – top-down, hierarchical and cooperative – there were as many women who chose for hierarchy as there were men who managed their teams in an amicable cooperative way.

EUROPE

What is Europe? A brilliant but miscarried idea of a clairvoyant who realized that collaborating with each other is better than to have parties waging war against each other. It is a marvellous idea. It may be wondered, however, if economic and monetary cooperation automatically leads to happiness and to the safeguard of human rights. In other words, it is a distorted idea, one that has become warped. It is distorted, warped, but we may be able to redress the balance, pull it back into position. . . . Europe is everywhere, but not where people need it. People are still unable to derive any direct rights from the EU. This can only be done indirectly, via committees. In the field of social policy, when it comes to cooperation on that level, on the issues of poverty and employment, there is still no collective answer from the Union, there is still no European responsibility, so a lot needs to be done there.

When you ask me 'Where is Europe?' I can give you another answer: 'Soon it will be in your purse!' certain groups (in Andalucía and other EU peripheral areas for instance, or others who are not doing that well, such as the unemployed) have an attitude of disbelief regarding the EU. Europe is very far away for those groups.

The EP can play a part in the field of health and safety, and in the field of equal consideration for men and women, etc. If issues are treated on a European level first, chances are they will subsequently be adopted by national member states.

CITIZENSHIP IN EUROPE

There is a shortage of jobs in the Union and there is a lack of responsibility for creating possibilities. In this respect, the EU has to become a lot more transparent and democratic. I would say then that it is a meagre citizenship, one in which people do not recognize themselves, especially when it comes to social and economic rights. The right of free movement of people is still far off for instance – a conclusion which I draw from my work in the Employment and Social Affairs committee. European citizenship is, in this sense, still an empty bottle, I would say. Much remains unclear on the issues of living and studying in Europe. A further example is cross-border workers – as an aside, and this is rather funny: one of the few rights which European citizens can claim is the right of petition. If a sufficient number of signatures have been collected the issue has to be treated by the EP, which then sends it to the Commission, which is obliged to deal with the issue – not to be sneezed at, not bad. In Belgium, people are rather jealous of this!

To come back to citizenship rights, civil rights in the Union cannot only refer to those originating from member states. They should be valid for all those who stay here and who are legally entitled to do so. Customs/ border controls between the EU and beyond may have been dropped, but controls within the EU continue. That this should change is intrinsic to my own principles of equality.

APPENDIX 3: LANGUAGES OF PROCESS AND MOVEMENT

Examples from the Plenary session of 14–18 November 1994. Quotations given in categories of issues, with male and female MEPs listed separately. Brackets after each quotation indicates the type of movement vocabulary being used in each quotation.

INTERNAL EU INSTITUTIONAL AFFAIRS

In the area of internal EU institutional affairs, the quotations provide examples (across nationality, party and gender) of movement as activity – 'fluctuating', 'being in two places at the same time', 'pursuing'; movement as process – 'extensive', 'increases', 'building', 'enlargement'; movement as journey – 'long and difficult journeys', 'long distances'; movement across frontiers – 'inter-institutional'.

MALE MEPS

'as the competence of our parliament BECOMES MORE EXTENSIVE, the power of each of the Members taken individually INCREASES' (Luxembourgeoise, PSE, 14.11.94, 4–453/5). ('becomes more extensive': PROCESS; 'increases': PROCESS).

'while we Members were making our long and DIFFICULT JOURNEYS to this Parliament' (Irish, EPP, 15.11.94, 4–453/27). ('difficult journeys': JOURNEY).

'should we not conclude a trilateral INTER-INSTITUTIONAL agreement between the EP, the Commission and the Council' (Belgian, ELDR, 16.11.94, 4–453/107). ('inter-institutional': ACROSS FRONTIERS).

'I know that the Members of this House are multi-talented, but BEING IN TWO PLACES AT ONE TIME is not a talent many of us possess' (British, PSE, 17.11.94, 4–453/189). ('being in two places at one time: ACTIVITY).

'the Commission is PURSUING its objective, which is the BUILDING of a federal Europe' (French, Ind., 18.11.94, 4–453/124). ('pursuing': ACTIV-ITY; 'building': PROCESS).

FEMALE MEP

[on a new translation centre] 'A centre of this kind could balance out the FLUCTUATING demand ... among the Union's various institutions. ... ENLARGEMENT of the EU ... coping with unusual language combi-nations and LONG DISTANCES' (German, EPP, 15.11.94, 4–453/29). ('fluctuating': ACTIVITY; 'enlargement': PROCESS; 'long distances': JOURNEY).

ECONOMIC ISSUES

In the economic areas debated, MEPs across lines of nationality, party and gender employ vocabulary of movement and change. Movement as activ-ity – 'movement', 'work towards', 'fast transmission', 'running around', 'complete the internal market', 'started off a vicious circle', 'leading to', 'no obstacles put in the way'; movement as journey – 'a good road to follow', 'further step towards integration'; movement as process – 'enlargement', 'development', 'extend', 'extension'; movement across fron-tiers – 'cross-border', 'cross-frontier'.

MALE MEPS

'FREE MOVEMENT of healthy goods ACROSS THE INTERNAL BOR-DERS ... seen in the context of the ENLARGEMENT of the EU' (Danish, ELDR, 16.11.94, 4–453/83). ('free movement': ACTIVITY; 'across the inter-nal borders': ACROSS FRONTIERS; 'enlargement': PROCESS).

'not just to work towards the future DEVELOPMENT of industrial Europe. ... I think that is A GOOD ROAD TO FOLLOW' (German, EPP, 16.11.94, 4–453/96). ('development': PROCESS; 'a good road to follow': JOURNEY).

'the right to EXTEND territorial waters ... is a national issue.' (Greek, EUL, 16.11.94, 4–453/116). ('extend': PROCESS).

'CROSS-BORDER bank payments.' (Dutch, ELDR, 16.11.94, 4–453/126). ('cross-border': ACROSS FRONTIERS).

[on the Poseima programme] 'wonder whether it should be DEVELOPED and EXTENDED to new areas . . . extended to certain areas' (Portuguese, ELDR, 16.11.94, 4–453/134). ('developed': PROCESS; 'extended': PROCESS).

'preparations for this FURTHER STEP towards integration into the EU . . . logical EXTENSION of the free trade area' (German, EPP, 18.11.94, 4–453/ 206). ('further step': JOURNEY; 'extension': PROCESS).

FEMALE MEPS

'interoperability of applications . . . the exercise of the four freedoms of MOVEMENT can only really be guaranteed with FAST TRANSMISSION of accurate information' (British, PSE, 16.11.94, 4–453/101). ('movement': ACTIVITY; 'fast transmission': ACTIVITY).

'In this Community of ours a lot of people are RUNNING AROUND with idealistic notions' (Dutch, EPP, 16.11.94, 4–453/102). ('running around': ACTIVITY).

'If we want to COMPLETE the internal market we must insist that NO OBSTACLES PUT IN THE WAY . . . in trade with services which involves CROSS-FRONTIER ACTIVITIES' (German, PSE, 16.11.94, 4–453/106). ('complete': ACTIVITY; 'no obstacles put in the way': ACTIVITY; 'cross-frontier activities': ACROSS FRONTIERS).

[agricultural set aside] 'we have STARTED OFF A VICIOUS CIRCLE LEADING TO the destructuring and even the collapse of European agriculture' (French, EDN, 18.11.94, 4–453/213). ('started off a vicious circle': ACTIVITY; 'leading to': ACTIVITY).

SOCIAL QUESTIONS

Social questions were relatively little debated in the 14–18 November Plenary, but the examples shown still provide illustrations of movement as activity – 'speed of change', 'move towards'; movement as journey – 'pave the way', 'forerunner'; and movement as process – 'development', 'changes'.

MALE MEPS

'The EU must PAVE THE WAY for the profound structural and social changes which will be needed to deal with the rapid development in technology ... KEEP PACE WITH the SPEED OF CHANGE' (Spanish, EPP, 16.11.94, 4–453/103). ('pave the way': JOURNEY; 'keep pace with': JOURNEY; 'speed of change': ACTIVITY).

FEMALE MEPS

'this shameless eugenics law may be the FORERUNNER of a MOVE TOWARDS eugenics in the West too' (German, Green, 17.11.94, 4–453/185). ('forerunner': JOURNEY; 'move towards': ACTIVITY).

FOREIGN AFFAIRS

The foreign affairs discussions on Bosnia and the enlargement of the EU to the East again show traces of the dominant institutional discourse of movement and change. Movement as activity – 'move off the sidelines', 'inexorable advance', 'progress', 'arrive at', 'go forward'; movement as journey – 'moving out of this impasse', 'on a different route', 'step on the way', 'embarking on the road'; and movement as process – 'union in the making', 'step in the process'.

MALE MEPS

[Bosnia] 'hopes that the EU will finally MOVE OFF THE SIDELINES. . . . Only by MOVING OUT OF THIS IMPASSE' (Italian, FE, 17.11.94, 4–453/169). ('move off the sidelines': ACTIVITY; 'moving out of this impasse': JOURNEY).

'inexorable ADVANCE and CONTINUOUS PROGRESS of the right of interference' (French, ARE, 17.11.94, 4–453/186). ('advance': ACTIVITY; 'continuous progress': ACTIVITY).

FEMALE MEPS

[Bosnia] 'we should ARRIVE AT a common position within our political UNION IN THE MAKING' (Italian, Ind., 16.11.94, 4–453/76). ('arrive at': ACTIVITY; 'union in the making': PROCESS).

[Bosnia] 'we must GO FORWARD ON A DIFFERENT ROUTE' (Belgian, PSE, 16.11.94, 4–453/80). ('go forward': ACTIVITY; 'on a different route': JOURNEY).

[Eastern Europe] 'STEP ON THE WAY for Lithuania to be fully integrated ... we are EMBARKING ON THE ROAD towards this area of freedom' (Spanish, EPP, 18.11.94, 4–453/205). ('step on the way': JOURNEY; 'embarking on the road': JOURNEY).

'an important STEP IN THE PROCESS of rapprochement between Western and Eastern Europe ... they must not just be seen as an extended market' (German, Green, 18.11.94, 4–453/208). ('step in the process': PROCESS).

REFERENCES

Agar, M. (1973) *Rapping and Running*, New York: Academic Press.

Agar, M. (1994) *Language Shock: understanding the culture of conversation*, New York: Morrow and Company.

Anderson, B. (1991) *Imagined Communities*, London: Verso.

Bakhtin, M. (1981) *The Dialogical Imagination*, Austin, Texas: University of Texas Press.

Ball, T., Farr, J. and Hanson, R. L. (1989) *Political Innovation and Conceptual Change*, Cambridge: Cambridge University Press.

Barker, R. (2000) 'Hooks and hands, interests and enemies: political thinking as political action', *Political Studies*, 48: 223–38.

Bataille, P. and Gaspard, F. (1999) *Comment les femmes changent la politique, et pourquoi les hommes résistent*, Paris: La Découverte.

Beasley, C. (1999) *What is Feminism?*, London: Sage.

Bédard, G. and Tremblay, M. (2000) 'La perception du rôle des femmes en politique au Canada: le cas des conseillères municipales au Québec en 1997', *Canadian Journal of Political Science*, 33(1): 101–131.

Behnke, A. (1997) 'Citizenship, nationhood and the production of political space', *Citizenship Studies*, 1(2): 243–65.

Bhabha, Homi K. (ed.) (1990) *The Nation and Narration*, London: Routledge.

Bock, G. and James, J. (eds) (1992) *Beyond Equality and Difference: citizenship, feminist politics and female subjectivity*, London: Routledge.

Braidotti, Rosi (1992) 'The exile, the nomad and the migrant: reflections on international feminism', *Women's Studies International Forum*, 15(1).

Bucholtz, M., Liung, A. C., and Sutton, L. A. (1999) *Reinventing Identities; the gendered self in discourse*, Oxford: Oxford University Press.

Burrell, B. (1994) *A Woman's Place Is in the House: campaigning for Congress in the feminist era*, Ann Arbor: University of Michigan Press.

Burrell, B. (1998) 'Campaign finance: women's experience in the modern era', in S. Thomas and C. Wilcox (eds), *Women and Elective Office*, New York: Oxford University Press, 26–37.

Burton, D. (1982) 'Through dark glasses, through glasses darkly', in R. Carter (ed.) *Language and Literature*, London: Allen and Unwin.

Butler, J. (1993) *Bodies that Matter: the discursive limits of 'sex'*, New York: Routledge.

Butler, J. and Scott, J. W. (eds) (1992) *Feminists Theorize the Political*, New York and London: Routledge.

Cameron, D. (ed.) (1998) *The Feminist Critique of Language: a reader*, London: Routledge.

Caraway, N. (1991) *Segregated Sisterhood: Racism and the politics of American feminism*, Knoxville: University of Tennessee Press.

Carey, J. M., Niemi, R. and Powell, L. (1998) 'Are women legislators different?', in S. Thomas and C. Wilcox (eds) *Women and Elective Office*, New York: Oxford University Press, 87–102.

Castle, B. (1993) *Fighting All the Way*, London: Macmillan.

Chilton, P. (1996) *Security Metaphors: Cold War discourse from containment to common house*, New York: Peter Lang.

Chilton, P. and Schaffner, C. (1998) 'Discourse and politics', in T. A. Van Dijk (ed.) *Discourse as Social Interaction*, London: Sage, 206–30.

Church, C. (1996) *European Integration Theory in the 1990s*. European Dossier Series 33, London: University of North London.

Citizen's Europe (1994) Luxembourg: Office for Official Publications of the EC.

Clark, J. (1998) 'Women at the national level: an update on roll call voting behavior', in S. Thomas and C. Wilcox (eds) *Women and Elective Office*, New York: Oxford University Press, 118–29.

Close, P. (1995) *Citizenship, Europe and Change*, London: Macmillan.

Coates, J. and Cameron, D. (1988) (eds) *Women in Their Speech Communities*, Harlow: Longman.

Cohen, C., Jones, K. B. and Tronto, J. C. (1997) *Women Transforming Politics*, New York: New York University Press.

Cook, E. (1998) 'Voter reaction to women candidates', in S. Thomas and C. Wilcox (eds) *Women and Elective Office*, New York: Oxford University Press, 56–72.

Corbett, R. (1998) *The European Parliament's Role in Closer EU Integration*, Basingstoke: Macmillan.

Council of Europe (1998) *Women in Politics in the Member States*, Strasbourg: Directorate of Human Rights.

Critical Social Policy (1998) 18(3).

Crystal, D. (1997) *English as a Global Language*, Cambridge: Cambridge University Press.

Daly, M. (1973) *Beyond God the Father: towards a philosophy of women's liberation*, London: Women's Press.

Darcey, R., Welch, S. and Clark, J. (1994) *Women, Elections and Representation*, Lincoln: University of Nebraska Press.

de Beauvoir, S. (1974) *The Second Sex*, trans. and ed. H. Parshley, New York: Vintage Books.

Delphy, C. (1984) *Close to Home: a materialist analysis of women's oppression*, trans. and ed. D. Leonard, Oxford: Basil Blackwell.

Denith, S. (1995) *Bakhtinian Thought*, London: Routledge.

Dietz, M. (1998) 'Context is all: feminism and theories of citizenship', in

A. Phillips (ed.) *Feminism and Politics*, Oxford: Oxford University Press, 378–94.

Easton, D. (1968) 'Political science', *International Encyclopaedia of the Social Sciences*, 12: 282–98.

Elshtain, J. (1981) *Public Man, Private Woman: women in social and political thought*, Oxford: Martin Robertson.

Elshtain, J. (1982) *The Family in Political Thought*, Brighton: Harvester.

Elshtain, J. (1998) 'Antigone's daughters', in A. Phillips (ed.) *Feminism and Politics*, Oxford: Oxford University Press, 363–77.

Eurobarometer (2000) No. 53, Spring, Brussels: DG Education and Culture Centre for the Citizen.

Europe from A to Z: guide to European integration (1997) Luxembourg: Office for Official Publications of the EC.

Europe in 10 Points (1998), Luxembourg: Office for Official Publications of the EC.

European Integration: the origins and growth of the European Union (1995), Luxembourg: Office for Official Publications of the EC.

European Journal of Women's Studies, Special issue, August 2002.

European Parliament (1999) *Citizens of the Union and Their Rights*, Europarl. Website: Fact Sheets.

Fairclough, N. (2000) *New Labour, New Language?*, London: Routledge.

Fawcett (1997) *Survey of Women MEPs*, London: Fawcett Society.

Fawcett (2000) *Towards Equality*, London: Fawcett Society.

Ferguson, K. (1993) *The Man Question: visions of subjectivity in feminist theory*, Berkeley: University of California Press.

Firestone, S. (1972) *The Dialectic of Sex: the case for feminist revolution*, London: Paladin.

Fontaine, N. (1994) *Les Députés Europeéns: Qui sont-ils? Que font-ils?*, Paris: CEIC.

Foucault, M. (1980) *Power and Knowledge*, Brighton: Harvester Press.

Gaffney, J. (1989) *The French Left and the Fifth Republic: the discourses of communism and socialism in contemporary France*, London: Macmillan.

Gaffney J. (1991) *The Language of Political Leadership in Contemporary Britain*, London: Macmillan.

Gaffney, J. and Drake, H. (1996) *The Language of Leadership in Contemporary France*, Aldershot: Dartmouth.

Gaffney, J. and Kolinsky, E. (1991) (eds) *Political Culture in France and Germany*, London: Routledge.

Gall S. (1995) 'Language, gender and power', in K. Hall and M. Bucholtz (eds) *Gender Articulated language and the socially constructed self*, London: Routledge.

Gamson, W. (1991) 'Commitment and agency in social movements', *Sociological Forum*, 6: 27–50.

García-Ramon, M. and Monk, J. (eds) (1996) *Women of the European Union. The politics of work and daily life*, London: Routledge.

Gaspard, F. (1999) *Comment les femmes changent la politique, et pourquoi les hommes résistent*, Paris: La Découverte.

Gilligan, C. (1983) *In a Different voice: psychological theory and women's development*, Cambridge: Harvard University Press.

Goddard, V., Llobera, J. and Shore, C. (1994) (eds) *The Anthropology of Europe: identity and boundaries in conflict*, Oxford: Berg.

Goetz, A.-M. (1981) 'Feminism and the claim to know: contradictions in feminist approaches to women in development', in R. Grant and K. Newland (eds) *Gender and International Relations*, Bloomington: Indiana University Press.

Greer, G. (1970) *The Female Eunuch*, London: MacGibbon and Kee.

Gubar, S. (2000) *Critical Condition: feminism at the turn of the century*, Columbia: Columbia University Press.

Guéraiche, W. (1999) *Les Femmes et la République: essai sur la répartition du pouvoir de 1943 à 1979*, Paris: Editions de l'Atelier.

Haas, E. (1968) *The Uniting of Europe: political, social and economic forces, 1950–57*, Stanford: Stanford University Press.

Habermas, J. (1986), in P. Dews (ed.) *Autonomy and Solidarity: interviews with J. Habermas*, London: Verso.

Habermas, J. (1990) *Moral Consciousness and Communicative Action*, trans. C. Lenhardt and S. Weber Nicolson, Cambridge, MA: MIT Press.

Habermas, J. (1992) *The Structural Transformation of the Public Sphere: an inquiry into bourgeois society*, trans. T. Burger, Cambridge: Polity Press.

Hall, K. and Bucholtz, M. (eds) (1995) *Gender Articulated: language and the socially constructed self*, London: Routledge.

Halliday, M. A. K. (1971) 'Linguistic function and literary style', in S. Chapman (ed.) *Literary Style Symposium*, Oxford: Oxford University Press.

Hirschkop, K. (2000) *Mikhail Bakhtin: an aesthetic for democracy*, Oxford: Oxford University Press.

Hirschkop, K. and Shepherd, D. (eds) (1989) *Bakhtin and Structural Theory*, Manchester: Manchester University Press.

Hobsbawn, E. J. (1992) 'Ethnicity and nationalism in Europe today', *Anthropology Today*, 8(1): 3–8.

Hoskyns, C. (1996) *Integrating Gender: women, law and politics in the European Union*, London: Verso.

Hoskyns, C. and Rai, S. M. Hoskyns (1998) 'Gender, class and representation: India and the EU', *European Journal of Women's studies*, 5: 3–4.

How Does the EU Work? (1998), Luxembourg: Office for Official Publications of the EC.

Hull, G. *et al.* (1982) *All the Women Are White, All the Blacks Are Men, But Some of Us Are Brave*, New York: Feminist Press.

Hutchinson, J. and Smith, A. D. (1994) *Nationalism*, Oxford: Oxford University Press.

Irigaray, L. (1977) *Ce sexe qui n'en est pas un*, Paris: Minuit.

Jack, D. and Jack, R. (1988) 'Women lawyers: archetypes and alternatives', in

C. Gilligan *et al.* (eds) *Mapping the Moral Domain*, Cambridge, MA: Harvard University Press, 263–88.

Jacobs, F., Corbett, R. and Shackleton, M. (1992) *The European Parliament*, Harlow: Longman.

Jamieson, K. Hall (1992) *Dirty Politics: deception, distraction and democracy*, Oxford: Oxford University Press.

Jamieson, K. Hall (1995) *Beyond the Double Bind: women and leadership*, Oxford: Oxford University Press.

Jamieson, K. Hall (1996) *Packaging the Presidency. A history and criticism of presidential campaign advertising*, Oxford: Oxford University Press.

Jamieson, K. Hall and Capella, J. N. (1997) *Spiral of Cynicism. The press and the public good*, Oxford: Oxford University Press.

Johnson, S. and Meinhoff, U. (1997) *Language and Masculinity*, Oxford: Blackwell.

Journal of European Public Policy (2000), Special issue, 'Women, power and public policy', 7: 4.

Kathlene, L. (1989) 'Uncovering the political impacts of gender: an exploratory study', *Western Political Quarterly*, 42: 397–421.

Kathlene, L. (1995) 'Alternative views of crime: legislative policy making in gendered terms', *Journal of Politics*, 57: 696–723.

Kathlene, L. (1998) 'In a different voice: women and the policy process', in S. Thomas and C. Wilcox (eds) *Women in Elective Office*, New York: Oxford University Press, 188–202.

Kauppi, N. (1999) 'Power or subjection? French women politicians in the European Parliament', *European Journal of Women's Studies*, 6: 329–40.

Kemp, S. and Squires, J. (1997) *Feminisms*, Oxford: Oxford University Press.

Kern, M. and Edley, P. (1994) 'Women candidates going public: the 30-second format', *Argumentation and Advocacy*, 31: 80–95.

Kofman, E. and Sales, R. (1998) 'Migrant women and exclusion in Europe', *European Journal of Women's Studies*, 5: 3–4.

Kristeva, J. (1974) *La Révolution du langage poétique*, Paris: Seuil.

Kristeva, J. (1981) 'Women's time' (1979), trans. A. Jardine and H. Blake, *Signs*, 7(1): 33.

Kristeva, J. (1984) *Revolution in Poetic Language*, trans. M. Waller, New York: Columbia University Press.

Lakoff, R. (1975) *Language and Woman's Place*, New York: Harper and Row.

Lakoff, G. and Johnson, M. (1980) *Metaphors We Live By*, Chicago: University of Chicago Press.

Landes, J. (1998) *Feminism. The Public and the Private*, Oxford: Oxford University Press.

Lister, R. (1997) *Citizenship: feminist perspectives*, Basingstoke: Macmillan.

Lovenduski, J. (1986) *Women and European Politics: contemporary feminism and public policy*, Brighton: Harvester.

Lovenduski, J. and Norris, P. (1993) *Gender and Party Politics*, London: Sage.

Lovenduski, J. and Norris, P. (1995) *Political Recruitment: gender, race and class in the British Parliament*, Cambridge: Cambridge University Press.

Lovenduski, J. and Norris, P. (1996) (eds) *Women in Politics*, Oxford: Oxford University Press.

Lovenduski, J. and Randall, V. (1993) *Feminist Politics: women and power in Britain*, Oxford: Oxford University Press.

Lyons, N. P. (1988) 'Two perspectives: on self, relationships and morality', in C. Gilligan *et al.*, (eds) *Mapping the Moral Domain*, Cambridge, MA: Harvard University Press, 21–48.

MacKinnon, C. (1987) *Feminism Unmodified: discourses on life and law*, Cambridge, MA: Harvard University Press.

Marshall, T. (1950) *Citizenship and Social Class*, Cambridge: Cambridge University Press.

Meehan, E. (1993) *Citizenship in the European Community*, London: Sage.

Millett, K. (1971) *Sexual Politics*, New York: Avon Books.

Mills, S. (1995) *Feminist Stylistics*, London: Routledge.

Mills, S. (1999) 'Discourse competence: or how to theorize strong women speakers', in C. Hendricks and K. Oliver (eds) *Language and Liberation: feminism, philosophy and language*, Albany: State University of New York Press.

Mitchell, J. (1986) 'Reflections on twenty years of feminism', in J. Mitchell and A. Oakley (eds) *What is Feminism?*, Oxford: Basil Blackwell.

Mitchell, J. and Oakley, A. (1976) (eds) *The Rights and Wrongs of Women*, New York and Harmondsworth: Penguin.

Moi, T. (1985) *Sexual/Textual Politics: feminist literary theory*, New York: Methuen.

Morgan, R. (1994) *The Times Guide to the European Parliament 1994*, London: The Times Books.

Mossuz-Lavau, J. and de Kervasdoué, A. (1997) *Les femmes ne sont pas des hommes comme les autres*, Paris: Editions Odile Jacob.

Mouffe, C. (1992) 'Feminism, citizenship and radical democratic politics', in J. Butler and J. W. Scott (eds) *Feminists Theorize the Political*, New York: Routledge, 369–84.

Pateman, C. (1988) *The Sexual Contract*, Cambridge: Polity Press.

Pateman, C. (1992) 'Equality, difference, subordination: the politics of motherhood and women's citizenship', in G. Bock and S. James (eds) *Beyond Equality and Difference: citizenship, feminist politics and female subjectivity*, London: Routledge, 17–32.

Phillips, A. (1991) *Engendering Democracy*, Cambridge: Polity Press.

Phillips, A. (1995) *The Politics of Presence*, Oxford: Clarendon Press.

Phillips, A. (1998) *Feminism and Politics*, Oxford: Oxford University Press.

Pillinger, J. (2000) 'Gender, trade unions and inequality in the public services', unpublished paper presented to the European Trades Unions 2000 conference, University of the West of England, March 2000.

Plutzer, E. and Zipp, J. (1996) 'Identity politics, partisanship, and voting for women candidates', *Public Opinion Quarterly*, 60: 30–57.

Procter, D., Schenck-Hamlin, W. and Haase, K. (1994) 'Exploring the role of gender in the development of negative political advertisements', *Women and Politics*, 14: 1–22.

Prodi, R. (2000) 'Shaping the new Europe'. Speech to European Parliament 15.02.00. DN: speech/00/41.

Rich, A. (1977) *Of Woman Born: motherhood as experience and institution*, London: Virago.

Rorty, R. (1989) *Contingency, Irony and Solidarity*, Cambridge: Cambridge University Press.

Rose, G. (1993) *Feminism and Geography* Cambridge: Polity Press.

Rosenthal, C. S. (1998) 'Getting things done: women committee chairpersons in State Legislatures', in S. Thomas and C. Wilcox (eds) *Women in Elective Office*, Oxford: Oxford University Press, 175–87.

Rowbotham, S. (2000) *Promise of a Dream: a memoir of the sixties*, London: Allen Lane.

Rupp, L. and Taylor, V. (1999) 'Forging feminist identity in an international movement: a collective identity approach to twentieth century feminism', *Signs*, 24, 2.

Rutherford, J. (ed.) (1990) *Identity, Community, Culture, Difference*, London: Laurence and Wishart.

Sapiro, V. (1998) 'When are interests interesting?', in A. Phillips (ed.) *Feminism and Politics*, Oxford: Oxford University Press, 161–93.

Sartori, G. (1984) *Social Science Concepts*, Beverly Hills, CA: Sage.

Schlesinger, P. (1994) 'Europeanness: a new cultural battlefield?', in J. Hutchinson and A. D. Smith *Nationalism*, Oxford: Oxford University Press, 316–25.

Segal, L. (1999) *Why Feminism?*, Cambridge: Polity Press.

Seven Key Days in the Making of Europe (1997), Luxembourg: Office for Official Publications of the EC.

Shapiro, M. (1981) *Language and Political Understanding: the politics of discursive practices*, Yale: Yale University Press.

Shapiro, M. (1989) 'Textualizing global politics', in J. Der Darian and M. Shapiro (eds) *International/Intertextual Relations: postmodern readings of world politics*. Lexington, MA: Heath.

Shapiro, M. J. (1992) *Reading the Postmodern Polity: political theory as textual practice*. Minnesota: University of Minnesota Press.

Shore, C. (2000) *Building Europe: the cultural politics of European integration*, London: Routledge.

Shore, C. and Black, A. (1994) 'Citizen's Europe and the construction of European identity', in V. Goddard *et al.* (eds) *The Anthropology of Europe: identity and boundaries in conflict*, Oxford: Berg, 275–98.

Sidjanski, D. (1992) *L'Avenir fédéraliste de l'Europe: la Commaunauté Européene des origines au traité de Maastricht*, Paris: Presses Universitaires de France.

Silverman, D. (1993) *Interpreting Qualitative Data*, London: Sage.

Sineau, M. (1997) 'Quel pouvoir politique pour les femmes? Etats des lieux et comparaisons européennes', in F. Gaspard (ed.) *Les femmes dans la prise de décision en France et en Europe*, Paris: L'Harmattan.

Singer, L. (1993) *Erotic Welfare: sexual theory and politics in the age of the epidemic*, New York: Routledge.

Spelman, E. (1990) *Inessential Woman: problems of exclusion in feminist thought*, London: Women's Press.

Spender, D. (1980) *Man-made Language*, London: Routledge and Kegan Paul.

Spradley, J. (1979) *The Ethnographic Interview*, Florida: Harcourt and Brace/ Jovanovich College Publishers.

Squires, J. (2000) *Gender in Political Theory*, Cambridge: Polity Press.

Steans, J. (1998) *International Relations*, Cambridge: Polity Press.

Stephenson, M.-A. (1996) *Winning Women's Votes: the gender gap in voting patterns and priorities*, London: Fawcett.

Straehle, C. *et al.* (1999) 'Struggle as metaphor in European Union discourses on unemployment', *Discourse and Society*, 10(1): 67–99.

Tannen, D. (1990) *You Just Don't Understand*, New York: Morrow.

Tannen, D. (1994) *Gender and Discourse*, Oxford: Oxford University Press.

Tannen, D. (1995) *Talking from 9 to 5*, London: Virago Press.

Tannen, D. (1998) *The Argument Culture*, London: Virago.

Taylor, P. and Groom, A. (1978) *International Organisation: a conceptual approach*, London: Francis Pinter.

Thomas, S. (1994) *How Women Legislate*, New York: Oxford University Press.

Tickener, J. Ann (1992) *Gender in International Relations*, New York: Columbia University Press.

Treaty on European Union (1997) *The Meaning of Amsterdam*, London: Representation of the EC in the UK.

Tronto, J. (1993) *Moral Boundaries: a political argument for the ethic of care*, New York: Routledge.

Uchida, A. (1998), in Cameron, D. (ed.) *The Feminist Critique of Language: a reader*, London: Routledge, 280–92.

Vallance, E. and Davies, E. (1986) *Women of Europe: women MEPs and equality policy*, Cambridge: Cambridge University Press.

Van Dijk, T. (1997) 'Describing others in Western Parliaments', in S. H. Riggins (ed.) *The Language and Politics of Exclusion: others in discourse*, London: Sage, 31–64.

Van Dijk, T. (1998) *Discourse as Social Interaction*, London: Sage.

Wallace, W. (1990a) *The Dynamics of European Integration*, London: Francis Pinter.

Wallace, W. (1990b) *The Transformation of Europe*, London: Francis Pinter.

Welch, S. (1978) 'Recruitment of women to public office', *Western Political Quarterly*, 31(3): 372–80.

Wessels, W. (1997) 'An ever closer fusion? a dynamic macropolitical view on integration processes', *Journal of Common Market Studies*, 35(2).

Whicker, M. L. (1998) 'The feminization of leadership in state legislatures', in

S. Thomas and C. Wilcox (eds) *Women in Elective Office*, New York: Oxford University Press, 163–74.

Wilkinson, H. and Diplock, S. (1996) *Soft Sell or Hard Politics: how can the parties best appeal to women?*, London: Demos.

Williams, L. (1998) 'Gender, political advertising, and the air waves', in S. Thomas and C. Wilcox (eds), *Women and Elective Office*, New York: Oxford University Press, 38–55.

Young, I. M. (1990) *Justice and the Politics of Difference*, Princeton: Princeton University Press.

Young, I. M. (1997) *Intersecting Voices: dilemmas of gender, political philosophy, and policy*, Princeton: Princeton University Press.

Young, I. M. (1998) 'Polity and group difference: a critique of the ideal of universal citizenship', in A. Phillips (ed.) *Feminism and Politics*, Oxford: Oxford University Press, 401–29.

Your Passport to Europe (1995), London: Representation of the European Commission.

Yuval-Davis, N. (1997) *Gender and Nation*, London: Sage.

INDEX